Contents

Foreword 11

Introduction 12

Clones 13

May 18th 2012 13

Animal Cloning (relevant articles): 13

Frozen mice brought back to life through cloning technology 13

May 19th 2012 14

Fake 'alien abductions' conducted through REM driven cloning technology 14

Tila Tequila's experience of '3 Dark Man-Made Greys' 14

Human Cloning 15

May 22nd 2012 15

The Trayvon Martin Conspiracy; human cloning & harvesting human organs 15

May 22nd 2012 18

How cloned Presidents are aged quickly & independent human clones 18

May 22nd 2012 19

Are people born into the Illuminati's REM driven human cloning subculture? 19

May 22nd 2012 21

How random civilians are recruited into the Illuminati's cloning subculture 21

May 22nd 2012 24

Alex Jones (American radio show host) discusses Secret human cloning projects 24

May 22nd 2012 25

The aims of Global Future 2045 and the reality of REM driven human cloning 25

May 22nd 2012 26

Celebrities and their doppelgangers, and the different types of human clones 26

Re-animated human clones and the soulstone microchip implant 26

Re-animated human clones WITHOUT the soulstone microchip implant 26

Re-animated human clones WITH the soulstone microchip implant 27

Replication clones 27

The reasons celebrities appear in public AS human clones 27

Celebrities appear in public as human clones to avoid dangerous stalkers 28

The original celebrity is dead and now lives on through cloning technology 28

How pain suffered as a REM driven clone affects a person's original body 29

The unlikelihood of a "Clone Army" 30

May 22nd 2012 30

Clones of Illuminati members: Supriem Rockefeller 30

May 23rd 2012 33

WHERE is the "HARD evidence" for human cloning / REM driven cloning? 33

May 23rd 2012...37

Public figures who attend the cloning centers as REM driven clones...........................37

May 24th 2012...38

REM driven Clone Sex (with celebrities)..38

May 23rd 2012...41

REM driven clone torture and victimisation...41

May 23rd 2012...45

Understanding REM driven cloning:...45

The same consciousness resides in the REM driven clone body................................45

May 23rd 2012...46

How do we know we are talking to the real Donald Marshall and not a clone?............46

May 23rd 2012...47

The Reality of Human Cloning...47

When did the Illuminati start to clone human beings?..47

Initial factors which stifle peoples' ability to accept the reality of human cloning..........47

The Environment..47

Technological Advancements...48

Personal Biases...50

Cloning Center...52

May 18th 2012...52

Visual image SIMILAR to the cloning center in western Canada................................52

May 21st 2012...54

Further comments on: the image SIMILAR to the cloning center in western Canada.....54

May 23rd 2012...54

Where is the location of the cloning center?..54

Donald Marshall's Health..56

May 22nd 2012..56

Mistaken identity: The "Donald Marshall" exposing the Illuminati still lives...............56

Donald Marshall's Mission..57

Facebook Posts: The progress of Donald Marshall's Mission..................................57

May 18th 2012...57

Donald Marshall promises to continue exposing the Illuminati..................................57

May 18th 2012...57

Donald Marshall informs the public he is doing his best to answer all questions...........57

May 18th 2012...58

Donald Marshall informs the public he likes Anonymous (We Are Legion)..................58

May 19th 2012...59

Donald Marshall makes preparations for his upcoming disclosures on the Illuminati...59

May 20th 2012...59

Tila Tequila may give false accounts about the cloning centers 59

May 20th 2012...60

Donald Marshall shares Tila Tequila's Facebook Post to his Facebook wall 60

May 20th 2012...60

Laser sight; Reincarnation and 'Caging the consciousness / soul'...........................60

May 20th 2012...62

Comments on: Tila Tequila's Truth Blog video...62

May 20th 2012...63

Tila Tequila blocks and deletes individuals helping to expose the Illuminati 63

May 20th 2012...63

Donald Marshall plans to make a video disclosure with the help of a friend 63

May 21st 2012...63

A whistleblower joins this cause to help expose the Illuminati 63

May 21st 2012...64

Celebrities are reading every single post on Donald Marshall's Facebook wall 64

May 21st 2012...65

"Secrets Revealed"; Phase One; Crisis Situations; Highlight Reel; & Human Clones..65

"Secrets revealed" according to Web Bot Computer Program 65

The importance of "Phase One" with regards to exposing the Illuminati 65

How people (generally) react in crisis situations 66

The highlight reel of Donald Marshall as a REM driven clone 67

The reality of human clones, explained by Donald Marshall...............................68

May 23rd 2012...69

Encourage Tila Tequila to tell the truth about REM driven human cloning...................69

May 23rd 2012...70

Wi-Fi internet installed & Further comments on Stephen Joseph Christopher 70

May 24th 2012...71

Personal reasons for the exposure of the Illuminati's REM driven cloning subculture...71

Psychological torment Donald Marshall MAY face once the Illuminati is exposed.....74

Revelations from Donald Marshall's MK Ultra PROBABLE simulations 74

Bernie Mac's death MUST be avenged!..77

May 24th 2012...77

Inform more people about this disclosure. Tell your friends & family.........................77

Donald Marshall informs the public that he will be making a video disclosure 77

Tila Tequila continues to delay in exposing the Illuminati's human cloning subculture.78

Document 2 79

Difficulties in exposing of the Illuminati's REM driven human cloning subculture 81

Discussions about the location of the cloning center & Talks of public protests............81

4 | P a g e

The Illuminati's REM driven human cloning subculture WILL end! 83

Discussions about movies imitating reality: "Eyes Wide Shut" & "Avatar" 84

Discussions about: "Eyes Wide Shut"; Bryan Adams; "Avatar" & Hollywood 85

Why it is difficult to express new information to others unaware of the information 87

"Eyes Wide Shut" & "Avatar" explained by Donald Marshall 87

Donald Marshall on: exposing the Illuminati & the danger he faces: "Megadeath" 88

Donald Marshall does NOT want attention once the Illuminati is fully exposed 90

The public is NOT in danger by sharing Donald Marshall's disclosures 91

Why Document 2 will take a considerable amount of time to compile 92

The Illuminati culprits deserve to be lynched 94

Being monitored & the last six months endured as a REM driven clone 94

   Monitoring 94

   Donald Marshall on: REM driven clone torture during the previous six months 95

Computer generated scenarios of PROBABLE outcomes by exposing the Illuminati 97

The main concern RIGHT NOW to ensure the Illuminati is FULLY exposed! 98

The LIES insisted by the Illuminati which Donald Marshall refused to tell the public 98

Donald Marshall explains why he must stay calm given the gravity of this situation 100

Tila Tequila MUST tell the TRUTH about the Illuminati's REM driven cloning 101

Document 2 102

  May 23rd 2012 102

   The Purpose of Document 2 102

Donald Marshall's life purpose 105

  May 19th 2012 105

   Pollution, Wildlife Preservation, Sustainability & Donald Marshall's main priority ...105

  May 20th 2012 106

   Donald Marshall expresses his views on his desire to have an ordinary life 106

Illuminati Factions 107

  May 23rd 2012 107

   Illuminati Bloodlines: Papal Bloodlines 107

  Aliens in the Illuminati 112

   May 23rd 2012 112

   Phil Schneider; Grey Aliens; Outer-Space Aliens & Ancient Sumer & Babylonia 112

   Revised Statements based on Donald Marshall's REM driven clone experiences 113

   Donald Marshall's perspective on the Illuminati in 2012 113

    Donald Marshall is sincere in his attempts to expose the Illuminati 113

    "Life" is a continual learning experience 114

    The downside of Donald Marshall's disclosures 114

    The upside of Donald Marshall's disclosures 114

    Donald Marshall's aim: with regards to FULLY exposing the Illuminati 115

Statements which have been revised in later years by Donald Marshall 115

Donald Marshall and his experiences with grey aliens and outer-space aliens 115

Phil Schneider's disclosures are legitimate WARNINGS to the public! 116

The Illuminati REM driven clones have made contact with outer-space aliens 116

The outer-space aliens are living underground right beneath your very feet! 116

The Purpose of this Document 117

Donald Marshall's current views on the Illuminati has changed since 2012 117

The authenticity of aliens being part of humanity's reality 117

Illuminati Symbolism 118

May 23rd 2012 118

Collage: German Chancellor Angela Merkel makes downward pyramid with hands ...118

Individuals hindering Donald Marshall's Mission 119

May 20th 2012 119

Trolls; Government agents; Cointelpro; and disinformation agents 119

May 21st 2012 120

Organisations hindering the progress of Donald Marshall's Mission 120

God Like Productions 120

Legitimacy 126

May 19th 2012 126

Are Donald Marshall's disclosures about the Illuminati fraudulent? 126

Where is the "hard evidence" for the Illuminati's REM driven cloning subculture? 127

Video testimonies from others will help to corroborate REM driven human cloning 128

Phase One of Donald Marshall's disclosures: REM driven human cloning 128

Donald Marshall wants YOU to expose the Illuminati & does NOT need your money .129

Disclosure must happen gradually to guarantee success 130

Remember to be kind towards Donald Marshall, because he has suffered immensely ..130

Polygraph tests will help to demonstrate the reality of REM driven human cloning 131

Use the BIGGEST & verifiable Illuminati secrets to save Donald Marshall & Others .132

Conspiracies are a fact of life; they happen all the time 133

Is Donald Marshall "Trolling" the public with his disclosures about the Illuminati? ..133

YOUR duty as a human being: GET to the bottom of this information! 134

More reasons REM driven human cloning MUST GAIN WORLDWIDE EXPOSURE! 135

You cannot ignore this undesirable information or remain ignorant on this topic! 135

It is rational to seek facts and evidence, than blindly believing something to be true ...136

"Condemnation without investigation is the height of ignorance" 137

There are two separate bodies in the narrative of REM driven human cloning 138

May 23rd 2012 139

Does Donald Marshall have a hidden agenda with the aim of creating a "cult"? 139

Individuals convinced by the belief that Donald Marshall aims to start a "cult" 139

Media..141
    May 22nd 2012...141
       Illuminati one-eyed symbolism referenced by a radio station in Winnipeg, Canada.....141
Movies...142
    May 18th 2012..142
       Eyes Wide Shut (1999)...142
    May 19th 2012..144
       Independence Day (1996)...144
Religion..145
    May 23rd 2012..145
       School girl who was kidnapped and used for Vatican sex parties.........................145
    May 23rd 2012..145
       Is a dead school girl the victim of Vatican sex parties? 145
People sharing Donald Marshall's Open Letter...146
    May 22nd 2012...146
Personal life...147
    May 20th 2012..147
       Donald Marshall gives video tour of his hometown: Halifax, Nova Scotia, Canada.....147
    May 20th 2012..147
       Donald Marshall takes a picture of a flower during his walk in Halifax.................147
    May 20th 2012..148
       Video footage of Halifax Harborside shot by Donald Marshall 148
    May 20th 2012..148
       Donald Marshall asks for opinions about having a new haircut 148
Song Making...151
    May 20th 2012..151
       Did Donald Marshall compose the song "Personal Jesus"?.............................151
    May 21st 2012...151
       "Heartless" made by Donald Marshall performed by Kanye West..............................151
    May 21st 2012...152
       Video footage of Donald Marshall rapping the song "Good Feeling".........................152
    May 22nd 2012...153
       "Edge of Glory" made by Donald Marshall performed by Lady Gaga.......................153
    May 23rd 2012..153
       Donald Marshall on: the song "Hero" performed by Nickelback & Chad Kroeger.....153
    May 24th 2012..153
       "Decode" by Donald Marshall performed by Paramore: "Twilight" soundtrack........153
       Donald Marshall on: the band Paramore & the meaning of the name "Paramore" 153

May 24th 2012 154
   Songs made by Donald Marshall performed by Cher 154
May 24th 2012 155
   "Someone Like You" made by Donald Marshall performed by Adele 155
Technologies 157
May 20th 2012 157
   Project Pegasus and the (CERN) Large Hadron Collider (LHC) 157
May 23rd 2012 158
Siri Technology 158
   Siri technology leaks Illuminati information 158
Television Shows 160
May 21st 2012 160
   I Cloned My Pet (2012) 160
Contact Information 162
   Facebook: 162
   Donald Marshall Proboards (Forum) 162
   Instagram: 162
   Twitter: 162
   Email: 162
Interviews 163
   Information about Donald Marshall's Interviews for Newcomers 165
   Links to Donald Marshall Interviews 170
      Vincent Eastwood (February 26th 2013) 170
      Lisa Phillips (CFR) (April 11th 2013) 170
      Jeanice Barcelo (March 8th 2013) 170
      Green Egg Radio Show (March 21st 2013) 171
      Greg Carlwood (THC) (February 26th 2016) 171
      Paranormal Central® (March 6th 2016) 171
      Paranormal Central® (May 29th 2016) 172
      Brett Wayne Pachmeyer & Cole Johnson (March 21st 2014) 172
      Donald Marshall's First Interview (May 10th 2012) 172
Radio Presenters –Contact Donald Marshall 173
Professionals who understand "Consciousness Transfer" –Contact Donald Marshall 173
Other Sources Corroborating Donald Marshall 174
   Astral 7ight Blogspot 174
   Donald Marshall Books: 174
   Donald-Marshall.com 175
   Donald Marshall Conspiratorium Room- Music Videos, Links, & News 175
   Donald Marshall Public Figure Facebook Page 175

The Reference Palace 176

whoisdonaldmarshall Instagram 176

Petitions 177

Stop Human Cloning 177

End Human Cloning. REM Driven Human Cloning. 177

Appendices 178

Appendix A: Steps YOU can take to help expose the Illuminati 178

Useful guidelines for understanding this disclosure 178

1) Know the information: 178

Listen to Donald Marshall's opening letter about the Illuminati 178

Watch George Green's interview 179

George Green interview: Part 1 of 2 179

George Green interview: Part 2 of 2 179

Phil Schneider's video lectures 180

Read: "Information about Donald Marshall's interviews for newcomers" 181

Watch Donald Marshall's interview with Vincent Eastwood 181

Vincent Eastwood (February 26th 2013) 181

Read Donald Marshall's Proboards Forum 182

Watch the remaining Donald Marshall interviews listed in this document 182

2) Tell your close friends and family about this information 182

Tell people about this information in person 184

Offer to answer any questions which others may have about this information 185

Information for your contacts who would like to know about this disclosure 185

Share Donald Marshall's Summary Disclosure document with loved ones 186

3) Read ALL of Donald Marshall's information: March 2012 to December 2015 187

Start by reading Donald Marshall's short documents 187

Get on a Laptop / Computer and start reading 188

4) Click "Like" on Donald Marshall's Facebook posts which you like 188

Click "Like" on Donald Marshall's Facebook 'Greeting Posts' 189

5) Share Donald Marshall's Facebook posts on YOUR Facebook Timeline 190

Start by SLOWLY sharing Donald Marshall's Facebook posts on YOUR Timeline ..191

Continue to read Donald Marshall's Facebook Timeline 192

Share Donald Marshall's posts to your Facebook Timeline 192

Share your FIRST Facebook post about REM driven human cloning 193

6) Join activist groups exposing the Illuminati's REM driven cloning subculture 194

Invite like-minded people to join activist groups helping to expose this information 194

7) Sign and share the petitions listed 194

8) Share Donald Marshall's video / audio interviews on multiple online platforms 195

9) Share videos, audio, and other sources which corroborate this disclosure 195

10) Make your own videos about this disclosure 195

11) Share Donald Marshall's document disclosures..196

12) Form groups with like-minded individuals to help expose the Illuminati................197

Closing words: What we MUST do to help with this exposure 198

Appendix B: Legislation 199

References 201

Foreword

Usually when a document such as this has been completed, which exposes the Illuminati, doubts raised by others who understand the gravity of the situation, but at the same time feel overwhelmed by the magnitude of the situation follows a pattern such as: **'I don't really know how to help the situation too much'; 'But we don't really know what to do at this point'; 'It's a big problem.'** You are not alone in this situation. Many people currently and actively helping to raise further awareness and expose the Illuminati to the point whereby the Illuminati's *REM driven human* cloning subculture is FULLY exposed and worldly known have all felt despair with regards to the severity of this situation at one point or another. You are not alone.

Keeping the above in mind, the following quote is paraphrased from "Conversations with Nostradamus Volume 3" (Cannon 1994, chapter 19) and presented here to anyone who has recently found this information, and has felt feelings of despair or hopelessness, as well as, to anyone who has felt feelings of despair or hopelessness despite actively taking necessary actions to help expose the Illuminati, and further remind us all: no matter how terrible a situation we are faced with, if we want the situation to change, "change" starts with the individual human effort, and the reason for this is because:

> It is extremely sad if we realise how terrible a situation is and we [as humanity] are not doing anything except feeling bad about the situation, the hopelessness that we feel about the situation is compounded [increased]. If we look at these things as too big for us to do anything about [such as looking at this information and thinking: 'What can "I" as one individual do to help expose the Illuminati's *REM driven human* cloning subculture? The problem is too big'] that means we have literally given up. Nothing is accomplished without individual human effort, which coalesces into group effort, and then action truly takes place. To give up is the worst thing that can happen to our world. It is essential while we are alive to **do whatever we feel is a positive helpful step**. To actually do it. Whatever it is!

With the above in mind, **"Appendix A"**, **pages 179 to 199** – is provided in this document with suggestions of positive helpful steps individuals can take to further help expose the Illuminati's *REM driven human* cloning subculture. Therefore, for the reader who needs guidance in terms of positive suggestions to help expose the Illuminati, you can skip to **Appendix A: pages 179 to 199** of this document– and take the necessary actions required, according to the suggestions presented. Every little helps, and at the very least, you can sign the **petitions (against human cloning)** mentioned in this document, **on page 178**—and you can also sign these petitions "Anonymously". Therefore, as the above suggests: Do whatever you feel is a positive helpful step in order to help with the divulgement and exposure of the Illuminati; whatever you feel is a positive and helpful step with regards to FULLY exposing the Illuminati's *REM driven human* cloning subculture, **DO IT!** Do whatever is a positive helpful step, because nothing is ever accomplished without individual human effort, and after all, humanity's fate depends on you!

Introduction

In this document Mr. Donald Marshall continues to answer questions relating to the Illuminati's *REM driven human* cloning subculture. Highlighted and noteworthy discussions points mentioned here and worth paying earnest attention to are: "Megadeath"; the psychological torment Donald Marshall MAY face once the Illuminati's *REM driven human* cloning subculture is fully exposed and worldly known; and the reality of human cloning. "Megadeath" is an extremely serious issue and deterrent for many insiders of the Illuminati's *REM driven human* cloning subculture who otherwise may voice their disapproval, if not for the deterrent of megadeath. Furthermore, if Mr. Donald Marshall was to die in his original (real) body, he too may face megadeath at the hands of the Illuminati, for revealing the BIGGEST Illuminati secrets to the world. Consequently, this is one of the main reasons Mr. Marshall must be successful in his quest to fully expose the Illuminati's *REM driven human* cloning subculture to the point where this information is worldly known and rectified. This document is a work of NON-FICTION!

Moreover, through the advent of MK Ultra technology, Mr. Donald Marshall was put through probable computer generated graphic scenarios as a *REM driven* clone duplicate version of himself, whereby the computer generated graphic scenarios feel "as real as real" to the conscious mind. The Illuminati wished to explore the likely probable course of actions Mr. Marshall will take once the Illuminati's *REM driven human* cloning subculture is fully exposed and worldly known. In each computer generated probable scenario (similar to immersive virtual reality) Mr. Marshall was under as a *REM driven* clone duplicate version of himself, Mr. Marshall committed suicide by shooting himself with a shotgun to the head in each scenario. The reasons Mr. Marshall took his life in the scenarios are because: ALLEGEDLY, and according to the Illuminati *REM driven* clones: Mr. Marshall will not be able to cope with the flashback memories of his *REM driven human* clone life, and all the evil Mr. Marshall has witnessed in this world as a *REM driven human* clone version of himself once the Illuminati are completely exposed. This suggests Mr. Donald Marshall may face psychological torment once the world rids itself of the Illuminati's *REM driven human* cloning subculture, and therefore it will be extremely beneficial for trustworthy qualified health professionals to pay extremely close attention to Mr. Marshall's mental health, for the express purpose that Mr. Marshall does not take his life once the Illuminati are fully exposed and the world continues to benefit from Mr. Marshall's genius.

Human cloning and REM driven human cloning are current realities of this world. However, this **extremely important** information is kept hidden from the majority of the world, to the point that, even when people have stumbled across this significant information, it is extremely difficult to believe initially, because of the conditioning most of us have become accustomed to. The factors which initially stifle peoples' ability to accept the reality of human cloning and REM driven human cloning is discussed at length in this document. Read / Print / Download / Share.

List of Abbreviations:
3SG1: = Third person singular (first respondent, etc.)
DM: = Donald Marshall

Frequently Asked Donald Marshall Questions

Clones

May 18th 2012

Animal Cloning (relevant articles):

Frozen mice brought back to life through cloning technology

3SG1 posts a link regarding how mice which were frozen for as long as 16 years were brought back to life as cloned versions of the original mice through a cloning method called "Nuclear cell transfer technique" (News 2008).

[Find the link to the article in the "References" section of this document, or press "Ctrl + (left mouse) Click" on the image below to be directed to the article (if you are reading this document on a device)].

May 19th 2012

Fake 'alien abductions' conducted through REM driven cloning technology

Tila Tequila's experience of '3 Dark Man-Made Greys'

3SG1 posts a link about Tila Tequila's experience of Man-Made Greys which were sent by the Illuminati to scare her (In5d 2010).

Never forget me for my love for you has always been true no matter what happens I don't care anymore I already died 7 times. Might as well let them finish the rest im not scared anymore. Lucky for me I saved 2 anti-seizure meds so swelling slowly coming down now but it hurts so bad. stop threatening me im not scared of u anymore. Come on then. Finish it off. fuck off you KNOW who's almost here and they are NOT happy with what u did to us at all! UR JUDGEMENT DAY IS COMING FASTER THAN U REALIZE! I'm one of the FEW who actually remembers "MY CONTRACT" before entering here. So I always knew before I was even born! You have always been there throughout my life watching haven't you" I remember you but Im not scared anymore. As for your litte gimmicks sending over 3 "DARK MAN-MADE" "GREYS to scare me: HA! u think I'm that dumb? well now the joke's on you! Your FAKE MAN MADE WANNA BE "GREYS" wont do shit. But at least I am friends with REALLLLL ONES FROM THE GOOOD LIGHT WHITE SIDE. THEY ARE REAL! Give it up with your pathetic fake greys! People are becoming a lot more stonger and smarte than you realize. They are cming for you and you know they are not happy. You cant keep BLOCKING THEM OUT of "GOOGLE EARTH" for much longer by using some lame dark square in attempts to keep the public from knowing the truth which they have a right to know! Ur all fucked anyway so I dont care. Come on baby! Ur real followers will chear you and welcome you back with open arms. Then together we, only the good ones will start

Tila Tequila: '3 Dark Man-Made Greys' Sent to Scare Her | in5d Alternative News

On her Facebook Fan wall, reality TV star Tila Tequila wrote about how three "man-made" Grey aliens were sent to scare her, although one can only infer that this was...

IN5D.COM

3SG2: Just as Donald describes in his letter (Donald Marshall Proboards 2012a).

DM: Yes. Tila Tequila was activated was a *REM driven* clone at the cloning center at the time when this happened to her. The Illuminati scared her by using short [*Mark 2 REM driven*] clones wearing full body grey-alien suits, and the short clones wore masks stretched over their heads to look like grey aliens. The Illuminati *REM driven clones*, were doing different scare tactics to Tila Tequila at the time whenever they activated her as a *REM driven* clone at the cloning center. The Illuminati, *as REM driven clone versions of themselves*, organise these types of fake alien abduction scenarios through *REM driven* cloning technology. Furthermore, the Illuminati do these types of fake alien abduction scenarios to many people they activate unwillingly as *REM driven* clones at the cloning center, to scare innocent people; making them believe they have been abducted by aliens, when in reality it is just the Illuminati members wearing full body grey-alien costumes, and using *REM driven* cloning technology to deceive the public. **May 20, 2012 at 10:07pm**

3SG3: Thank you Donald! I've learned so much from you!

Human Cloning

May 22nd 2012

The Trayvon Martin Conspiracy; human cloning & harvesting human organs

3SG1 posts a link to a video regarding the conspiracy of Trayvon Martin [African American, aged 17] *being sacrificed, so that Dick Cheney* [American Politician] *could have Trayvon Martin's heart, via heart transplant surgery* (Human Beings –vs- Psychopathic Entities 2012).

3SG2: Whoa!

3SG3: If the government wanted to, people in high positions of power can choose any random person they wish, and murder that person without the public knowing the real perpetrators behind that random person's murder. The government also have the option to prevent the random person they chose to murder, becoming a "high profile case".

3SG2: Oh really?! [The government can do that?] I mean the government could do, as you describe above, however, the murdered individuals have family that will investigate the whereabouts of his / her child. It is not easy erasing someone off the face of the world, believe me.

3SG1: Well... apparently, Trayvon Martin's dad is a Freemason.

3SG3: [The argument you make is a good one 3SG2, however] what about all the people around the world that vanish and are never found (?) or the people who do not have a family to investigate the whereabouts of their missing child (or children)? Unfortunately mass groups of the public are **not** taunting the government for the whereabouts of the hundreds of thousands of people who go missing without a trace each year; and who is to say that governments did not have the people who go missing without a trace each year eliminated (?), for the simple reason that people in government and high positions of power felt like it [eliminating these people]?

3SG3: Anything is possible; however, it just seems [to me] that everything which happens to be reported in the [mainstream] media...; someone [usually on the internet] makes it their mission to tie what has been reported in the [mainstream] media into some conspiracy. Not everything which is reported in the [mainstream] media is a conspiracy. We [the public] have to separate fact from fiction; imagination from reality, to be able to filter out the things we should really be caring about and paying attention to. I do not fully trust Donald Marshall and his disclosures yet either, so no; I am not enforcing [supporting] Donald Marshall, by saying this.

3SG2: I could tell since the beginning, that you [3SG3] do not truly trust Donald Marshall. Nonetheless, there are so many corroborations, pointing to the reality of *REM driven* human cloning, and how *REM driven* cloning is really connected to the Illuminati. However, if you refuse to see the corroborations you will not see it [the reality of *REM driven* human cloning]; the truth is there; make an effort to see the corroborations, and you will start to see that the reality of *REM driven* human cloning, and the connection REM driven human cloning has to the Illuminati, is all around us.

3SG4: A person does not have to trust Donald Marshall to realise if *REM driven* human cloning is true or not. All a person must do is watch, wait, and see what happens in terms of the progress of Donald Marshall's disclosures in fully exposing the Illuminati's *REM driven* cloning subculture, and the corroborations which are made through articles, songs, media and other popular culture to support or debunk his claims. At the very least, whatever happens, a person will be entertained.

3SG4: I can confirm that Trayvon Martin's father was indeed a Freemason. This is a fact. Donald, was Trayvon Martin sacrificed for the cause? [In other words, was Trayvon Martin sacrificed for a heart transplant, and to meet the Luciferian agenda of "human sacrifice"?].

DM: It is true [Trayvon Martin was sacrificed, and his organs were harvested]...
Duplicate clone organs are not viable for transplant. The organs of Mark 1 – Mark 4 clones are not viable for transplant into an original human's body because the cells of Mark 1 – Mark 4 duplicate clones are different in comparison to an original human's organs. With regards to organ transplantation: the better option involves receiving organs from natural born human donors, where the blood type of the donor (O, A, B, AB) and the "HLA typing" (UC Davis Health System 2016a; UC Davis Health System 2016b) [Human leukocyte antigen (HLA); "antigens" are cells in the body] match and are compatible with the recipient who receives the new organ from the donor. The HLA typing (cells) in Mark 1 – Mark 4 clones are different in comparison to the HLA typing of a natural born human; therefore, because the cells of Mark 1 – Mark 4 clones are different, and do not match the cells of a natural born human being, nor are the cells of Mark 1 – Mark 4 clones compatible with that of a natural born human being, transplanting the organs of Mark 1 – Mark 4 duplicate clones, for a natural born human being to receive is **not** a viable option. The organs received from the Mark 1 – Mark 4 clones will be rejected in the body of a natural born human being, because the cells are incompatible. Consequently, it is better to find and use the organs of a natural born human being where there is compatibility between blood type and HLA typing (UC Davis Health System 2016a; UC Davis Health System 2016b) for organ transplant.

DM: Moreover, Mark 2 *REM driven* clones, which are grown via the process of duplication cloning (*agitating cells until a fully formed duplicate of an original human is grown*) are grown very quickly (*it takes five months to form a fully grown Mark 2 REM driven clone duplicate of an original*) and therefore the cells of Mark 2 *REM driven* clones are also different, and not compatible or viable for organ transplantation into a natural born human being.

However, **replication cloning** on the other hand, which involves growing a clone of an original person, where the clone starts life off as a baby, is a viable method for organ transplantation. Nevertheless, the replicated clone (*which starts off life as a baby*) of an original person, must age, and the organs must grow, and this takes many years. Consequently, although replication cloning is a viable method for organ transplantation, the process of gaining a fully functioning, matching and compatible organ for transplant, into a natural born human being, is a slow process.

[Furthermore, harvesting the organs of replicated human clones, crosses many ethical and moral grounds; this is because, replicated human clones start life off as a baby, and develop a mind and thinking pattern of their own, shaped by their life experiences and environment, as they age and grow over many years, and as a consequence, replicated human clones develop different personalities and world views in comparison to the original person they were cloned from. Therefore, growing a clone from an original person, only to have the replicated clone as a "back-up plan" or "insurance", with a possibility the replicated clone will be harvested for his or her organs at a future date once the replicated clone's organs have matured, is ethically incorrect and for many people, morally inappropriate].

Moreover, the Illuminati harvest organs from plenty of natural born human beings; the Illuminati also obtain plenty of human organs from [patients in] psychiatric hospitals (mental hospitals), and [from prisoners in] prisons etc... The Illuminati harvest lots and lots of human organs... Harvesting human organs is Phase Two information... and we are almost there. **May 22, 2012 at 10:03pm**

May 22nd 2012

How cloned Presidents are aged quickly & independent human clones

3SG1: I wonder how they [the Illuminati] age cloned Presidents so quickly. It makes a person think (whether the Illuminati do have the technology to age cloned Presidents quickly, and we suspect they may do).

DM: Those types of clones [that Presidents use] are Mark 3 or Mark 4 clones also known as "independent clones" (because they can function on their own independently). Independent clones (Mark 3 and Mark 4 clones) are also grown via the process of duplication cloning, and are grown very quickly. Duplicate clones (Mark 1 – Mark 4 clones) develop rashes and warts on their skin after a period of time... Presidents, and other members of the Illuminati, who use Mark 3 and Mark 4 clones (independent clones) need new Mark 3 and Mark 4 clones all the time, because duplicate clones degrade quickly... The Illuminati grow multiple independent clones (Mark 3 and Mark 4) in batches at a time... the Illuminati will then keep the best looking independent clones which look most similar to the original person.

DM: Duplicate clones are always similar looking to the original person, but duplicate clones **never** look **exactly** like the original person, and there are slight differences between the duplicate clones and the original person; such as: the eyes of a duplicate clone will look a little different in comparison to the original person sometimes; the shape of the head of a duplicate clone may be thinner or wider, in comparison to the shape of the original person etc. Furthermore, the Illuminati can only use a duplicate clone (Mark 1 - Mark 4 clone), and an independent clone (Mark 3 and Mark 4 clone) for approximately, a period of **six months to a year**. After a period of six months to a year, the duplicate clone will start to degrade and become faulty, and usually have to be "tuned-up" [fixed] or replaced with a new duplicate clone. Moreover, when duplicate clones are starting to degrade, sometimes one eye (either left or right) starts to protrude ("pop out") much, much further out of the eye socket than the other eye, and this is one of a few indicators, that a duplicate clone is losing its functionality and may need to be "tuned-up" [fixed] or replaced, with a new duplicate clone. There is plenty of information I must divulge about human cloning and the Illuminati... soon, you will know everything. **May 22, 2012 at 10:09pm**

May 22nd 2012

Are people born into the Illuminati's REM driven human cloning subculture?

3SG1: I thought you said people were born into the Illuminati's *REM driven human* cloning subculture? However, you have also said that anyone off the street [which also means: any random civilian] could be part of the Illuminati's *REM driven human* cloning subculture. Are you also saying that the Illuminati grab people randomly [*to be a part of the REM driven cloning subculture*]?

DM: If a person's parents are part of the *Illuminati's REM driven human* cloning subculture, then their children are usually brought up in the *REM driven human* cloning subculture. In other words, when the children go to sleep, and enter REM sleep, the children are activated in cloning centers, worldwide, as *REM driven* clone versions of themselves, and the children substitute having dreams and nightmares whenever they sleep, to be activated as *REM driven* clone versions of themselves, at cloning centers during their sleep. The parents involved in the Illuminati's *REM driven human* cloning subculture, usually arrange for their children to have a position, in an easy high paying job, in an organisation somewhere, and their children become loyal agents for the Illuminati.

HOWEVER, if a person is a random civilian, 'off the street', and Illuminati members believe such a person can sing remarkably or rap exceptionally, the Illuminati send for the blood records of that random person and have that random person grown as a duplicate clone; five months later, a fully formed duplicate clone body of the random person is complete, and the next time that person who can sing amazingly, or rap outstandingly, enters REM sleep, the Illuminati transfers that person's consciousness to their *REM driven* clone duplicate, located at a cloning center.

Once that person who can sing or rap wonderfully is activated as a *REM driven* clone duplicate at the cloning center by the Illuminati, the Illuminati, who are also *REM driven* clone versions of themselves, at the cloning center, will show the random person videotapes of people who have been murdered by the Illuminati; and once the Illuminati (*as REM driven clone versions at the cloning center*) are satisfied and confident that the random person who can sing or rap excellently, will comply with the Illuminati's decisions; and that she or he will **never talk** or reveal any secrets pertaining to the Illuminati's *REM driven, human* cloning subculture, the Illuminati, *as REM driven clone versions of themselves, at the cloning center*, will introduce the random person, *who is also activated as a REM driven* clone, *at the cloning center*, to *a REM driven clone version of* "the song-freak" (me); the Illuminati then instructs the random person to: "Hurt him until he sings you something!"

DM: Moreover, say for example, a person is cute and of Asian ethnic origin, however, that person does not have money...; nonetheless, if this person *of Asian ethnic origin*, is funny and attractive, the Illuminati will activate this person as a *REM driven* clone *version of himself or herself* at the cloning center; and *as REM driven clone versions of themselves*, the Illuminati *REM driven* clones, will offer this person *of Asian ethnic origin*, a reality TV show, money, and the opportunity to have their image promoted (by the Illuminati), in exchange for this person *of Asian ethnic origin*, who is attractive, to be a *REM driven* clone sex slave, whenever this person enters REM sleep, and is activated as a *REM driven* clone by the Illuminati.

In exchange for money, a reality TV show, and promotion, (in the person's waking life) the Illuminati will want the person, *of Asian ethnic origin*, to give their consent to be a *REM driven* clone sex slave, for ugly, fat, smelly and rich people, as well as, give their consent to be a *REM driven* clone sex slave, to directors, producers and 80 plus year old royalty figures who wish to have *REM driven* clone sex with this cute and attractive person *of Asian ethnic origin*, whenever the person *of Asian ethnic origin* goes to sleep in their original body, and is activated as a *REM driven* clone by the Illuminati.

However, once the reality show is over, and the person *of Asian ethnic origin*, who initially agreed to be a *REM driven* clone sex slave for the Illuminati, in exchange for money and promotion, wants to leave the Illuminati's *REM driven human* cloning subculture, because he or she is disgusted with the Illuminati, and what they do as *REM driven* clone versions of themselves, the Illuminati will tell this person *of Asian ethnic origin*: "NO! We [the Illuminati] made you what you are" [in other words: the Illuminati are the ones who promoted the person *of Asian ethnic origin*, and gave the person the opportunity to earn a substantial amount of money]. "You're staying [in our *REM driven* cloning subculture, to be used as a *REM driven* clone sex slave –because the person *of Asian ethnic origin*, initially gave his or her consent for this] until we tell you that you can leave" [our *REM driven human* cloning subculture, and you no longer have to be a *REM driven* clone sex slave]. "Talk about us [*the Illuminati's REM driven human cloning subculture*] and you will have an aneurysm [in your original body] like we [the Illuminati] gave this guy Bernie Mac, who tried to start talking about us"

> [In other words: the person *of Asian ethnic origin* is threatened, that if he or she does not put an end to his or her rebellious attitude, and conform once again to being a *REM driven* clone sex slave, the Illuminati will end his or her life, just like the Illuminati ended Bernie Mac's life. In other words: if this person has the slightest inkling of speaking publicly, his or her life will end, similar to how the Illuminati ended Bernie Mac's life. These are the types of threats made to individuals who want to leave the Illuminati's *REM driven human* cloning subculture, after initially agreeing and giving their consent in exchange for money, fame, promotion etc. to be part of the Illuminati's *REM driven human* cloning subculture]

DM: Furthermore, if the person *of Asian ethnic origin*, does decide to speak publicly against the Illuminati's *REM driven human* cloning subculture, despite the threats made against him or her, by the Illuminati (during the time when him or her, and the Illuminati members were *REM driven* clone versions *of original people, at the cloning center*); the next time the person *of Asian ethnic origin* goes to sleep, and enters REM sleep, the Illuminati will activate him or her as a *REM driven* clone version (*through the process of consciousness transfer*), and torture multiple *REM driven* clones of the person *of Asian ethnic origin*, while simultaneously transferring that person's consciousness to the multiple *REM driven* clones to, be tortured; clone death, after clone death; until the person *of Asian ethnic origin* has a heart attack or aneurysm in their original (real) body and dies (during sleep, or even after waking up) because consciousness is linked (Petkova and Ehrsson 2008; Ehrsson 2013), and the person's original body will have registered all the pain suffered as a *REM driven* clone version, because consciousness is linked (Petkova and Ehrsson 2008; Ehrsson 2013).

People have a higher chance of surviving *REM driven* clone torture, and not dying in their original bodies, from torture suffered as a *REM driven* clone version, when they are young. Agreeing to be a part of the Illuminati's *REM driven human* cloning subculture is more or less, "selling your soul" –because every time a person sleeps and enters REM sleep that person has given their consent to be activated as a *REM driven* clone *version of themselves at a cloning center*. Nonetheless, the Illuminati say it is not the soul which is sold or transferred to the *REM driven* clone; it is only a person's consciousness. **May 23, 2012 at 3:43am**

May 22ⁿᵈ 2012

How random civilians are recruited into the Illuminati's cloning subculture

3SG1: [Thanks for answering my question, Donald]... But, where 'on the streets', do the Illuminati find random civilians who can sing or rap amazingly? Are these people who can sing and rap found through talent shows, or through other people? Do plenty of people initiated into the Illuminati's *REM driven, human* cloning subculture, want to leave after a while [of experiencing life as REM driven clones]?

DM: The Illuminati find random civilians who have a skill for singing or rapping from all over the world, to join their *REM driven* cloning subculture. Some people **do** want to leave the Illuminati's *REM driven human* cloning subculture after having been a part of it; others think their lives will benefit from staying in the Illuminati's *REM driven* cloning subculture and are therefore are compliant with the wishes of the Illuminati. Others, including random civilians, are purposefully activated by the Illuminati to serve the function of being *REM driven* clone slaves, at the cloning center (while their original body, is asleep at home; this can include *REM driven* clone sex slaves, as well as, *REM driven* idea clone slaves); some of these people who are activated at the cloning center to serve the purpose of being a *REM driven* clone sex slave, retain the memories of their experiences as a *REM driven* clone sex slave. Some people do **not** have their experiences of being a *REM driven* clone slave suppressed, and are purposefully left with their experiences and memories intact by the Illuminati, in order for some people to retain memories of their experiences as a *REM driven* clone slave; other *REM driven* clone slaves are kept memory suppressed.

DM: Furthermore, the Illuminati victimise the people they purposefully bring to the cloning centers, who are there to serve the function of *REM driven* clone slaves; the Illuminati victimise these random civilians, as *REM driven* clone versions of original people, for the Illuminati's own amusement...; the random civilians who are activated as *REM driven* clones for the Illuminati's amusement, are raped, as *REM driven* clones, while other Illuminati members *as REM driven clone versions of themselves*, watch the rapes of random civilians from the stands of the arena.

The Illuminati activate children as *REM driven* clone versions of themselves at the cloning center too, for the children to be victimised in terrible ways, as *REM driven* clone versions of original children. The Illuminati believe 'messing with' or harming [real] children, as well as, 'messing with' or harming *REM driven* clones of children will help make and keep a person young [this is a Luciferian ideology; it is **not** true; it does **NOT** keep anyone young; rather, such a standpoint is a **pathetic excuse** to be paedophiles]. The Illuminati are exceptional losers! Their actions and behaviours are beyond disgusting! You will see [what I mean once this is all proven unequivocally...]. The Illuminati are awaiting an angry mob of the public demanding answers about their *REM driven human* cloning subculture. The Illuminati will beg for mercy... once they are faced with an angry mob; it is the Illuminati's plan to beg for mercy from the angry public once the public starts demanding answers about *REM driven* human cloning. The information about the Illuminati's *REM driven human* cloning subculture has spread too far now... the Illuminati have said to me *as REM driven clone versions* at the cloning center, that "Even if I died, they are still done!". Once the Illuminati and their *REM driven human* cloning subculture are done, I will never be activated as a *REM driven* clone again, and I will have saved so many people, who also do not want to attend the cloning centers as *REM driven* clone versions of themselves but cannot speak out publicly about their situation.

The celebrities involved in the Illuminati's *REM driven human* cloning subculture are going to try to save themselves too; soon celebrities are going to suddenly or unexpectedly, start hinting / talking about cloning and cloning centers when the celebrities figure it is safe, and the hinting and talking about cloning and cloning centers cannot be stopped –because there is safety in numbers; the celebrities will start talking and hinting about cloning and cloning centers when they believe it is safe to do so, this way they do not get an aneurysm or heart attack as a result of *REM driven* cloning technology, as Tila Tequila experienced [an aneurysm]. **May 23, 2012 at 5:34am**

3SG1: I hope you are correct! [I don't think] celebrities will ever admit to the public what they have done [*as REM driven clone versions of themselves at the cloning centers*]. How will the celebrities save themselves?

DM: Once the Illuminati's *REM driven, human* cloning subculture is reaching its culmination point, towards full public exposure, the celebrities will voice that "They wanted to leave the Illuminati's *REM driven human* cloning subculture" and will begin to voice their disdain for *REM driven* human cloning and the cloning centers in the very last second, to save themselves [from public hatred]... It's all part of the celebrities, who have been involved in the Illuminati's *REM driven* cloning subculture, last resort plan. **May 23, 2012 at 7:35pm**

3SG2: Yes, once there is one celebrity who says "Yes it happened to me, I was activated as a *REM driven* clone at the cloning centers" (such as Tila Tequila); other celebrities will join and also start saying, "Yes that [*being activated as a REM driven clone at the cloning center*] happened to me too!"

3SG1: I cannot wait to see that [*celebrities admitting their involvement in the Illuminati's REM driven human cloning subculture*]! The celebrities would never admit the evil things they have done [*as REM driven clone versions of themselves at the cloning centers*] for fame and greed!

DM: Once the exposure of the Illuminati's *REM driven human* cloning subculture is reaching its peak and nearing full public exposure, and it is safer for the celebrities to speak publicly and openly, the celebrities will most like say "They were afraid of the consequences they would have suffered, as *REM driven* clones, and in their original bodies, and because of fear, they complied because they did not want to be punished". The celebrities acted "evil" exceptionally well, as *REM driven* clone versions of themselves at the cloning center. The Illuminati, (as well as the celebrities), never thought I would succeed in my efforts to disclose the Illuminati's *REM driven human* cloning subculture.

Let's get this information regarding the Illuminati's *REM driven human* cloning subculture to the point where we are nearing full public exposure, and stop the Illuminati before the Illuminati passes anti-protest laws or pass internet censorship laws; –these are a few plans of the Illuminati; it is a plan, in attempt to halt the progress of fully exposing their *REM driven human* cloning subculture. Nonetheless, if the Illuminati are to proceed with anti-protest laws and internet censorship laws, the Illuminati, and their *REM driven human* cloning subculture will still reach a point where it is fully exposed, worldwide. The Illuminati have said that "Nothing can be done to stop the worldwide exposure of their *REM driven human* cloning subculture"; the Illuminati have even mentioned that "My death will quicken the process, to the point where the information about the Illuminati's *REM driven human* cloning subculture is worldly known". However, the Illuminati believe that once the world learns of their *REM driven human* cloning subculture; they will still be able to hold power, somehow; they said to this to me *as REM driven clone versions of ourselves* at the cloning center; I responded (*as a REM driven clone version of myself unwillingly activated by the Illuminati, at the cloning center*) "That would be like a dictatorship... your own military would rise up against you". *As REM driven clone versions of themselves*, the Illuminati replied "We know..." and this was followed by plenty of crying by the Illuminati *REM driven* clones...

There have been plenty of tears shed by the Illuminati *as REM driven clone versions*, at the cloning center these days; whereas, in the past the Illuminati *REM driven* clones would strut around the cloning center confidently, with their chins in the air, because they felt they were untouchable and had ultimate power. This is a wonderful time for me; I cannot express the feeling to you... I am nearly free [*of ever being activated as a REM driven clone, at cloning centers*] and the delay is bothering me because I am itching to be completely free with **NO** chance of ever being cloned and activated as a *REM driven* clone... as well as, justice for all...
May 23, 2012 at 9:24pm

May 22nd 2012

Alex Jones (American radio show host) discusses Secret human cloning projects

3SG1 posts Alex Jones' video regarding human cloning (The Alex Jones Channel 2011) *on Donald Marshall's Facebook Timeline.*

3SG1: Have fun with this one.

DM: *Laughter*. Careful, you do not have an aneurysm [*at the hands of the Illuminati, by saying too much about "human cloning"*] Alex... **May 22, 2012 at 11:39am**

DM: More information regarding cloning will be released, as we edge closer to the Illuminati's *REM driven* cloning subculture becoming fully exposed and worldly known. Do you notice all the "cloning" posts being released these days? [It is being released by the Illuminati]. Do you notice how there are posts about all sorts of animals and pets which have been cloned, and other post which reference "cloning"? The Illuminati are getting ready to tell the world about human cloning by themselves... perhaps... and if they do tell the world about human cloning themselves... they will sugar-coat the extent to how far their scientific and technological understanding has developed with regards to "human cloning". Nonetheless, then there is me, I tell the complete truth from my firsthand experiences *as a REM driven clone version of myself, unwillingly activated* at the cloning centers *by the Illuminati*, and I disclose everything I have seen the Illuminati do, and what the Illuminati continues to do as *REM driven* clone versions of themselves, as well as, divulge the Illuminati's technologies and secrets which have been unequivocally proven to me on more than one occasion [as technology which exists today], and because of this, now many people know what the truth is regarding the Illuminati, and what they do in complete secrecy (*REM driven human cloning*). The Illuminati are currently scrambling for a solution... the exposure of the Illuminati's *REM driven human* cloning subculture is **THE BIGGEST THING** happening in the world right now... **I'M ON THE EDGE OF GLORY... AND I'M HANGING ON A MOMENT OF TRUTH...** (LadyGagaVEVO 2011) performed by Lady Gaga written by Donald Marshall [*as a REM driven clone version of himself, at the cloning center*]...

[I am almost at a point where I will be completely freed from the Illuminati's *REM driven human* cloning subculture and I'll never have to be activated as a *REM driven* clone version of myself at the cloning center, again ("I'm on the edge of glory...") and I'm hanging on for the moment when the Illuminati's *REM driven human* cloning subculture is fully exposed and worldly known, and stopped by the populace ("and I'm hanging on a moment of truth")] **May 22, 2012 at 9:58pm**

May 22nd 2012

The aims of Global Future 2045 and the reality of REM driven human cloning

3SG1 posts a video about the GF2045 Avatar project (Канал пользователя gf2045 2012) *which seeks to make it a public reality of downloading human consciousness to Avatar bodies.*

Dmitry Itskov: Welcome to the Global Future 2045
Dmitry Itskov. GF2045 General chair
http://www.gf2045.com/

YOUTUBE.COM

3SG1: The "code word" in this presentation is: "Avatar body", which sounds suspiciously like *REM driven* human cloning.

DM: The Illuminati MADE the movie "Avatar" (2009) and based the concept of the movie Avatar (2009) from *REM driven* cloning technology, which the Illuminati have. I was speaking about REM driven cloning and consciousness transfer, as a reality, and as something the Illuminati do on a daily practice, long before the movie Avatar (2009) was ever made or thought of for a movie concept... REM driven human cloning and consciousness transfer, is similar to the concept of what is depicted in the movie Avatar (2009); however, in reality, a person's consciousness is not transferred to a blue-skinned avatar, as depicted in the 2009 James Cameron movie, but consciousness is transferred to a duplicate clone of the person; and the clone looks almost identical to the original person... However, there are subtle differences between the physical appearance of the REM driven clone, and the physical appearance of the original person. **May 23, 2012 at 3:30am**

May 22nd 2012

Celebrities and their doppelgangers, and the different types of human clones

3SG1 posts an article about celebrities and their doppelgangers (The Chive 2012) *to Donald Marshall's Facebook Timeline.*

Celebs and their doppelgangers (30 Photos)

THECHIVE.COM

3SG1: Wow! How much do Heath Ledger and Joseph Gordon Levitt look alike? Are they Clones? Check out the rest of the pictures.

DM: "Doppelgangers" as is mentioned in the title of the article, is what the German people, and German faction of the Illuminati at the cloning center call clones. I will explain later... I currently have a backlog of messages which I must reply to... I must reply to messages and email too [as well as, post on Facebook]... **May 23, 2012 at 5:48am**

DM: OK... well there are a few different types of clones... there are "duplication clones", such as the *REM driven* clones which I deal with; "re-animated clones" and "replication clones". **May 23, 2012 at 6:19am**

Re-animated human clones and the soulstone microchip implant

Re-animated human clones WITHOUT the soulstone microchip implant

DM: "Re-animated clones" (which can be referred to as 'dead people clones') –which are clones of original people which once lived; these re-animated clones (dead people clones) are clones of original people which previously lived on this earth; without the "soulstone microchip" (which is a microchip invented by the Illuminati, containing a flawed recording of an entire person's consciousness) re-animated clones develop a mind and personality of their own, different from the original person who previously lived. Without the soulstone microchip, the personalities of re-animated clones are shaped by the **circumstances** experienced, in the life of the re-animated clones, as well as, the **environments** experienced, in the life of re-animated clones. Although re-animated clones develop a personality of their own without the soulstone microchip, re-animated clones without the soulstone microchip tend to be dumber than original natural born human beings, because essentially clones are dumber, and this is just a side effect of human cloning.

Re-animated human clones WITH the soulstone microchip implant

DM: WITH the soulstone microchip inserted into the brain of a re-animated clone, the re-animated clone remembers the previous life experience of the original dead person, who lived on this earth. Although the re-animated clone can now remember her / his previous life experience as a consequence of the soulstone microchip inserted into the brain of the re-animated clone, a major side effect of the soulstone microchip inserted into the brains of re-animated clones is that: because there is a flawed recording of consciousness, of a dead person's consciousness overriding the consciousness of a clone, this tends to make re-animated clones WITH the soulstone microchip more impulsive; more negative than an original natural born human would be; as if there is "something missing"; and essentially, re-animated clones with the soulstone microchip inserted into their brains have a tendency to be: **rapists, child molesters, and paedophiles**. These re-animated clones with the soulstone microchip inserted into their brains have a tendency towards negativity, and impulsivity and believing "doing evil is good", whereas they may not have had such a tendency when they were originally a natural born human being (before death).

Re-animated clones WITH the soulstone microchip inserted into the clone's brain, relive life, **BUT**, re-animated clones WITH the soulstone microchip implant, relive life as a flawed, and negative version, of the original person who once lived; whereby the mind of the reanimated clone is not the same as the mind of the original person because it is a flawed recording of consciousness, operating the mind of the re-animated clone. This is similar to the movie "Pet Sematary" (1989), which is adapted from the Stephen King novel, with the same title (King 1983). Furthermore, I also refer to re-animated clones with the soulstone microchip in their brains as "Dead chip-heads" –because these are clones of dead people with microchips in their heads.

Replication clones

DM: "Replication clones" are clones of original people, which start life off as a baby, and go through the entire gestation process (9 months), similar to natural born human beings. Replication cloning can be achieved through surrogacy; -where a woman is implanted with the embryo containing the DNA of the person to be cloned; OR, replication cloning can also be achieved through the use of artificial wombs.

The reasons celebrities appear in public AS human clones

DM: Sometimes celebrities do appear in the public domain (television appearances, concerts, award shows etc.) **AS** cloned versions of themselves. For example, if the celebrity's original body has pimples on her or his face, OR, she or he has a cold sore, and physically does not look her or his best, then they may chose to appear in public as a cloned version of themselves. **May 23, 2012 at 6:19am**

DM: Moreover, Nicki Minaj was considering doing a music award show as a clone version of herself, because she had a cold sore, and she could not cover up the cold sore with makeup... However, clones are dumber than the original person, and Nicki Minaj was going to have to do plenty of talking at the music award show. *As REM driven clone versions of ourselves at the cloning center,* Nicki Minaj asked a *REM driven* clone version of me for a solution to her dilemma. The only thing which I could think of, and which I told *a REM driven clone version of* Nicki Minaj *when I was unwillingly activated as a REM driven clone at the cloning center,* was that she should wear a bandana over the lower part of her face during the award show, as if she was 'going to rob a bank'... Nicki Minaj actually took my advice, and appeared at the award show in her original body (and **NOT** as a clone) with a bandana covering the lower half of her face to hide her cold sore... Nicki Minaj looked ridiculous, but Lady Gaga does weirder things, so nobody thought twice to question why Nicki Minaj was wearing a bandana covering the lower half of her face.

Celebrities appear in public as human clones to avoid dangerous stalkers

DM: Other times when celebrities appear in public as cloned versions of themselves, is because they have a stalker who may kill the celebrity, and therefore it is safer for the celebrity to appear as a clone version of themselves rather than their original body.

The original celebrity is dead and now lives on through cloning technology

DM: Another example where celebrities may appear in the public as cloned versions of themselves includes times where the original celebrity may have died due to unforeseen circumstances. In such cases, the public are not informed that the celebrity did die. However, the celebrity who dies in actuality, is not seen or heard of in the public for some time, while at the same time that the celebrity who is not seen or heard of in the public, is revived through cloning technology, whereby the Illuminati grow (multiple) duplicate clones of the dead celebrity, because the celebrity who died makes the Illuminati too much money for the Illuminati to end that celebrity's image, and proclaim the celebrity as dead at the time the celebrity actually died. Consequently, sometimes the public are REALLY seeing a clone of the original celebrity who has died (but it has not been publicly announced that said celebrity did in fact die), walking around in public, and these re-animated clones (clones of dead people), grown via the process of duplication cloning are dumber, because this is a flaw of human cloning; everyone is slightly dumber as a clone version, than natural born humans. Furthermore, clones grown via the process of duplication cloning need to be replaced every six months to a year.

Therefore, because duplicate clones must be replaced at least once or twice a year, the Illuminati grows multiple clones at a time of celebrities who have actually died, so that the Illuminati can still have the celebrity appear in the public as a duplicate cloned version, in the place of the original celebrity who actually died, and continue to make money from the celebrity's image, although the celebrity is now a (permanent) clone. The Illuminati grows multiple clone bodies of the dead celebrity via duplication cloning, and handpick the clone bodies which resembles the physical appearance of the original person as closely as possible.

DM: Duplicate clones have small differences in their faces in comparison to the original person; sometimes the eyes of the duplicate clone are slightly different in comparison to the original person's eyes; sometimes the shape of the nose of the duplicate clone is different in comparison to the original person, and sometimes the wrinkles on the face of the duplicate clone is different from the original person etc. Sometimes duplicate clone bodies which are grown in the tanks filled with salty water end up being deformed. Deformed duplicate clone bodies do not bother the Illuminati; the Illuminati scraps deformed cloned bodies by throwing deformed cloned bodies into the wood-chippers at the cloning center, and start once again, to grow duplicate clone bodies of the original person who in actuality, died.

There is another way to live life again, which involves human cloning and microchip implants [the "soulstone microchip" –as briefly explained above]; however a detailed explanation of the soulstone microchip is for later... you will know all the information I have acquired through REM driven cloning technology, all in due time. I have to share the information about the Illuminati's *REM driven human* cloning subculture correctly and in the right order. **May 23, 2012 at 6:29am**

How pain suffered as a REM driven clone affects a person's original body

3SG2: Donald, you have a really good memory.

DM: Yes, my memory regarding the Illuminati's *REM driven human* cloning subculture is impeccable. Furthermore, with REM driven cloning and consciousness transfers, from the original person's body to the *REM driven* clone duplicate, your original body remembers and registers the pain suffered as a *REM driven* clone duplicate, in your original body too (because consciousness is linked (Petkova and Ehrsson 2008; Ehrsson 2013)). Moreover, while a person's consciousness resides in their *REM driven* clone duplicate, pain suffered as a *REM driven* clone hurts **JUST** the same as pain suffered in a person's original body in real life... overtime, pain suffered as a *REM driven* clone version of a person will give the person heart damage (in their original body), like I currently have (in my original body)... or continuous *REM driven* clone torture, will cause a person to have an aneurysm within hours while their consciousness resides in their *REM driven* clone duplicate... The Illuminati have secretly murder MANY people via REM driven cloning technology; **many**. **May 23, 2012 at 6:48am**

The unlikelihood of a "Clone Army"

3SG1 posts a link to an article about the possibility of the Pentagon having a secret cloning program (Unconfirmed Sources 2004) (although the source is unconfirmed).

> **Pentagon Reveals Secret Cloning Program - Unconfirmed Sources**
> Breaking twenty years of carefully guarded silence, the Pentagon's chief medical officer, Army Maj. Gen. Anne S. Thesia, admitted today that research has been conducted since the 1980's at Ft. Detrick, the Army's secret biowarfare laboratory, on stem cell technology, ...
> UNCONFIRMEDSOURCES.COM

3SG1: Donald, please have a look at the link above. It says that the Pentagon reveals a secret cloning program [I'd like to hear your thoughts].

DM: *As REM driven clone versions of themselves*, the Illuminati members have discussed the possibility of a clone army in front of me *when I have been unwillingly activated as a REM driven clone* at the cloning center. However, human clones are so dumb; I doubt a "clone army" would be effective. The Illuminati *REM driven clones*, are not telling me any secrets when they activate me as a *REM driven* clone at the cloning center lately... **May 24, 2012 at 12:13am**

May 22ⁿᵈ 2012

Clones of Illuminati members: Supriem Rockefeller

3SG1 posts an excerpt of an article taken from "Armageddon Conspiracy" [the full article can no longer be found on Armageddon Conspiracy, but is available on Hiduth (Hiduth 2015) or by clicking the image of the article below] *which discusses the aims "elite scientists" wish to achieve by perfecting human cloning, on Donald Marshall's Facebook Timeline.*

Supriem Rockefeller - Hiduth.com
Supriem Rockefeller - Is it possible for a human being to be possessed by Satan? The idea has been explored in a number of horror films, but there's a group
HIDUTH.COM | BY HIDUTH - CAN YOU HANDLE THE HIDDEN TRUTH ?

3SG1: Is Supriem David Rockefeller **ACTUALLY** an Illuminati mind controlled clone?

"The ancient mission of the Brotherhood of the Shadows was to master every aspect of the golem [which in Jewish legend is a clay figure brought to life by magic; "golem" can also be thought of as an "automaton" (a moving mechanical device made in imitation of a human being) or robot; and in this respect, "golem" can also be thought of as a "clone"] and its interactions with humans. In modern times, they have become experts in artificial intelligence, cybernetics, the human genome, genetic engineering, **CLONING** etc: every aspect of the "science of the double". Many are elite scientists, being paid vast salaries. They desire to produce a perfect simulacrum of a human being, like the "replicants" of the film Blade Runner. Many of them see it as purely a scientific endeavour, but the higher ranks of the Brotherhood have very different aims.

They want to create 1) "Manchurian Candidates" (perfect, disposable assassins), 2) "doubles" to take the place of leaders in dangerous situations or to produce airtight alibis for leaders while they are engaging in nefarious activities elsewhere, 3) simulacra of soldiers who can be sent on the most dangerous missions, 4) doppelgangers for use in psy-ops [Psychological Operations] against chosen targets (nothing is more psychologically disturbing than to suddenly encounter your own double), 5) young clones of old, dying members of the Old World Order into which their minds can be transferred so that they can be "reborn" in their prime."

DM: Oh my goodness! Where did you find this [information]? Everything you have quoted in the excerpt is ALL true... what on earth?! Whoever wrote that article must know [about the extent of the Illuminati's secret projects, and the Illuminati's *REM driven human* cloning subculture]! **May 23, 2012 at 5:22am**

DM: I knew I had seen that stupid looking guy [in reference to the coloured picture displayed above, on this page, of supposed "Supriem David Rockefeller" (with glaring blue eyes) – most likely as *REM driven* clone versions at the cloning center] somewhere before... and it is not Supriem... it's more like "Supreme" like "Supr-eeum" [David Rockefeller]. **May 23, 2012 at 7:13am**

DM: Yes, sometimes these Illuminati members are walking around, in public, as clones of themselves [Mark 3 clones or Mark 4 clones -which are independent clones; or they are replicated clones (grown from a baby upwards) of an original person who has died] and not as REM (sleep) driven clones (in public). **May 23, 2012 at 7:11pm**

3SG1: Wow! I did not know people could still see this photo [picture on page 31 in this document above, posted on Donald Marshall's Facebook Timeline], since Donald deleted me [off his friends list on Facebook]. I guess I was freaking him out [with my posts]!

3SG2: [That picture of Supriem David Rockefeller, looks like a] Hybrid or clone.

DM: No 3SG1, I did not remove you off my Facebook friends list because your posts were disturbing me; I removed you from my Facebook friends list because you and your malicious wife wanted to have a chat with me when we were activated by the Illuminati, as *REM driven* clone versions of ourselves at the cloning center. **April 25, 2013 at 10:49pm**

3SG3: So 3SG1, you and your wife visit the cloning center as *REM driven* clone versions? Please can you explain to us all what Donald is speaking of [with his disclosures *concerning the Illuminati's REM driven human cloning subculture*]?

3SG4: There is plenty of information on this site (Hiduth 2016). It seems I will be spending most of my nights reading. Thank you.

3SG3: Yes, I heard the same thing [which is referenced by Hiduth and Armageddon Conspiracy] about Supriem Rockefeller on the A.M.M.A.C.H Project website [when Supriem Rockefeller was mentioned in an interview]

3SG5: Supriem [David Rockefeller; pictured above, page 31] has got the same type of eyes as the corporate head of Nestlé [Paul Bulcke, Chief Executive Officer, Nestlé]. Having those types of eyes must be a "droned" thing [referring to "parasite human hosts", as a result of Vril; Vril and parasite human hosts will be explained at length in upcoming documents] or an obnoxious or rude person thing [to have those types of eyes]!

3SG6: And no more words from 3SG1!

3SG4: Have a read of someone else's [James Casbolt's] experiences regarding clones in Wales United Kingdom (Project Avalon 2008).

James Casbolt:Underground U.K. bases! -
Page 5 - Old Project Avalon Forum...

PROJECTAVALON.NET

3SG7: I have to catch up here. I also need to Google 'Who is James Casbolt?', as well as, 'Who is Supriem David Rockefeller?'

3SG8: I have had visions of nano women being created. When I have visions, I see myself creating these nano women or being part of the nano creations. I could share quite a few insights with you too Donald; it is too bad you do not live closer. I am in Washington State.

3SG9: There is some degree of Photoshop here [in reference to the picture of Supriem Rockefeller on page 31 of this document]; look at that neck and body!

3SG10: 3SG9, it is possible that the above photo of Supriem Rockefeller is edited using the photo editing software "Photoshop"; however, one of Photoshop's greatest attributes is that: nearly everything now, can be put down to 'Photoshop'.

3SG1: Paranoia [is a] big destroyer!

May 23rd 2012

WHERE is the "HARD evidence" for human cloning / REM driven cloning?

3SG1: Where is the evidence [for human cloning / REM driven cloning]?

DM: I have [hard] evidence... but I need more eyes to see the circumstantial evidence of human cloning / REM driven cloning which is evident and surrounds us at all times; to read and educate themselves on the science and technology of "cloning", "consciousness" and "the stages of sleep", and reach a point where they KNOW with certainty this is occurring, or at least reach a point, given what they have learned regarding "cloning", "consciousness" and "the stages of sleep" that they can accept there is a high probability all I am disclosing is in fact happening right underneath our very noses, covertly.

"Trans-humanism" also provides a great key for helping the casual observer who may not have come across such topics before, to understand the reality of what I am disclosing, regarding the Illuminati and their high advances in medicine, science and technology, because the trans-humanists do not hide their aims: which is mainly that they want to download consciousness to avatar bodies. People should also be **objective**, and not delude themselves in believing something is real, when it is not, and they should reach a point where they have plenty of verifiable evidences to form their own conclusions.

Therefore, for the casual observer who is unsure, and wants to know whether human cloning / REM driven cloning and the cloning centers are real or not, the first questions they really should be asking are: do I know and understand the science of "cloning" (even at a basic to intermediate level)?; do I know and understand the science of "consciousness" (even at a basic to intermediate level)?; do I know and understand the stages of sleep (even at a basic to intermediate level)?; and do I know and understand the concepts and ideologies of "Trans-humanism" (even at a basic to intermediate level)? -because most people have never heard of "Trans-humanism" and therefore the experiences I am divulging regarding REM driven cloning and the high advances in technology the Illuminati use in secret is well beyond some people's understanding because they do not have this foundation.

DM: I understand that hard evidence such as seeing video footage of the cloning center will help people accept this as reality much faster, but I have never visited the cloning center in my original body... nor are the Illuminati going to allow me to film video footage from inside the cloning center as a *REM driven* clone version of myself, and send video footage to my personal email for me to show the world. Furthermore, I don't know the exact location of the cloning center, because I have never been told exactly where it is by the Illuminati *REM driven clones*. Moreover, people should pay attention to the experiences they have while they sleep, because firsthand experience where people retain memories of the cloning center and all that I am disclosing, such as Gabriela Rico Jimenez (explained fully in "Experiences from the Cloning Center" Volume 1, pp. 33 - 35 (Marshall 2016a)) did when Gabriela Rico Jimenez was activated as *a REM driven* clone by the Illuminati, will be one of the greatest proofs for anyone who does not understand the science and technology involved in REM driven human cloning which I discuss, to be convinced that REM driven human cloning is indeed a reality.

Furthermore, I am **NOT** advocating that people should consider being activated as *REM driven* clones where they retain memories of their experiences, for them to be convinced that this is all true, because quite frankly: the cloning of human beings, especially unsuspectingly while they sleep is disgusting and abhorrent! However, I am suggesting that a practice carried out by the Illuminati, is that the Illuminati activate many random civilians worldwide as *REM driven* clone versions of original people... and in the unforeseen circumstance where a person may have experienced something very peculiar during their sleeping hours such as Gabriela Rico Jimenez did (Q69573 2012; Marshall 2016a, pp. 33 - 35), such an experience could possibly be a *REM driven* clone experience, and therefore it is important to pay attention to experiences which occur personal to oneself during sleep. I also need more eyes to see the circumstantial evidence regarding REM driven human cloning, otherwise, we'll never have an angry crowding demanding that low level Illuminati members submit to independent polygraph tests to prove the reality or the Illuminati's *REM driven human* cloning subculture unequivocally once and for all; nor will we have the opportunity to force the high level Illuminati members, such as [Former] Prime Minster Stephen Harper to tell the public the exact location of the above ground cloning center and the remaining cloning centers, if there isn't a large percentage of the population who are aware of the information I am disclosing, and **KNOW** it is a reality...

Besides some people know the Illuminati's *REM driven human* cloning subculture is real anyway... Anonymous (We Are Legion) were already aware that the Illuminati were cloning humans somehow [before these disclosures regarding the Illuminati's *REM driven human* cloning subculture]... However, Anonymous (We Are Legion) thought that the Illuminati were only involved in "replication cloning" (human cloning from a baby stage upwards), and Anonymous could not understand HOW cloning humans, where human clones start life off as babies would BENEFIT the Illuminati... However, Anonymous were overjoyed to have met me and heard and learned about "duplication cloning" and "REM driven technology" as well as, the many other different types of clones. Anonymous (We Are Legion) now understood that the Illuminati have the technology and capability to grow fully formed clones, whereby the clones are aged through the process of duplication cloning, to the point where the duplicate clone looks similar in likeness to the age of the original person.

DM: Anonymous (We Are Legion) were also pleased to learn that through *REM driven* cloning technology, the Illuminati communicates their biggest secrets at an undisclosed location as *REM driven* cloned versions of themselves. Furthermore, because of *REM driven* cloning technology, and consciousness transfer, this gives the Illuminati the functionality, of being in two places at once: their original body is asleep in one location, while the Illuminati members are active and walking around the same earth as cloned versions of themselves in a different location. *REM driven* cloning technology also gives the Illuminati the perfect alibis, because they can, and have done terrible things as *REM driven* clone versions of themselves in one location, but have the alibi of being at a completely different location to the places where the crimes were committed, and as a consequence, Illuminati members have escaped prosecution of many crimes because of this concealed advancement in technology.

The Illuminati also do their most deplorable acts as *REM driven* clone versions of themselves to innocent Canadians and Americans, as well as, many people of differing nationalities, worldwide. However, sometimes the Illuminati have real people in their original bodies, kidnapped and brought to the cloning center, to be victimised in front of the on-looking crowd of *REM driven* clones sitting in the arena. Many children are also cloned by the Illuminati, and used by the Illuminati for many aspects, for the Illuminati's amusement. I made the [Former] Canadian Prime Minister Stephen Harper cry (*as a REM driven clone version of himself*). *As a REM driven clone version of himself at the cloning center,* Stephen Harper believes he is going to be pulled (in his original body) from his home and lynched in the street by an angry large mob... *As a REM driven clone version, at the cloning center,* [Former] Canadian Prime Minister Stephen Harper expressed that "He wants to leave the country" as tears were flowing down his *REM driven* clone face... **May 23, 2012 at 10:09am**

3SG2: Where is this proof [*about human cloning / the Illuminati's REM driven human cloning subculture*]? I have been reading your accounts for a while and still no proof [*of human cloning or REM driven cloning*]. Children are being tortured daily, for real, by real cults, and they not being tortured "as clones"; they are being tortured as **REAL** children [*in their original bodies*].

3SG3: The situation Donald describes about the Illuminati's *REM driven* cloning subculture, is not so cool if you are a victim. The Illuminati's *REM driven* cloning subculture is **NOT** a joke! I have been investigating such phenomenon for many years, and the information Donald is divulging, fits into my years long worth of investigations.

3SG4: Donald, I have a suggestion: rather than sparring with the Illuminati [going back and for with the Illuminati *REM driven* clones], demand the location of the cloning center the next time the Illuminati activate you as a *REM driven* clone. Nobody in their right mind is going to 'confront' [Former Canadian Prime Minister] Stephen Harper based on your letter (Donald Marshall Proboards 2012a) [*regarding the Illuminati's REM driven human cloning subculture*] alone. Courts of law require evidence, therefore demand the location of the cloning center next time you are activated as a *REM driven* clone, and I will get someone to go to the cloning center.

3SG3: I will [go to the cloning center, in western Canada, once we have the exact location] 3SG4; I am also working on getting a lie detector machine to Donald as we speak, for Donald and his evil mother.

3SG4: [OK, it is great that you are doing that, however] we still need the exact location of the cloning center [in western Canada]. What if the Illuminati decide to close the cloning center in western Canada which Donald describes and move to a different location? We will still need live video footage of the cloning center [or one of these cloning centers] because a lie detector can prove Donald's experiences either happened, OR, Donald truly **'believes'** it happened.

3SG3: Fine [I understand 3SG4]... Nevertheless, I have a lot of allies here in British Columbia [Canada], where I have a sense this cloning facility is. My allies and I will either find this cloning center in western Canada, OR, we will destroy it after we have video evidence of the existence of the cloning center in western Canada. Either the above shall happen or we will force the low level Illuminati members to tell the truth, and in that respect I mean the local bad guys who protect these high level freaks. Hell, the Illuminati members are so into "torture", maybe we will use their own methods against them to get the information needed to destroy them [*and the Illuminati's REM driven human cloning subculture*]. I'm just joking [about the torture comment].

DM: OK 3SG4, [I understand what you are saying, however]...I do **NOT** just **'BELIEVE'** that the Illuminati's *REM driven* cloning subculture is happening, I **KNOW** wholeheartedly that this **IS** happening! I have my consciousness transferred on many occasions when I go to sleep, and I am unwillingly activated as a *REM driven* clone version of myself at the cloning center by the Illuminati; this is not something I BELIEVE is happening; I **KNOW** it is happening from firsthand experience, you only have to watch Gabriela Rico Jimenez (Q69573 2012; Marshall 2016a pp. 33 - 34) and the explanation I have given about Gabriela Rico Jimenez's *REM driven* cloning experience to realise there is something more happening in the background of this world, which is very disturbing... yes that something is the Illuminati's *REM driven human* cloning subculture!

3SG4, I can understand your argument, however, once a large majority of people understand the Illuminati's *REM driven human* cloning subculture, and what the Illuminati do with *REM driven* cloning technology and as *REM driven* cloned versions of themselves, members of the public can go to [Former Canadian] Prime Minister Stephen Harper and demand the exact location of the cloning center from Stephen Harper; Stephen Harper will crack under the pressure from the public and the cloning center will be found. Furthermore, other people involved in the Illuminati's *REM driven human* cloning subculture will have to give up the locations of the cloning center in western Canada, as well as, the location of other cloning centers, worldwide. I only know of cloning centers in the following places: western Canada, Mexico, Russia, America, and China. The Illuminati did not activate me as a *REM driven* clone version of myself, through the process of consciousness transfer, when I went to sleep, and entered REM sleep in my original body last night. We are winning! Moreover, 3SG2, the Illuminati members kidnap real children [natural born children], and bring these real children to the cloning center, to have the children tortured to death... **May 23, 2012 at 7:13pm**

3SG3: These Illuminati members are going to die! After the Illuminati members are dead, I will personally grab their dark souls and put their souls in a special hellish prison, just for them!

DM: The Illuminati members, as *REM driven clone versions of themselves*, torture real children to death at the cloning center(s) ... the Illuminati members also torture real children to death in other places, other than the cloning centers, in their original bodies and not as clones, in their waking life too... I'll explain the Illuminati members' motives, but I am worried I will lose people, and people will not believe what I have to say regarding the Illuminati's motives in regards to why the Illuminati torture people (clones and real people) to death, because as I have already said, it is so outrageous to think a human could do what the Illuminati members do to a defenceless animal, yet alone defenceless humans! Unless a person has witnessed what I must describe as the motives behind the Illuminati members' reasons for torturing humans to death, it is extremely difficult to fathom... but soon... I will disclose this information regarding the Illuminati's motives for human torture and human sacrifice soon... do not worry; in time, people will completely understand why I had to explain everything gradually, regarding the Illuminati's *REM driven human* cloning subculture. **May 23, 2012 at 7:16pm**

May 23rd 2012

Public figures who attend the cloning centers as REM driven clones

3SG1: Donald, I need to know if these people are at the cloning center too, or if they are Illuminati [members]: Tony Robbins [Anthony Robbins] (Self development Guru); Richard Branson (English Billionaire, and owner of Virgin); Tony Blair, as well as any other high profile British politicians and people aside from Queen Elizabeth II of course. Moreover, are Oprah Winfrey; Israeli Prime Minister Benjamin Netanyahu and other Israelis at the cloning center too?

DM: Okay. Yes, Richard Branson attends the cloning center as a *REM driven duplicate* clone version of himself. Richard Branson wanted to meet the "Song Guy". I've only seen a *REM driven* clone version of Tony Blair once (*while I was also activated as a REM driven clone duplicate, at the cloning center*). As a *REM driven clone version of himself*, Tony Blair said to *a REM driven clone version of* Queen Elizabeth II "Elizabeth is a deplorable woman for what she does, and he does not want to participate" –and Tony Blair's consciousness was deactivated from his *REM driven* clone; Tony Blair's *REM driven* clone fell limp [to the ground of the dirt arena], and Tony Blair was no longer active as a *REM driven* clone version of himself, at the cloning center. Moreover, before [Former British Prime Minister] Tony Blair was deactivated as a *REM driven* clone, at *the cloning center, as a REM driven clone,* Tony Blair actually said "Sorry" to me (*a REM driven clone version of me*) and mentioned that "He would be killed, if he tried to help me" –this experience happened many years ago.

DM: Oprah Winfrey also attends the cloning center *as a REM driven clone version of herself.* The leadership of Israel attends the cloning center *as REM driven cloned versions of themselves;* there are too many Israeli leaders who attend the cloning centers *as REM driven clone versions of themselves,* and this includes Israeli Prime Minister Benjamin Netanyahu... *As a REM driven clone version of myself,* I have seen a *REM driven* clone of Benjamin Netanyahu at the cloning center once. However, there are many, many, many, Jewish people who attend the cloning centers *as a REM driven cloned versions of themselves...* I am **not** racist... I do not like Nazis or Adolf Hitler, but as a matter of fact, there are more Jewish people who attend the cloning centers as *REM driven* cloned versions of original people than any other social class of people. **May 23, 2012 at 11:03am**

3SG1: So, some people CAN choose to be deactivated as *REM driven* cloned versions of themselves! They do not have to attend the cloning centers *as REM driven clone versions of themselves* against their will! [Yes, this has already been covered: some privileged members or some high profile people can choose, if they wish, to be activated as *REM driven* clone versions of themselves or not]. I hate all forms of genocide; the Holocaust was one of many genocides. However, the Jews seem to have gotten a monopoly on the world's sympathy for the Holocaust.

Moreover, thanks to the Jewish ownership of Hollywood, the Jews have also gained control of our media, and our financial structure. Ironically, it is the Jews who follow "The Talmud" and worship the devil [follow Luciferian philosophies and ideologies], whereby the Talmud inculcates ["inculcate" [in-Kuhl-keyt] -to implant by repeated statement; teach persistently or earnestly] in them a lust for blood, and they have the most gruesome rituals for **REAL** torture on **REAL** babies and people. Therefore, it is not surprising that the cloning centers are full of Jews, who attend cloning centers *as REM driven clone versions of themselves*!

3SG2: 3SG1, the Jews have the monopoly on the world's sympathy yet you hate ALL forms of genocide? What kind of double speak is that? Give me a break.

May 24th 2012

REM driven Clone Sex (with celebrities)

3SG1: Which celebrities have you had [*REM driven clone*] sex with?

DM: HAHA! THERE IS NOT ENOUGH TIME TO TYPE ALL OF THE CELEBRITIES WHO I HAVE HAD REM DRIVEN CLONE SEX WITH! HAHA! Having sex with celebrities as a *REM driven* clone version of oneself is not as exciting as people would think it would be. The *REM driven clone versions of the* celebrities STANK BADLY! The celebrities did not shower or wash themselves when they were activated as *REM driven* clone versions of themselves at the cloning center. OH MY GOODNESS what a stench!

DM: The celebrities would have their consciousness transferred to the same *REM duplicate driven* clone body for months at a time... and because they did not shower or wash the *REM driven* clone duplicate body they would have their consciousnesses transferred to, and have sex with multiple guys without showering or deodorising their *REM driven* clone duplicate body, the celebrities smelled awfully (*as REM driven clone duplicate versions*). *As a REM driven clone version of myself,* the Illuminati *REM driven clones* would kill me as a *REM driven* clone *version of myself* in some strange way at least once every two days at the cloning center... and then it turned into killing *me as a REM driven clone version of myself* everyday or every time I was unwillingly activated as a *REM driven* clone *version of myself* at the cloning center. Consequently, I had fresh and new *REM driven* clone duplicate bodies which my consciousness resided in, and my *REM driven* clone duplicate bodies were more or less 'literally fresh from the cloning tubes', and therefore I did not smell as *REM driven* clone *version of myself* like the celebrities did, because my consciousness was inhabiting new *REM driven* clone duplicate bodies whenever I was activated unwillingly by the Illuminati as a *REM driven* clone, unlike the celebrities who had their consciousnesses reside in the same *REM driven* clone body for months at a time.

The celebrities figured that it was a waste of time to shower, and concluded that if they began showering and washing themselves then they would have to shower and wash themselves as *REM driven* clone duplicate alternatives every night they were activated as *REM driven* clone versions of themselves at the cloning center, and therefore the celebrities became slack and lazy in regards to basic hygiene as a concern. It was nice and fun to have *REM driven* clone sex with a *REM driven* clone version of Whitney Houston earlier on in her career when she was young... however, after having *REM driven* clone sex with someone like Whitney Houston (*a REM driven clone version of Whitney Houston*), a random *REM driven* clone version of an old woman would want to have *REM driven* clone sex with me [oh god!]... Or Queen Elizabeth II *as a REM driven clone version of herself,* would want to have *REM driven* clone sex with me... If I said "No I do not want to have [*REM driven clone*] sex with an old woman or Queen Elizabeth II" for that matter, I would be tortured by the Illuminati *REM driven* clones *as a REM driven clone version of myself,* and would be **forced** to have *REM driven* clone sex with the old women (who are REM driven clones of original people) anyway, as well as, Queen Elizabeth II *as a REM driven clone version of herself.*

Therefore *as a REM driven clone version of myself at the cloning center,* whenever I was forced into a position where I had to have *REM driven* clone sex with old women or Queen Elizabeth II for example (*as a REM driven clone of herself*), I would breathe through my mouth and clamp my eyes shut [tightly]. I asked Queen Elizabeth II *as a REM driven clone version of herself,* when I was older and activated as a *REM driven* clone *version of myself* at the cloning center "Why would you want to [*have REM driven clone sex with me*]?" I had a child's sized genital, back in the days when Queen Elizabeth II *as a REM driven clone version of herself* forced me into positions to have *REM driven* clone sex with her and I told her "It could not have been that fun for her [*to have REM driven clone sex with me as a REM driven clone version of myself, when I had a child's sized genital*]" and as a *REM driven clone version of herself* Queen Elizabeth II replied "It is the knowledge that you are doing [something] wrong and you will not be caught... it makes you feel ultimately powerful!... Also, it is having power over another human being!"

DM: Queen Elizabeth II *as a REM driven clone version of herself* wanted to have *REM driven* clone sex with me *whenever I was activated unwillingly as a REM driven clone* because of all the songs which I made as a *REM driven* clone version of myself. The Illuminati *REM driven* clones, the celebrities, the politicians, the wealthy, and just about anyone who attended the cloning center(s) as *REM driven* clone versions of themselves were awestruck towards me... they were fascinated by me beyond belief... I was the only person the Illuminati had ever found through the process of transferring original peoples' consciousnesses unsuspectingly while they slept (*at home in their beds*) to their *REM driven* clone duplicates and activated as *REM driven* cloned alternatives, at the cloning center(s), who could make songs consistently... and super songs consistently [which the public enjoys, which unfortunately the Illuminati profits from]! **May 24, 2012 at 10:14pm**

3SG2: I guess that is where Justin 'Beaver' [Justin Bieber] came from.
[In other words, 3SG2 implies Justin Bieber got the songs which he sings from attending the cloning center *as a REM driven clone version of himself*].

DM: Yes, Justin Bieber attends the cloning center *as a REM driven clone version of himself*, as does Selena Gomez. I made all the songs Justin Bieber and Selena Gomez perform since the start of both their careers, *as a REM driven clone version of myself* from the cloning center. *As a REM driven clone version of myself*, I made all of Justin Bieber's and Selena Gomez's official and super-hit songs... Justin Bieber TRIED to be evil like the Illuminati *REM driven* clones, when he was activated as a *REM driven* clone *version of himself* at the cloning center; *as a REM driven clone version of himself*, Justin Bieber hurt me a little as a *REM driven clone version of myself*, but then he said "He felt like a coward for hurting me [as a *REM driven* clone], and that he would **not** participate in harming me [as a *REM driven* clone *version of myself*]". Phil Reece on the other hand, who is a Commissionaire (doorman in uniform) for the Canadian Security Intelligence Service (C.S.I.S), was always looking for an excuse to talk and be seen at the cloning center whenever Phil Reece was activated as a *REM driven* clone *version of himself*. Consequently, when Justin Bieber as a *REM driven* clone said "He did not want to harm me, and would not participate..." during that moment, Phil Reece *as a REM driven clone* jumped over the hockey boards in the arena and ran at me in haste, as if I was going to get away, however, *as a REM driven clone version of myself*, I was chained to the same black wooden cross which the Illuminati *REM driven* clones have chained me to, multiple times, when they wish to torture me *as a REM driven clone version of myself*; therefore I wasn't going to escape in any direction. Justin Bieber *as a REM driven clone version of himself* had to jump out of the way *as a REM driven clone version of* Phil Reece dashed towards me and proceeded to hammer (punch) me in the face repeatedly... until Phil Reece *as a REM driven clone* got tired in his efforts and was out of breath... Although Justin Bieber does not participate in harming me *as a REM driven clone version of myself*, Justin Bieber still basically sold his soul to "the cloners" [the Illuminati] and Justin Bieber has given permission for the Illuminati to transfer his consciousness to his *REM driven* clone duplicate, whenever Justin Bieber's original body sleeps, and enters REM sleep... just like the other celebrities have given the Illuminati permission to transfer their consciousnesses to their *REM driven* clone duplicate alternatives whenever their original bodies sleep, and enter REM sleep... Justin Bieber, however, is not as bad as most of the other celebrities who attend the cloning center *as REM driven clone versions of themselves*. **May 25, 2012 at 1:33am**

May 23rd 2012

REM driven clone torture and victimisation

3SG1: Donald, how do you [*as an original, natural born person*] feel victimisation, if it is your [*REM driven*] clone that is the one being victimised?

DM: Okay. I will explain. When a person is activated as a *REM driven* clone through the process of consciousness transfer from their original body to the *REM driven* clone located at the cloning center (*which is at a different location far from a person's home or where a person's original (real) body is sleeping*), the experience of being a *REM driven* clone is nothing like a dream or nightmare, where the scenarios and events are fuzzy, incoherent or nonlinear. In actuality, it is the same consciousness which belongs to a person, which temporarily inhabits the *REM driven* clone body, while the original person's body is still asleep, and therefore, a person is simultaneously asleep and awake, at the same time, walking around the SAME earth at the SAME time. A person is asleep in their original body, however, they are awake, and walking around the same earth, only in a different location from where their original body is sleeping, as a *REM driven* human clone version of themselves... and it is the consciousness of the person which controls the *REM driven* clone.

Moreover, the experience of being a *REM driven* clone at the cloning center is exactly like it is now; the experience is **CLEAR** as daylight... and the difference between having an original person's consciousness inhabit their *REM driven* clone version temporarily while they original person sleeps, in comparison to waking life where a person's consciousness resides in their original body, is that: as a *REM driven* clone version of oneself, experiencing life and the same earth, people are dumber as *REM driven* clone versions of themselves; it is a side effect of *REM driven* human cloning technology that nobody is immune from. **May 24, 2012 at 7:54pm**

[The fact that people are slightly dumber as *REM driven* cloned versions, in comparison to when consciousness resides in their original body, may be a result between the frequencies between REM states of consciousness while a person sleeps, and the frequencies manifesting in awake states of consciousness during a person's waking life. REM frequency is similar in wave-like pattern, to the wave like pattern and frequencies when a person is awake, but not exactly. REM frequency appears erratic in its wave-like pattern in certain instances, and this could possibly lead to one explanation of the dumbness and impulsivity of clones and REM driven clones: frequency plays a vital role. See Krugman (2008) and National Sleep Foundation (2016) for more information about the different states of frequencies, and the similarities between REM frequency and awake-state frequency. It is **highly recommended** that the reader seeks the two aforementioned sources above, to gain further understanding of brainwave frequencies during REM stage consciousness and awake-state consciousness. The two sources mentioned above contain graphs, tables and figures, which help to easily understand the discussion being presented regarding brainwave frequencies].

DM: Moreover, the Illuminati have the option of turning the pain sensors of *REM driven* clones completely off or turning the pain sensors past the normal threshold of pain, a person will experience in their original body. Furthermore, because the Illuminati, can turn the pain sensors of *REM driven* clones past the normal threshold for pain, a person will experience in their original body, the Illuminati can make the experience of *REM driven* clone torture excruciatingly painful, when a person's consciousness resides in a *REM driven* clone, and more painful, than the pain a person would feel if their consciousness was inhabiting their original body. **May 24, 2012 at 7:55pm**

DM: The torture I suffered at the cloning center *as a REM driven clone version of myself* was excruciatingly painful, to the point that: in approximately 90% of the incidences where I was tortured as a *REM driven* clone *version of myself*, the Illuminati had my *REM driven* clone pain sensors on at the normal threshold of pain a person will experience in their original body, or at a lower threshold of pain than a person will feel in their original body, as the Illuminati tortured me as a *REM driven* human clone *version of myself.*

Accordingly, because it is the same consciousness of a person which gets transferred from their original body to their *REM driven* clone duplicate, whereby a person experiences life on the SAME earth while their original body sleeps, "time" (as a construct measured in hours minutes, seconds, etc.) ticks away at the same interval, because a person is experiencing the SAME earth, only in this instance, as a *REM driven* clone version of themselves. Therefore, six hours spent asleep (*after a person has reached REM sleep, and had her / his consciousness transferred to their REM driven clone*) in a person's original body, is equivalent to six hours of spent at the cloning center as REM driven clone version, (*if a person had their consciousness transferred to their REM driven clone when she or he went to sleep*). Therefore "time" such as hours, minutes, seconds etc. progresses at the same interval, when a person becomes activated as a *REM driven* clone version of themselves, because it is the same earth a person experiences, as a *REM driven* clone, and therefore "time" passes at the same intervals during *REM driven* human cloning experiences, as it does during a person's waking life –whereby consciousness resides in a person's original body, during waking life. **May 24, 2012 at 7:56pm**

DM: The "Relative time" (Fuller 2008) spent getting tortured as a *REM driven* clone version of oneself, causes a "time dilation" (Fuller 2008) which appears to make "time" or the experience spent as a *REM driven* clone, go much slowly and lasting much longer, when one is getting tortured as a *REM driven* clone of oneself, although "time", in actuality, continues to proceed at the same interval, of hours, minutes, seconds etc. **May 24, 2012 at 7:56pm**

["Relative time" is the difference between two events (or objects), measured by observers, and personal to the observers, and from these movements, observers infer 'a passage of time' (Fuller 2008). For example: two people talking with each other where both are having a wonderful experience, could spend four hours talking in real time, but when asked 'How long did the passage of time feel like?' The people involved could say something like 'Time went by very quickly; it feels like we were only in each other's company for half an hour'.

Or, in a different example: if a person is performing a task considered boring, menial and monotonous, then the passage of time will feel much longer to the person whose duty it is to perform said task, although in actuality, time still progresses at the same intervals: hours, minutes, seconds etc. This is why the passage of "time" feels much longer to the observer (the person getting tortured as a *REM driven* clone), when one is getting tortured as a *REM driven* clone version of themselves, because it is the event (*getting tortured*), which makes the "relative time" (or passage of time) seem much longer to the observer (*the person getting tortured as a REM driven clone version of themselves*) in comparison to the actual time, which still ticks at the same intervals, of hours, minutes, seconds etc.]

DM: Moreover, when a person is getting tortured as a *REM driven* clone version of themselves, and because relative time is progressing at a much slower rate, it is common for people to start to pray that they wake up in their original bodies, so that the torture suffered as a *REM driven* clone version will end for them (and their consciousness), because the awake consciousness of an original person, overrides the consciousness in a *REM driven* clone body. With me, as time is passing when I am being tortured as a *REM driven* clone version of myself, the Illuminati *REM driven* clones get bored of torturing me *as a REM driven clone version* after a while and then the Illuminati *REM driven human* clones wish to talk to me, as *REM driven* clone version of ourselves at the cloning center.

"New Donny, please." –they will say; which is an order for someone in the control-room of the cloning center to transfer my consciousness into a new *REM driven* clone body belonging to me. The Illuminati have made more *REM driven* duplicate clone bodies of me than anyone else, and they have killed me as a *REM driven* clone version (*while my consciousness resided in the REM driven clone bodies*), **over several thousand times.** Sometimes the Illuminati *REM driven* clones **killed FIVE** *REM driven* clone duplicate bodies **of me, a night,** whereby my consciousness was transferred to each of the five *REM driven* clone duplicate bodies, in one night, where I died five times in one evening, as a *REM driven* clone version of me. Furthermore, because consciousness is linked (Petkova and Ehrsson 2008; Ehrsson 2013), I would suffer the consequences of being tortured as a *REM driven* clone version of myself in my original body with either heart lurches, or massive and painful headaches and head rushes, in my original body. **May 24, 2012 at 7:58pm**

DM: Oh my! I am sweating (*in my original body*) just thinking about and explaining how I feel victimisation in my original body, as the real me, when it is my *REM driven* clone which suffers torture at the hands of the Illuminati (*REM driven clones*). Furthermore, when a person wakes up in their original body from sleeping and having experienced being activated as a *REM driven* clone version of themselves, whereby the person suffered *REM driven* clone torture, the experience of *REM driven* cloning, is not like remembering a dream [or nightmare]. The experience of *REM driven* cloning is **clear as daylight**, and therefore the experience of being a *REM driven* clone **is like remembering the previous day's events**. As a reader, can you picture what you did yesterday, or even just the highlight of your day (?) and seeing and experiencing everything happening clearly in a sequential and logical order (?) –well that is what it is like to experience life as a *REM driven* clone version of oneself (after waking up in your original body from the experience of being a *REM driven* clone).

Moreover, when a person suffers the experience of *REM driven* clone torture, provided the person is not "memory suppressed" as a *REM driven* clone version of themselves: once a person wakes up, and gets out of bed, in their original body, they will have a memory which follows a **linear and sequential sequence on this earth, clear as daylight**, and the person will also experience the world again in their original bodies clear as daylight (just like you are experiencing the world, clear as daylight, at this very moment, while you read this document). However, because a person suffered tortured when she / he was activated as a *REM driven* clone version of themselves at the cloning center, once the person wakes up from sleep and is experiencing life in their original bodies, she / he will begin to have heart lurches or heart palpitations in their original bodies. Other times, as a consequence of suffering *REM driven* clone torture, a person will experience the side effect of having massive and painful head rushes and headaches in their original body, which may lead them to question whether the heart palpitations are early warning signals of a heart attack, and whether the intense headaches or head rushes will lead to the person suffering an aneurysm or not in their original bodies during waking life (as a result of *REM driven* clone torture). **May 24, 2012 at 7:59pm**

May 23rd 2012

Understanding REM driven cloning:

The same consciousness resides in the REM driven clone body

3SG1: I am sorry Donald, but I am still confused [by the narrative]... when the Illuminati 'clone you [in]' [Donald Marshall]... do you [Donald Marshall] feel what the Illuminati are doing to your [REM driven] clone, a [REM driven] clone that is located at the facility [cloning center, and different to your real body]?

DM: When I use the term 'clone me in' I am referring to the Illuminati growing a *REM driven* duplicate (clone) body of me, through the process of regenerative medicine, science and technology, and transferring my consciousness from my original, natural born body, to my *REM driven* clone. Where you may find confusion is that you may be thinking of two different bodies, and asking how does pain experienced in a body separate to a person's original body, affect a person's original body? The answer to that question is simply: it is the **same consciousness** which resides in the *REM driven* duplicate clone body during REM sleep. Furthermore, because consciousness is transmutable, adaptable and linked (Petkova and Ehrsson 2008; Ehrsson 2013), my consciousness perceives my experiences to be as "real as real" (and they are) when I am experiencing the world in a *REM driven* human clone body, and because it is the **same consciousness** residing in the *REM driven* clone body (which allows me to be in two places at once: asleep at home in my original body, and awake as a *REM driven* clone at the cloning center), pain felt as a *REM driven* clone, means I display biological and physiological responses in my original body, because my consciousness is registering the pain suffered as a *REM driven* clone, as IF it were pain suffered in my original body, which leads to the side effects suffered in my original body during my waking hours. It is the CONSCIOUSNESS which registers the pain, therefore leading to physiological and biological responses and side effects in my original body, although I am tortured as a *REM driven* human clone version of myself and not in my original body.

[Readers should review Ehrsson's (2013) video documentary, to further understand how consciousness is transmutable, adaptable and linked, as well as, how it is possible to experience the world through a different body, reviewed through scientific experiments. The video documentary (Ehrsson 2013) also highlights how pain suffered in a body, different from a person's original body, can cause a person to display physiological and biological responses in a person's original body, because it is the perception, that a person's consciousness is no longer in their original body, but their consciousness is actually in a different body that is experiencing pain, which causes people to display physiological and biological responses in their original bodies –although the original body is not being harmed. This is similar to how *REM driven* human clone torture, can cause a person to suffer a heart attack or aneurysm in their original body. It is the consciousness which registers the pain].

May 23rd 2012

How do we know we are talking to the real Donald Marshall and not a clone?

3SG1: Is it possible I am talking to one of your [*REM driven*] clones now [via Facebook]... and not to the real [original and natural born] Donald Marshall?

DM: [No. You are **not** talking to a *REM driven* clone version of me. I am a natural born person, posting on Facebook about the Illuminati's *REM driven human* cloning subculture, during my waking hours of life.

I am only ever a clone, *a REM driven clone version of me*, while my original body sleeps, and reaches REM sleep, whereby I have my consciousness transferred, from my original body to my *REM driven* clone. This means I must reach REM sleep (*for which rapid eye movement (REM) sleep, is a brainwave frequency, and brainwave state the body gets into; 90 -110 minutes after first falling asleep*) before I unwillingly have my consciousness transferred into a different body, a *REM driven* clone body (*operating on REM frequency*) by the savagery of the Illuminati].

May 23rd 2012

The Reality of Human Cloning

When did the Illuminati start to clone human beings?

3SG1: How long [how many years] have the Illuminati been cloning human beings?

DM: [The Illuminati first started to clone humans after World War II; approximately 1944 / 1945; so over 70 years ago. REM driven human cloning technology was perfected after World War II (1944 / 1945)]

Initial factors which stifle peoples' ability to accept the reality of human cloning

[When most people first hear of the statement that human beings have been cloned as early as 1945, and in complete secrecy, they find that statement very disparaging and difficult to accept, and there are many, many reasons for this]

The Environment

[Firstly, the current environment we live in does not overtly demonstrate or reveal the reality of human cloning; however, very subtly and covertly, our environment does demonstrate, and reveal the reality of human cloning. When one begins to really pay attention and focus on this topic, as well as, hone in on this topic; one's reticular activation system (RAS) (make-your-goals-happen (no date); innovateus c.2013; TimeMasteryCoach 2013) will then start to show her / him many, many instances in this world regarding the reality of human cloning; inferences which one may have seen thousands of times before, but one never paid much attention to, which will now grab one's attention like never before, and demonstrate to her / him many more instances of the reality of human cloning. This happens, because, a person's reticular activation system is now focused on seeing if there is truth to the disclosure of the Illuminati's *REM driven human* cloning subculture, and there is truth to this disclosure, however the truth about the reality of human cloning is conveyed subtly, and discreetly, in our environment. Reticular activation system (RAS) is one of the most important parts of our brains, and RAS has a great influence over cognition (our abilities to process or acquire knowledge, and understand through thought, experiences and our senses). The RAS is considered the brain's "attention center" and acts like the filter between a person's conscious mind and their subconscious mind. At anyone one time there are millions, upon millions of data and information around us; our brains can only process so much information at any one time, and therefore the RAS acts as a filter against the data which is around us, and ensures we (consciously) process information deemed 'important', while other information gets 'filtered out' (make-your-goals-happen (no date); innovateus c.2013; TimeMasteryCoach 2013). Consequently, when one starts to focus on the topic of the Illuminati's *REM driven human* cloning subculture, his / her reticular activation system will begin to reveal to him / her, the many, many instances in songs, movies, books, television, etc. and more or less the whole of human culture, where there are hints and references to human cloning or REM driven human cloning]

Technological Advancements

[Secondly, the public is **thousands of years** behind in terms of technological advancements. This is another statement which is difficult for most people to accept at first; it is not hundreds of years worth of technological advancements, but **thousands of year's worth of technological advancements**, that the military (and the Illuminati) have and use in comparison to the technology the public is accustomed to and uses on a regular basis. Therefore topics such as "consciousness transfer to a substrate body"; "sleep (REM) driven cloning" (where a person goes to sleep, only to "wake up" in a clone body of themselves); "human cloning" (even if it is just "replication cloning": growing clones of humans, where the human clones start off life from a baby and mature to adulthood) all seem like 'science-fiction' to anyone who has **never** considered the occult (hidden) world; or paid **extensive attention** to technological advancements in this world, as well as, the directions of research and development opportunities, technology wise, and has come to the realisation, through **extensive attention and research:** that many, many technological advancements are withheld from the public during their initial inception, as well as initial completion. Furthermore, there are patents for many, many advances in technology, which were invented, or were being researched many decades ago, which demonstrates there were research and development opportunities being undertaken, with the hope to create certain technologies many decades ago.

Consequently, a difficult reality to accept, for the casual observer who has stumbled across this information initially: is that all the technology which the public sees around themselves in their environment, on a daily basis, is **not** the pinnacle of humanity's technological capabilities; and in reality, the highest advances in technology are kept underground, in deep underground military bases, far removed from the senses, imaginations, and perceived reality of what is technologically capable; the general public are kept uniformed or misinformed in regards to such technological advancements. Although, having said the above, it is easier for most people to accept that advances in technologies are usually trialled, tested, used and weaponized by the military first, before said technologies ever become available for public consumption; that is IF said technologies ever do become available for public consumption. Therefore, for the reader who truly desires to know and understand that human beings have been cloned since as early as the 1940s, it is best to seek George Green's interview (Project Camelot 2008a; 2008b) whereby Green corroborates the disclosure of the Illuminati's *REM driven* human cloning subculture by confirming he too, knows from firsthand experience that human beings have been cloned since the 1940s. Furthermore, readers should also seek Phil Schneider, who through his whistle-blowing disclosure, informed the public that, military technology advances at a rate of 44 years for every 1 year (12 months) which passes in comparison to the technology the public sees, uses, and is accustomed to (Schneider 1995; 1996; Open Minds 2011). Therefore at a ratio of 44:1, this vindicates that every 8 days (1 divided by 44 = 0.023; 0.023 multiplied by 365.25 days in a year = 8.40 days; "365.25" accounts for leap years), the military achieves 1 years worth of technological advancements equivalent to what the public realises after every 12 months which passes]

[The fact that the military is capable of accomplishing such technological advancements rapidly, at a rate of every 8 days equivalent to what the public realises technologically, after every 12 months, helps to vindicate the Illuminati's *REM driven human cloning* subculture, consciousness transfer to substrate bodies; sleep (REM) driven human cloning; and human cloning as realities which currently exist today. Furthermore, such a rapid rate in technological advancement achieved by the military, vindicates that such realities mentioned above, have existed for many decades (since the 1940s, in complete secrecy) and are **NOT** concepts relegated to the genre of science-fiction, because in truth, humanity's technological capabilities advances at a rapid rate; at a ratio of 44:1, in terms of military technological advancements in comparison to the technological advancements the public sees and is accustomed to. Therefore, it must be the will of the reader, which drives him or her, to realise the truth about the Illuminati's *REM driven human* cloning subculture, as well as, his or her will, which drives him or her to know and realise the rapid rate of humanity's technological capabilities, because such an examination will further help to demonstrate to the reader the reality of the Illuminati's *REM driven human* cloning subculture; it will also help to reveal to the reader that there are many, many advances in technologies, available today, which are **WITHELD**, which would benefit humanity as a collective, and further demonstrate to the reader that the technologies which he or she sees, in his or her environment, is not all that is currently available technologically, or the pinnacle of humanity's technological accomplishments.

Furthermore, by exploring sources such as George Green (Project Camelot 2008a; 2008b), who confirms through his first hand experience, that humans have been cloned since then 1940s; and Phil Schneider who explains the military's might, in terms of technological advancements achieved, compared to the technological accomplishments the public realises (Schneider 1995; 1996; Open Minds 2011), this will help one to better understand that human cloning (and more) is a reality which has already been achieved. Moreover, in reality and practicality, humanity is **NOT** at the stage of debating whether humanity should clone humans or not, because such a reality was achieved over 70 years ago in complete secrecy. Presently speaking, humanity **IS** at a stage whereby the cloning of human beings **MUST** end!]

[Human beings have been grown as human clones, in complete secrecy and used for the most abhorrent purposes conceivably imaginable, to the point where natural born humans are even in danger of being victims of REM driven human cloning (which is a form of human cloning), or natural born people are **already** victims of REM driven cloning, whereby these natural born humans are activated against their will, through the process of consciousness transfer, whenever they sleep, and enter REM sleep, to REM driven clone duplicate version of themselves, whereby, as a REM driven duplicate clone version of themselves, these victims of REM driven cloning, must bend to the Illuminati's will. This is how far technology has advanced today in complete secrecy; this is why we as "humanity" can no longer debate whether humanity should clone humans or not, because it is a reality which has already happened! Consequently, we **ARE** at a stage where we must realise the reality of such advances in science and technology involved with the Illuminati's *REM driven human* cloning subculture, and bring an end to such an injustice on earth, and end the Illuminati's *REM driven human* cloning subculture!]

Personal Biases

[A third reason why some people may find difficulty accepting the reality of the Illuminati's *REM driven human* cloning subculture, and the fact that human beings have been cloned as early as the 1940s, is to do with the issues of personal biases. The topic of human cloning being a current reality which exists today, and has existed in secrecy for over 70 years, and is indeed a reality, just makes people feel initially uncomfortable, fearful, disgusted, offended, angry, and a whole myriad of emotions. Some people do not like to even conceive the idea of human cloning, yet alone realise it is a reality which currently exists, because for them, the reality of human cloning removes the "uniqueness" of the human experience, and therefore a topic and a reality such as this, offends them]

[The key and most important factor here is to **be objective**; we all have personal biases and opinions, as well as, beliefs which we adhere to. It is **NOT** the intent of the messenger (Donald Marshall) or messengers (people helping Donald Marshall to expose the Illuminati's *REM driven human* cloning subculture) to offend the opinions, and belief systems personal to individuals; rather it is the intent of the messengers to **ALERT** the people they care most about in their lives, in regards to a reality which affects the livelihood and wellbeing of their close family and friends. Donald Marshall and his messengers are **NOT** the ones who took away the 'uniqueness of the human experience' (as some have suggested) by growing human beings as clones; activating human beings as *REM driven* clone versions while they sleep and making human beings perform tasks to a third-party's demands etc. Therefore, **be objective**, and make the distinction between the person informing you of bad news; and the people committing the actions detailed in the unfavourable news; it is the people committing the actions detailed in the unfavourable news we must concentrate our efforts on; and as the old adage goes: "Do not shoot the messenger" (Do not blame the messenger(s), as being the one(s) responsible for sharing the unfavourable information received; **make the distinction**)]

[Moreover, for individuals who still have strong personal biases, and find it difficult to accept the reality of the Illuminati's *REM driven human* cloning subculture and the fact that human beings have been cloned since the 1940s.... it is best to **CALM DOWN**, and look at this information **objectively**. Try as best as possible to put your personal biases to one side, until you have reached a place where you can categorically debunk this information, or categorically conclude that this information is indeed true. Once you have reached a stage where you can categorically conclude that the information regarding the Illuminati's *REM driven human* cloning subculture is in fact true; concentrate the anger and hurt that you feel against the Illuminati, and help humanity expose the Illuminati's *REM driven human* cloning subculture, so that eventually, humanity can bring an end to such injustice!]

Cloning Center

May 18th 2012

Visual image SIMILAR to the cloning center in western Canada

3SG1 posted the following comment and photo (below) on Donald Marshall's Facebook Timeline.

3SG1: After a long and gruesome sword fight [*as REM driven clone versions*] at the cloning center, [*as a REM driven clone*] Donny looks back to make sure all the [*other REM*] clones he just slayed are really dead. The victory is hollow because [*as a REM driven clone version*] Donny will most likely be chained to a black wooden cross and will be very painfully tortured to death [*as a REM driven clone version*] for no other reason than for the pleasure of the evil Illuminati members *as a REM driven clone versions of themselves* at the cloning center. At the cloning center arena, it is either: kill, or be killed; obey evil or die! Some *REM driven* clones sitting in the stands whistle and cheer for Donny, other *REM driven* clones boo and hiss. Phil Reece, Commissionaire (doorman in uniform) for the Canadian Security Intelligence Service (C.S.I.S), *and also a REM driven clone version at the cloning center*, anxiously awaits the indication from *the REM driven clone version of* the old, fat and ugly Queen "Evil-lizard-breath's" [Queen Elizabeth II's] signal. *As a REM driven clone version*, Commissionaire Phil Reece, can hardly wait to show the on-looking crowd of *REM driven* clones just how evil he really is, by painfully, and slowly torturing, and brutally raping, and killing more people, as *REM driven* clone versions...

DM: The picture you have posted is nearly identical to the cloning center in Canada, which I attend when I am unwillingly activated as a *REM driven* clone by the Illuminati. The ceiling of the cloning center in Canada is different, in comparison to the picture posted. At the cloning center in Canada, there is a concourse which can be found at the top on the upper bowl of the arena... I'll have to draw this place [the Canadian cloning center]... Thank you 3SG1. **May 18, 2012 at 9:51pm**

3SG1: It's the closest thing I could find according to your description [of the cloning center]. I think it gives one an idea of what it's like there [at the cloning center in Canada]; makes it more real.

DM: The picture you posted, scared me... the cloning center in Canada is so LIKE that too... the stands are filled though... oh man! **May 19, 2012 at 12:02am**

3SG2: Am I correct in assuming the far wall should have stained glass windows?

DM: I haven't seen any stained glass windows [at the cloning center in Canada]. **May 19, 2012 at 12:06am**

3SG2: Okay. What about the dirt in the arena? Is it black, almost obsidian?

3SG1: Maybe it is intermission. Time to get rid of the old *REM driven* clone audience, who will soon be waking up from REM sleep [*in their original bodies*] and bring the new audience of *REM driven* clones [to the arena], of people who are now just going into REM sleep [*in their original bodies*].

3SG3: Wow! Now I see what you mean Donny! Freaky s***! Oh my God!

3SG3: From what I understand, only the consciousness is transferred [and the consciousness goes to the new *REM driven* clone body at the cloning center].

3SG3: I am currently in contact with Donald... I have heard many more things which Donald has discussed. Donald has so much more to tell... he also has some very creepy stuff to detail that people are unlikely to believe... I told Donald to go easy, and have one subject of discussion per day to make it easier to focus and evolve as a big united family... we can all have our thoughts about this, and everyone is welcome to ask and know the TRUTH! Once and for ALL!

3SG4: So, is this an actual photo of the cloning center?

[No, this is not an actual photo of the cloning center in Canada. However, the image depicted is almost identical to what the cloning center in Canada actually looks like.]

3SG5: The picture posted, surely does look like your description of the cloning center, Donald.

May 21st 2012

Further comments on: the image SIMILAR to the cloning center in western Canada

3SG1 reposts the above picture [bottom of page 52, above] *of the arena at the Cloning Center as described by Donald Marshall, on Donald Marshall's Facebook Timeline.*

3SG2: The cloning center is much smaller than the picture displayed above, and seats approximately 400 people, Donny said!

DM: The above ground cloning center is in western Canada... somewhere... there are many other cloning centers worldwide. I have mostly been to and have *REM driven* clone experiences from the above ground cloning center in western Canada. **May 22, 2012 at 10:16pm**

3SG3: Have people from the UK been to the cloning centers?

DM: Yes [people from the UK do attend cloning centers, *as REM driven clone versions of themselves*]. Queen Elizabeth II owns the above ground cloning center in western Canada. **May 22, 2012 at 10:16pm**

May 23rd 2012

Where is the location of the cloning center?

3SG1: Where is the location of the cloning center?

DM: I don't know. People should **DEMAND** the location of the above ground cloning center in western Canada from [Former] Canadian Prime Minister Stephen Harper... Stephen Harper attends the cloning center located in western Canada *as a REM driven clone version of himself, through the process of consciousness transfer,* and Stephen Harper is someone who knows the exact location of the cloning center in western Canada. I need an angry crowd to go and **confront** Stephen Harper and demand the exact location of the above ground cloning center in western Canada from Stephen Harper... an angry crowd demanding the location of the above ground cloning center in western Canada from Stephen Harper, will work... Stephen Harper will crack under the pressure... he is terrified. Stephen Harper literally said, while *he was a REM driven clone version of himself* at the cloning center, with tears streaming down his *REM driven* clone face, crying, "I want to flee the country, I know what is coming!"

DM: Furthermore, **I do not know** the location of the above ground cloning center in Canada because I have my consciousness transferred to my *REM driven* clone duplicate located at the cloning center in western Canada *when I reach REM sleep in my original body at home in bed*, and I have not been told the exact location of the above ground cloning center in western Canada by the Illuminati *REM driven* clones, when I have been activated as a *REM driven* clone *version of myself* at the cloning center located in western Canada. What happens with me is that: I go to sleep in my original body, and 90 - 110 minutes after first falling asleep, I enter REM sleep, the Illuminati then transfer my consciousness to my *REM driven* clone, and I open my eyes as a *REM driven* clone version of myself, and I am laying down on a stainless steel rack at the cloning center... and because of this advancement in technology, people do not travel to the cloning center physically, but rather, they are activated as *REM driven* clone versions of themselves through the process of consciousness transfer, while their original body sleeps, and they experience life from a first person perspective as a *REM driven* clone version of themselves (just like people experience life from a first person perspective in their original bodies), **ON THE SAME EARTH**. People have a first person perspective experience as a *REM driven* clone version of themselves, and walk around the same earth.

Not many people, even willingly members, as well as, celebrities, who like being part of the Illuminati's *REM driven human* cloning subculture know of the exact location(s) of the cloning center(s). However, high rank Illuminati members such as Stephen Harper know the exact location of the above ground cloning center in Canada and therefore, Stephen Harper will be an ideal person to **confront**. *As a REM driven clone version of myself, unwillingly activated by the Illuminati,* I have seen the outside of the cloning center as *REM driven* clone, and there is nothing surrounding the above ground cloning center located in western Canada for approximately 50 yards... beyond that there are trees... after that, there is a road which is rarely used [leading to and from the above ground cloning center, supposedly], the road is not paved, and the road is covered with dirt. The above ground cloning center has to be as far away as possible from civilisation because of the screaming which can be heard coming from the cloning center... and as a consequence, the public are oblivious to any strange noises, such as screams which can be heard at a distance...

The Illuminati torture people for their own amusement. The Illuminati grows duplicate clones of random civilians only to have these people tortured as *REM driven* clone versions of themselves for some sick amusement, as the Illuminati members watch from the stands as *REM driven* clone versions of themselves. The Illuminati also grow duplicate clones of original children and have these children activated as *REM driven* clone versions while they sleep in their original bodies, to be tortured as *REM driven* cloned children at the cloning center for a "disgusting pain and theatre spectacle", for the rich, famous, and politically powerful.... However, the Illuminati are afraid now because, the public now knows what they do in complete secrecy with their hidden high advances in technology, and moreover, Anonymous (We Are Legion) knows about the Illuminati's *REM driven human* cloning subculture, and this information is spreading around the world. **May 23, 2012 at 9:57am**

Donald Marshall's Health

May 22nd 2012

Mistaken identity: The "Donald Marshall" exposing the Illuminati still lives

3SG1 posts a link to an article about a "Donald Marshall" (Native Indian) who is wrongfully convicted and dies (CBC News Canada 2009), *to Donald Marshall's Facebook Timeline.*

3SG1: Donald, what is this [in reference to the article displayed above]?

3SG2: That's just a guy with the same name [as the NWO whistle-blower]; no relation.

3SG3: Yes, this is what I was researching before... Donald [the NWO whistleblower] told me they are not related; however people should investigate more! It is kind of strange, because they have the same name!

DM: The "Donald Marshall" referred to in the article is Native Indian, a Mi'kmaq, I am not. It is just a coincidence. **May 22, 2012 at 10:05pm** ["Mi'kmaq" also referred to as "Micmac" are people indigenous to Canada's Maritime Provinces. The Micmacs are original natives of the Nova Scotia / New Brunswick region. They also settled in locations in Quebec (Canada), Newfoundland (Canada), and Maine (United States)]

3SG1: Thanks.

3SG4: This person has the same name and is also from Nova Scotia? That is quite the coincidence...

DM: The person referred to in the article is Native Indian, I am not; unfortunately, he is dead, and I am not... it is a coincidence... **May 23, 2012 at 3:44am**

3SG4: I am not saying the person referred to in the article is you. I am saying it makes sense that people who are new to finding your information would assume that the identity belongs to you because it refers to a "Donald Marshall" who died from Nova Scotia [and you are also from Nova Scotia, in Canada].

DM: I understand. There were plenty of times others assumed, situations concerning different people named "Donald Marshall" was referring to my identity, even when I was young. **May 23, 2012 at 6:08am**

3SG5: I too, researched "Donald Marshall", there are plenty of people with that name. Remember the white man forced "white man names" on my people [Native Indians].

Donald Marshall's Mission

Facebook Posts: The progress of Donald Marshall's Mission

May 18th 2012

Donald Marshall promises to continue exposing the Illuminati

DM: Soon I will have unlimited internet connection. I will then make videos and write documents containing everything I have ever seen or heard as a *REM driven* clone version of myself at the cloning center. I will also detail who has visited the cloning center as a *REM driven* clone version of themselves; what they have done, as well as, highlight people that have remotely dispatched their wives [by applying a constant electrical currents to their wives *REM driven* clones until their wives died in their original bodies] to avoid giving their wives half their money in divorce settlements when there wasn't any arranged prenuptial agreements. I will also disclose just about everything the Illuminati members do as *REM driven* clone versions of themselves at the cloning center, as well as, disclose the Illuminati's attitudes, outlooks, leadership and organisational setup. I will disclose what is true about the Illuminati and what is not. I really wish Tila Tequila would join me and this cause; it would make things a lot easier; hopefully she will join. Many celebrities do not want to attend the cloning centers *as REM driven clone versions of themselves whenever they go to sleep* and do not want to go to the cloning centers anymore; this includes non famous people. My relatives will **NOT** submit to lie detector tests (independent polygraph tests) if confronted. They have told me *as REM driven clone versions of ourselves* at the cloning center: "They won't bury themselves further; they will just say I'm telling the truth." It will be done then, and I will be free from the Illuminati's *REM driven human* cloning subculture, and the world will know about REM driven human cloning. Then the world can go after [Former] Prime Minister Stephen Harper and ask him why he allows people to clone Canadian children assembly line style for the rich Illuminati members and celebrity figures to molest daily as *REM driven* clone versions, whenever they sleep. Stephen Harper told me *when we were both activated as REM driven clones at the cloning center*, that "He is afraid he will be lynched in the street, and hung from a light pole..." ...many of the Illuminati members have expressed their fears *as REM driven clone versions* at the cloning center and they are all afraid of a massive public uprising, and the public demanding answers regarding the Illuminati's *REM driven* cloning subculture.

May 18th 2012

Donald Marshall informs the public he is doing his best to answer all questions

DM: I apologise that I do not have enough time online a day to answer the flood of questions from the concerned public. I try to answer all messages and threads in my limited time, but there are too many questions to answer in such a limited amount of time. I will have Wi-Fi internet connection 24/7 on Wednesday and I will answer all questions then. I will make many more informative videos too. Remember to be vigilant and watch the multitude of rooms for trolls and people trying to serve their own agendas. Soon the information will flow and will be smooth.

3SG1: Don't worry about it Donny. Just as long as you are safe, that's all that matters.

DM: The Illuminati have said *as REM driven clone versions of themselves at the cloning center*: killing me now [in my real body] will only make it worse [for the fate which they shall suffer]. Many, many, big people are watching to see if this 36 year old has a heart attack or aneurysm... and they will take my premature death as proof positive. Even at the cloning center recently... the Illuminati *REM driven clones* are NOT TORTURING ME [when they activate me as a *REM driven* clone version against my will]! *Smiling*. *As REM driven clones at the cloning center,* the Illuminati have said they do not want to risk the chance, and I die... You've already saved me in a way... *As a REM driven clone version of myself, unwillingly activated at the cloning center,* I started shouting and freaking out at the Illuminati *REM driven* clones and screaming at Queen Elizabeth II, *who is also a REM driven clone version of herself at the cloning center.* I got very worked up [emotional] and *as a REM driven clone version*, my voice started cracking. My *REM driven* clone's heart was beating fast and hard... it was a strange occurrence... *As a REM driven clone* Queen Elizabeth II looked concerned, and even worried... and then she said "Turn him off, turn him off!" –and my consciousness inhabiting the *REM driven* clone body began to fade to black... However, just before my consciousness faded completely, the Illuminati *REM driven* clones said "They are just waiting...", "It's too late now, and it is inevitable"... You have already somewhat saved me... Thank you so much... I will message again soon. Spreading my disclosures is working my friends. **Share; share, share**! I need more people, and then I can move to Phase Two of disclosure. **May 18, 2012 at 10:57pm**

May 18th 2012

Donald Marshall informs the public he likes Anonymous (We Are Legion)

DM: LASTLY TODAY: It has been brought to my attention that some think that I am anti-Anonymous (We Are Legion)... I am NOT anti-Anonymous. I really like the Anonymous people; they are needed now more than ever before... The people in Anonymous are helping me against the Illuminati in a major way. Also the Illuminati / NWO fear the Anonymous people... So Anonymous are cool in my book.

3SG1: Yessir [Yes sir].

3SG2: Slowly, but surely, Donny, you are closing in on the Illuminati, and the Illuminati know it more than ever. You must be careful brother!

3SG3: We do not forgive. We do not forget.

3SG2: No retreat. No surrender!

3SG4: This IS the BUG in the MATRIX!

3SG3: It is inevitable the same way that the Illuminati blind many to believe they have a choice; we will make the Illuminati believe they have a choice... before we strike!

DM: I'm going home now. Hopefully I will not be activated as a *REM driven* clone, at the cloning center tonight. I will share updates when I'm next online. **May 19, 2012 at 1:06am**

May 19th 2012

Donald Marshall makes preparations for his upcoming disclosures on the Illuminati

DM: I'm chilling at home with a friend and checking out his technology... [and] setting up [a few things]... this will be much easier now... it is going to get hectic soon... my mail box is 'blowing up' [receiving many messages] more than ever before.

DM: One of the next videos I make will contain small proof about REM cloning and the cloning centers. It will feature the experiences of someone else who has been activated at the cloning centers as a *REM driven* clone when they went to sleep in their original body and retained their memories from their experience. **May 20, 2012 at 4:55am**

3SG1: Have you seen that some people are saying you are Anti Anonymous?

DM: I READ that ['I am anti-Anonymous']... I love Anonymous (We Are Legion)... [because] the Illuminati hates Anonymous and therefore Anonymous have become my best friends... that [article / post] was made by an angry person named Steven [Joseph Christopher] trying to be negative... I need Anonymous' help with exposing the Illuminati / NWO and their *REM driven* cloning subculture. **May 20, 2012 at 5:06am**

3SG2: *sarcastic comment, not to be taken seriously*: Steven [Joseph Christopher] is the best. He is god, you know? He made stuff in a few days... even though life has been co-existing before Steven [Joseph Christopher] created his Facebook page in one of those days...

May 20th 2012

Tila Tequila may give false accounts about the cloning centers

DM: TILA TEQUILA... is going to talk about the Illuminati's *REM driven human* cloning subculture, but she will give false accounts about the cloning center and what the Illuminati members have done as *REM driven* clone versions and what they continue to do at as *REM driven* clone versions the cloning center... It is a plan of the Illuminati's to have Tila Tequila give false accounts regarding the cloning center and the Illuminati's *REM driven human* cloning subculture. I **WILL** tell you the truth about the cloning center(s)...

3SG1: I trust you with all this [*disclosing the Illuminati's REM driven human cloning subculture*] not Tila Tequila. I made a post about the cloning center on Tila Tequila's Facebook page, for which I wrote: "I know about the cloning center [and what happens there] and that some people do know about cloning center(s)"; after making such a post on Tila Tequila's Facebook page, I am now blocked from seeing her Facebook page or commenting on her Facebook page. Tila Tequila blocked me, simply because I wrote something about the cloning center.

DM: I've messaged Tila Tequila about disclosing the cloning centers; she hasn't blocked me... Tila Tequila also does not want to be activated as a *REM driven* clone version of herself at the cloning center; she wants freedom from the cloning centers she and will join us. Tila Tequila is scared to speak out against the Illuminati's *REM driven human* cloning subculture... I am scared too when it comes to speaking out against this filthy business; anyone would be... Tila Tequila has seen my Facebook posts and my private messages... I am not going to harass her. She knows it is time to say "clone" [and speak the truth about the cloning centers]. **May 20, 2012 at 10:51am**

3SG1: Tila Tequila did not block you because she knows you are true and can help her.

DM: Precisely... she can help me too... **May 20, 2012 at 10:57am**

May 20th 2012

Donald Marshall shares Tila Tequila's Facebook Post to his Facebook wall

DM: Almost...; Say "clone". Just say it... "Cloning": it is two syllables.

> "**Tila Tequila**
> **May 20, 2012**
> [Are] you still here? It is taking me a while because I'm getting closer and closer to letting you all know, what've I've been dying to share with you! But before I go any further I'd better re-launch my own websites to prevent any of my pages getting deleted... Which I still think is messed up seeing how we do have FREEDOM OF SPEECH! OK, I am uploading the video now, with more information, and more content to my "TRUTH BLOG" revealed soon! Be Right Back!"

May 20th 2012

Laser sight; Reincarnation and 'Caging the consciousness / soul'

DM: I am currently walking around [Halifax, Nova Scotia, Canada], and I hope no glowing red dots appear on my chest... *winking smile*

[In reference to "Laser sight" –which is a small, usually visible, light laser placed on firearms (guns) and aligned to emit a beam parallel to the barrel of the firearm. Laser beams have a low divergence and usually appear as a small (red) spot on a target, even at long distances. The user places the (red) spot to the desired target and the barrel of the firearm is aligned. Therefore, Donald Marshall is referring to the fact that he hopes there are no laser sights on his chest, because it could imply –he is about to get shot!]

3SG1: It is better than a thousand red eyes glaring at you from the other side of other veil. [Getting shot, is also better than] seeing something from a "Dungeons and Dragons" (Dungeons and Dragons 2016) book in real life or in a spiritual manifestation. When one starts getting harassed by the Illuminati's "string pullers" (also known as the reptilian forefathers of the hidden empire; the "rulers" of mankind [the previous comment refers to underground aliens who are currently more technologically advanced than humans, and are therefore top of the Illuminati hierarchy; these underground aliens will be covered separately in upcoming documents]), that is when one has to be very wary for their life. Being Dragon-blood [refers to the Chinese Zodiac; a person born in the year of the "Dragon" and whichever blood type (O, A, B, AB –either positive or negative) that person may be; see (Travel Guide China 2016) for further details] and part of the Royal line [having ancestry which traces back to a monarch] makes a person a significantly damned target; *points to himself*.

I would prefer a red dot [being shot], rather than the psychological warfare the Illuminati use by pulling strings of fate through "magick" ["Magick" is the science and art of using forces (natural or artificial) to cause change (in consciousness) to occur in conformity with will, which can be achieved by directing one's own personal energy and the energy of surrounding elements, as well as, achieved through the means of using advances in science, medicine and technology (for which today's Illuminati uses concealed advances in science, medicine and technology, against the public) to cause change in consciousness. Magick (and with regards to "technology") is neutral; it is neither good, nor evil. The practitioner decides how they would like to focus their personal energy, and the energy of surrounding elements to cause change in consciousness] to keep me locked up, and broken down. However, the Illuminati know that if they killed me that way [physically, such as with firearms], I would just come back [to this plane of existence] reborn [refers to reincarnation]. Therefore the Illuminati work on keeping me, and many others like me, severed, as best as they can.

DM: What you have said is very true; there are some fates which are worse than death. __May 21, 2012 at 12:20am__

3SG1: I know [there are some fates worse than death]. I've experienced them; such as the void... or the lowest ring of "hell". [Another worse fate is] living in a world, where, by blood and authority you are meant to protect others from the tyrants, and yet you can do nothing as you watch many suffer needlessly [is also a worse fate than death].

DM: Have you been a clone? __21 May 2012 at 12:23am__

3SG1: Technically [I have been a clone], but not quite the way you have [*where you are activated as a REM driven clone version of yourself whenever you enter REM sleep*]. I suffer reincarnation. The cloning process [for reincarnation] is different. I've been here since... Well, a long time...

[This person's above comments refer to capturing / trapping a person's consciousness with the Illuminati's technology (which can be done) and placing the same consciousness into a new body.

In Donald Marshall's May 2016 interview with Paranormal Central (Paranormal Central 2016b), Marshall alludes that the Illuminati have now told him (*as REM driven clone versions of themselves at the cloning center*) they have the technology to trap the consciousness after death (the Illuminati term as 'caging the soul') and an interviewer on the show further alludes to the fact that such technology implies this is the ultimate battle of the universe: "the war on consciousness". An interesting thought is also the fact that REM driven cloning, is also a temporary trap of the consciousness, because a person's consciousness inhabits a clone version of themselves for the period of time they sleep after entering REM sleep.

There will be further lengthier discussions regarding different methods of how consciousness is trapped / captured by the Illuminati in upcoming documents].

<u>May 20th 2012</u>

<u>*Comments on: Tila Tequila's Truth Blog video*</u>

3SG1 posts a video titled "TRUTH BLOG: Cover-Ups, 2012 & More They Won't Tell You!" to Donald Marshall's Facebook Timeline. The video features Tila Tequila. [Unfortunately this video has been deleted on YouTube, and cannot be found].

3SG1: Here we go.

DM: There are all kinds of veiled messages to me in her latest [video] blog. Tila Tequila also puts a picture of Jay Z making the "triangle symbol sign" for half a second in her [video] blog... at the of the end of the [video] Tila Tequila says "Keep up the good fight and keep spreading the love [Donald Marshall's open letter to the public (Donald Marshall Proboards 2012a)]". Watch it. Listen [to what she is saying]; she hints at me, REM driven cloning; the cloning centers, and us. **May 21, 2012 at 7:18am**

3SG2: I have a bad feeling about this [Tila Tequila's] video... Please be careful, and only listen. Do not stare at the strobe lighting in this video!

DM: Tila Tequila titled this video "Truth Blog"?! That is kind of funny... um how about you [Tila Tequila] tell the truth in the video?! Tila's delay in talking about REM driven human cloning and the cloning centers; will look like she is delaying because of "fear"; however, Tila Tequila's delay of corroborating the cloning centers is just dragging it out... When Tila Tequila does corroborate the disclosure of [human] cloning centers, Tila Tequila is likely to sugar-coat events which happen at the [human] cloning centers... Tila Tequila wants to be sure that I will also sugar-coat events which happen with the Illuminati *REM driven* clones at the cloning center, with her, so that Tila Tequila does not look like a "lying villain"...when I tell the **real deal** about everything which I have experienced as a *REM driven* clone version of myself at the cloning center(s)... **May 22, 2012 at 10:43pm**

May 20th 2012

Tila Tequila blocks and deletes individuals helping to expose the Illuminati

3SG1: On Thursday [May 17th 2012] at 6:43 Tila Tequila posted this: "We were all born to the Earth and became part of a species called "Human Beings", to which by natural law of the Universe, is where our TRUE rights derive. As long as we don't harm others or do anything destructive to the Earth, then with that, no one else has the right to tell us what rights we have and do not have. We are all human beings, born under the Earth and the higher power of God, not the Government. -Just my thought of the day. ~Miss Tila"

I posted a comment in reply to her above post, saying: "Right! Just like the cloning center". Tila Tequila deleted my comment and blocked me from posting on her page.

DM: She'll come around. **May 20, 2012 at 10:52am**

May 20th 2012

Donald Marshall plans to make a video disclosure with the help of a friend

DM: I am going home to make a longer, special, video... I will upload the video tonight.

DM: Actually, I will make the video tomorrow; I am too tired right now. The video will be a special one. **May 21, 2012 at 7:19am**

3SG1: We're working on the video right now!

May 21st 2012

A whistleblower joins this cause to help expose the Illuminati

3SG1: [Donald] we need to talk...

3SG2: Okay. I will inform Donny, and make sure Donny makes time to speak to you via personal message (email / Facebook inbox messenger). Please hold on, if you can, Donny is so busy trying his best to reply to everyone! However, I will make sure Donny gets in touch with you as soon as possible my friend...

DM: Welcome aboard the good ship, whistleblower. **May 22, 2012 at 10:35pm**

May 21st 2012

Celebrities are reading every single post on Donald Marshall's Facebook wall

3SG1: Donald, so all these celebrities [politicians, royalty and others etc.] are reading everything on your Facebook wall?

DM: Yes. They are all reading my Facebook wall like a Soap Opera. *As REM driven clone versions of themselves at the cloning center*, the celebrities, politicians, royalties etc. have called the disclosure of the Illuminati's *REM driven* cloning subculture as: "Front row seats to the end of the world". However, the world will not end once the Illuminati's *REM driven human* cloning subculture is fully exposed and worldly known though... What needs to happen is that once the Illuminati are fully exposed and their *REM driven* cloning subculture is worldly known: some government heads will have to be replaced; some monarchies in the world will have to be ended; and there must be a shutdown of ALL the cloning stations worldwide, as well as, a complete ban on the science and practice of REM driven cloning, as well as an end to any form of human cloning.

As REM driven clone versions of themselves, the Illuminati have been showing me on a big screen at the cloning center what is likely to happen with the decisions I undertake, when I am *unwillingly activated as a REM driven clone version of myself* at the cloning center; do this and this will happen (they tell me); tell the world about this and this will happen. *As REM driven clone versions of ourselves*, the Illuminati have been schooling me on what to say and when to say it... I know how I must disclose the Illuminati's *REM driven* human cloning subculture... and it must happen in **Four Phases**... so that the world will keep spinning, nuclear war does **not** happen; and anarchy and chaos does not happen on the streets...

The celebrities, politicians, royalty and others are all following my lead, *as REM driven clone versions of themselves* from the cloning center now... these celebrities, politicians, royalty and others will beg for mercy from the angry populace when the time comes and the Illuminati's *REM driven human* cloning subculture is fully exposed, and worldly known. Stay tuned... anything can happen now. This really is one of the most critical times in earth's history, at this very moment. It is "heavy" [profound and serious]. **May 23, 2012 at 3:56am**

May 21st 2012

"Secrets Revealed"; Phase One; Crisis Situations; Highlight Reel; & Human Clones

"Secrets revealed" according to Web Bot Computer Program

3SG1: According to "Web Bot" (Web Bot Forum c.2012) [which is an "internet bot" computer program whose developers, Clif High, and George Ure, claim the software is able to predict future events by tracking key words entered on the internet], the month of June is a really big month in regards to having huge subsets of words which have been tracked and recorded such as "The beast will rot from the inside"; Clif High calls the Illuminati the "entrenched elite", because they are. Clif High has a report which he will soon be releasing. My point is: I believe June [2012] will be a huge month for you, Donald. The theme highlighted by the creators of "Web Bot" for June [2012] is "Secrets Revealed".

DM: Well as long as people do not rise up with torches and pitchforks and march on Stephen Harper's house and demand to know the exact location of where this above ground cloning center is in Canada... Err... wait a minute... That would be **a great thing to happen** if people do in fact rise up by next month and march on Stephen Harper's house and do demand to know the exact location of where the above ground cloning center in Canada is! *Smiling*.

The importance of "Phase One" with regards to exposing the Illuminati

DM: We are currently in Phase One in regards to exposing the Illuminati's *REM driven human* cloning subculture. Phase One involves gathering as many eyes and ears possible, in order to increase our numbers and reach the point where we do have a large parentage of the public informed about the Illuminati's *REM driven human* cloning subculture, and disgusted by the Illuminati's *REM driven human* cloning subculture, to the point where a large percentage of the public will actively demand and protest the shutdown of the cloning centers, publicly. There is strength in numbers, and we need a large percentage of the public, before we will gain an advantage, otherwise, without the strength of the populace, and public support we simply will **not** achieve the closure of the human cloning centers in our lifetime; this situation really is this serious. This is why it is important to inform as many people as possible and gather as many eyes and ears as possible, in order to increase our numbers and reach a stage where there is a large percentage of the public who are informed and actively support the shutdown of the cloning centers.

How people (generally) react in crisis situations

DM: Although, it is imperative that we must inform as much of the public as possible in order to reach a stage where we are close to realising the shutdown of the cloning centers, it is also imperative to keep the following in mind: in crisis situations, psychologically speaking, only 1-3 percent of people will feel compelled to do the right thing etc. in the face of adversity (TED 2008). Therefore, do not become too discouraged if, initially the message you have to convey to your friends and family regarding the Illuminati's *REM driven human* cloning subculture is met with indifference, silence, fear, disagreement, apathy etc... This is a crisis situation, and as such, you should expect approximately 1 to 3 people out of every 100 people, to feel the weight of the situation such as you do, and feel legitimately compelled to help rectify the problem straight away. With the above in mind, there is another 1-3 percent of individuals on the opposite tail end of the spectrum, who, when witnessing crisis situations etc. will want to exacerbate [make worse or intensify] and join in on the adverse situation (TED 2008) [just like the example of Lenny Bloom and Jane Steele, who sided with the Illuminati, when the duo realised the Illuminati really exists (Marshall 2016a, pp. 41 - 46)].

Moreover, in terms of exposing the Illuminati's *REM driven human* cloning subculture, we have witnessed examples where people have written in, after realising the "Illuminati" is indeed real, requesting to be a part of the Illuminati and "They would do anything if the Illuminati can make them rich". The point being made here is that: there are also a small percentage of people in crisis situations who CHOOSE to worsen the situation (TED 2008). The majority of population 97 - 99% will choose to sit back, observe or avoid the situation, and in a situation such as this: although many people know the truth regarding the Illuminati's *REM driven human* cloning subculture, there will be a large percentage of the population which initially partakes in a phenomenon known as "The Bystander Effect" or "Bystander apathy" [which is a social phenomenon that refers to cases in which individuals do not offer any means of help to a victim when other people are present] (Brandon Gaille 2014), and will only join this cause and actively help to expose the Illuminati's *REM driven* cloning subculture, when our numbers have increased significantly; or, it becomes 'socially acceptable' to be a part of this cause.

Therefore, if you are currently a person who is in the category of 1-3% of people who feel COMPELLED to correct wrongs, and rectify (put right) crisis situations, then the best thing to do is to continue informing as many people as you can, regarding the Illuminati's *REM driven human* cloning subculture, with the aim of reaching others who also fall into the 1-3% of people who feel compelled to act immediately when they see or hear of a crisis situation. Do not feel too discouraged by the initial low turnout willing to actively help end the Illuminati's *REM driven human* cloning subculture, initially, because when it is more socially acceptable and most evident for those who have their reservations, the people who sat back and watched the drama unfold, will also join our cause to help expose and end the Illuminati's *REM driven human* cloning subculture!

The highlight reel of Donald Marshall as a REM driven clone

DM: There are currently, clusters of people worldwide, who now know about the Illuminati's *REM driven human* cloning subculture, so that is positive. These days when the Illuminati activate me as a *REM driven* clone *version of myself* at the cloning center, *through the process of consciousness transfer*, the Illuminati *REM driven* clones try and negotiate with me (*as REM driven clone versions of ourselves*); the Illuminati *REM driven* clones ask me to sugar-coat the exposure of their *REM driven human* cloning subculture, and in return the Illuminati promises to show the world, publicly, the best video highlights of me as a *REM driven* clone at the cloning center, and promise me that I will become rich, famous and loved by the public. However, if I continue to tell the world the truth about the Illuminati's *REM driven human* cloning subculture, the Illuminati will choose to show the world selected edited video footage, of me as a *REM driven* clone *version of myself at the cloning center* doing disgusting things, and saying and doing terrible things, in order for the world to hate me as much as the Illuminati members, when in reality, as a *REM driven* clone version of myself, I was under MK Ultra technology (mind control technology) as a *REM driven* clone version of myself, and it was a third party who was controlling my *REM driven* clone, and making me do and say disgusting things via the use of MK Ultra technology on my REM driven clone. REM driven clones are very susceptible (easily influenced) by MK Ultra technology, and there is no force of will which can prevent a *REM driven* clone, acting against their mind control programming run by a third person, when a person is activated as a *REM driven* clone version and under MK Ultra (mind control) technology.

The Illuminati's back-up plan is to show the world highlighted video footage of me as a *REM driven* clone, saying and doing disgusting things, in an attempt to make world hate me, as much as the Illuminati, and drag me down with the Illuminati members. *As a REM driven clone version of myself, unwillingly activated via the process of consciousness transfer at the cloning center*, I told the Illuminati *REM driven* clones "Show the world whatever you want, people will know exactly what is going on!" When I said the above *as a REM driven clone version of myself,* the Illuminati *members as REM driven clone versions of themselves*, agreed with me and then they begged me to sugar-coat events regarding their *REM driven human* cloning subculture to the world.

People of the world are going to freak out [lose control of their minds] when the exposure of the Illuminati's *REM driven human* cloning subculture reaches its culmination point, and it is widely and publicly know [because this situation is one of the most deplorable things to happen in human history, and when the public witnesses all the appalling things the Illuminati have done with the use of REM driven cloning technology, well... for now, it is best to say: we will worry about that possible future outcome when we get to it]. Once the world learns about the Illuminati's *REM driven human* cloning subculture and the Illuminati's *REM driven human* cloning subculture is widely and publicly known, the world will **NOT** end. This situation is easily fixed once the Illuminati's *REM driven human* cloning subculture is worldly and publicly know: the world will have to replace a few government officials (individuals complicit in the REM driven cloning subculture); shutdown a few monarchies and bulldoze every cloning station and ban the science and practice of human cloning and REM driven human cloning.

The reality of human clones, explained by Donald Marshall

DM: Furthermore, organs from duplicate clones (clones grown via duplication cloning) are not compatible for transplantation into natural born humans / real humans; the organs from duplicate clones are grown too quickly, and therefore these organs are rejected in the bodies of real humans. Only organs from replicate clones (clones which start life off as babies) via the process of replication cloning are viable for transplantation into the body of the original, natural born person the clone was grown from. However, replication cloning is a very long process, and the replicate clone must grow and mature, for the organs to mature, and this takes many years. We also thread into many moral and ethical grounds if we are to consider growing replicate clones as "insurance policies" for the purpose of organ transplantation for original humans, because as it has already been discussed, replicate clones, develop a mind and personality, much different than the original person they were cloned from, and for many people it is morally and ethically unsound to grow replicate clones of ourselves, simply to harvest their organs at a future date, because the original person is in need of a transplant. Furthermore, because replicate clones develop minds and personalities much different from the original, it also becomes morally and ethically unsound to grow a sentient conscious entity solely for the purpose of organ harvesting, and this leads to many, many ethically and moral considerations with regards to replicate clones.

Overall, human clones are not good for much... human clones are always dumber than the original person they have been cloned from; whether this is a Mark 1 REM driven clone (also known as an "Organic Robotoid") or Mark 2 REM driven clone a person has their consciousness transferred to while they sleep; the person will be dumber as a clone version, while they are activated as a Mark 1 or Mark 2 REM driven clone. It is the same situation with Mark 3 and Mark 4 clones; although Mark 3 and Mark 4 clones are independent clones which operate on their own consciousness, via a microchip. Furthermore, given the fact that Mark 3 and Mark 4 clones also allow simultaneous consciousness or duality consciousness, between the original person and the independent clone (in other words, through thought alone, the original person can control his or her Mark 3 or Mark 4 clone), these independent clones (Mark 3 and Mark 4 clones) are STILL dumber than the original person. On some occasions replicate clones (clones which start life off as a baby) are also dumber than the original, natural born person; this is more evident with re-animated clones (clones of dead people who once lived on earth). Re-animated clones tend to display, different psychological and behavioural traits, and ways of thinking much different than natural born human beings, especially re-animated clones who have been created from remains of individuals who lived thousands of years ago. The DNA gene print is ancient and therefore, these re-animated clones tend to be dumber than naturally born humans. The reduced intelligence, as well as, the reduced decision making aptitudes of human clones is a side effect nobody is immune to. It doesn't matter how intelligent an original person is; their human clone equivalent, is always slightly dumber than the original person... Tila Tequila is reading my posts as we speak. *Smiling*; *Laughter* **May 21, 2012 at 10:52pm**

3SG2: I am so happy you are not like Tila Tequila Donny... We are so lucky; you will not be bought, or bribed by the Illuminati... You rock! [You are really great!] *Smiling*

May 23rd 2012

Encourage Tila Tequila to tell the truth about REM driven human cloning

3SG1: Please support Donald's comments on Tila Tequila's [Facebook] wall by 'Liking' them. It might encourage her to tell the truth [*about the Illuminati's REM driven human cloning subculture*]. Thank you.

DM: Feel free to ask Tila Tequila about *REM driven* cloning and the cloning centers too. Tila Tequila has a *REM driven* clone, and she too is activated as a *REM driven* clone *version of herself* at the cloning center *via the process of consciousness transfer whenever her original body enters REM sleep*, and Tila attends the cloning center *as REM driven clone version of herself*. Tila Tequila knows about the cloning centers, and she knows many things about me, that I have done *as a REM driven clone version of myself* at the cloning center. **May 24, 2012 at 2:02am**

3SG2: *Posts a link to Tila Tequila's Public Facebook Page.*

3SG2: Scroll down to the first post [on Tila Tequila's Facebook page], and read what I wrote to her! All my posts have been DELETED and Tila Tequila BLOCKED me!

DM: Tila Tequila has not blocked me on her public Facebook page and I have said the word "clone" on her page many times. Tila Tequila may still want to join forces [*with me in order to help expose the Illuminati's REM driven human cloning subculture*]. It is the only reason I can think of for why Tila Tequila has not yet blocked me, even though I have commented on her public Facebook page and I have said "clone" in a few comments I have posted to Tila Tequila's Facebook page. Tila Tequila keeps putting cryptic hints about the Illuminati's *REM driven human* cloning subculture in (online) blogs, poems, and her Facebook posts... I believe Tila Tequila did not block me because she wants me to decipher her cryptic hints [*about the Illuminati's REM driven human cloning subculture*]... Is Tila Tequila warning me about the possible actions of the Illuminati which may be carried out unfavourably against me?! What on earth is going on?! **May 24, 2012 at 8:52am**

3SG3: Tila Tequila has not blocked me either, or erased my posts on her Facebook wall... yet!

3SG4: Donald, did Queen Elizabeth II [or her representatives] block you on her public Facebook Timeline? *Laughter*

DM: No. Queen Elizabeth II [or her representatives who run her Facebook page] has not blocked me on her Facebook public page. I have also sent a private message to Queen Elizabeth II's public Facebook page. **May 24, 2012 at 6:06pm**

May 23rd 2012

Wi-Fi internet installed & Further comments on Stephen Joseph Christopher

DM: I have Wi-Fi internet connection installed in my place now, and therefore I have the internet 24/7 now. The disclosures regarding the Illuminati's *REM driven human* cloning subculture is going to go faster now.

3SG1: Hi Steven [Joseph Christopher] *shocked faced*

DM: You are welcome back on my Facebook friends list Steven (messiah) [Joseph Christopher; the "messiah" part in this sentence is said jokingly and in endearment, because Steven Joseph Christopher believed himself to be a messiah when he is **NOT**, and therefore the above comment should **not** be taken seriously], however, if you cause problems, I will block this account [on Facebook] which you have registered as "Ed Hollow" too. Moreover, Steven [Joseph Christopher], you are **NOT** God... you discredit me whenever you say that. Furthermore, 3SG1 is good, he is helping with the divulgement of the Illuminati's *REM driven human* cloning subculture majorly... **May 23, 2012 at 6:44pm**

3SG2: [Stephen Joseph Christopher]... you became "Ed Hollow", that is pretty cool, you are about to "Walk like an Egyptian" next ["Walk like an Egyptian" (TheBanglesVEVO 2013) is a song reference].

3SG3: Donald, now that you have Wi-Fi internet connection in your place, at last, you have once less problem... all systems are "Go", now!

3SG1: [In response to comments made by Stephen Joseph Christopher on a Facebook account registered as "Ed Hollow" which has now been deleted off Donald Marshall's Facebook Timeline]: Steven [Joseph Christopher] I am a proud father and I have absolutely nothing to hide... and you [Steven Joseph Christopher] are here to bring confusion! I will no longer reply to you, and I ask you to stop harassing me please. Furthermore you have NO permission to use any of Donald's materials or Donald's videos [or video testimonies]. You are just making this situation worse than it needs to be, and Donald is now very stressed, all because of you! Thank you 3SG3! You are awesome!

3SG3: Thank you for all you are doing for Donald, 3SG1... you are a godsend.

3SG4: Hey Ed / Steven [Joseph Christopher], did you not ask Donald to tell everyone that you are Jesus / God / Messiah? Whether you beLIEve that you are Jesus / God / Messiah or not, you do not ask someone else to be your Public Relations (P.R.) agent in exchange for your support. Talk about being a "handler" with an agenda.

[A "handler" is a person who manages and represents another individual, or, a person who tends to the emotional and physical needs of another; a person who handles. Furthermore, 3SG4 emphasises the word "Lie" in the word "believe" above to suggest that Stephen Joseph Christopher is lying in his assertions of being 'Christ like']

3SG5: Ed / Steven, it is not conceivable that ANYONE would believe that you are God / Messiah. Your behaviour and words [Steven Joseph Christopher] are disturbing, and Donald has already asked you to leave [his Facebook friends list, as well as this cause]. Please do not come here [Donald Marshall's Facebook friends list, as well as, this cause] with other names and violate [Donald Marshall's or anybody else's] boundaries. Hasn't this world had enough of that [violating other's boundaries]? God or Messiah does not need ANY announcement or proclamation by anyone else. The energy of God speaks for itself.

3SG4: "God or Messiah does not need ANY announcement or proclamation by anyone else." -Not to mention ego and idol worship!

3SG5: Amen! It is called "Narcissism" and it is blatant!

May 24th 2012

Personal reasons for the exposure of the Illuminati's REM driven cloning subculture

3SG1: They [the Illuminati] have cultist scum [individuals who support the Illuminati, whether directly or indirectly] sending negatives [individuals who reject Donald Marshall's disclosures *regarding the Illuminati's REM driven human cloning subculture*] to your Facebook page Donald; do not fall for their ploys, which I am sure you are aware of Donald. The Illuminati started sending these negatives yesterday. Donald, remove any individuals on your (Facebook) friends list who speaks against the overthrow and imprisonment of these abominations. Stand strong, and continue this path, as I will. I am coming to the East Coast, to confront the Anti-Christ's lapdog [possibly, referring to Former Canadian Prime minster Stephen Harper]... Your courage reminds me of myself Donald. You are brave and I admire bravery in anyone. All supporters of Donald Marshall and his divulgement of the Illuminati's *REM driven human* cloning subculture, do **NOT** believe the naysayers; these naysayers are directly or indirectly supporting the very guys we are going after [the Illuminati]. Oh look at the eyes of this one guy... his eyes give him away; he is one of them [an Illuminati supporter, whether directly or indirectly].

3SG1: I have a soul, which I know of. However, I must admit: I have met people without souls, without light in their eyes. So yes, there are some who walk around this planet without souls.

3SG2: If someone completely envelopes themselves into such a bizarre idea [that science and technology is really that advanced and hidden to the point where the Illuminati do in actuality have a *REM driven human* cloning subculture], such a person will not have much of themselves left [which is one of the main reasons people choose **NOT** to look any further to discover for themselves whether the Illuminati's *REM driven human* cloning is indeed fact or fiction, because initially, the reality of such an abomination is horrifying]. Stop being an extremist, 3SG1! [Do] You want to remove people from this cause who have doubts [about Donald Marshall's disclosures regarding the Illuminati's *REM driven human* cloning subculture]? It seems to me that you, 3SG1, have your own agenda than saving mankind.

3SG1: Yes [I do have an agenda], it is securing the children of the world's futures; and yes, it is personal with me too. I was tortured for 11 years in the "Luciferian" Child Protective Services in Alberta (Canada). [There have been many cases informing the public that Child Protective Services do not protect children, but have rather led to the continual abuse of many children (CESSqc 2011; Salem News 2012)]. They [the Illuminati] even tried to set me up [arrange an event by deceptive purposes so that a specific person suffers the consequences of that event], because they had foreknowledge that I would rise up against them. They [the Illuminati] even had a woman torture me who was similar in appearance to the image of the Anti-Christ Queen Lillibet [Queen Elizabeth II], so yes, this cause is very personal for me. They [the Illuminati] even killed my younger brother. You do not know me or why I spend my time exposing the Illuminati [*and their REM driven human cloning subculture*]; I do this for very good and powerful reasons, which I have been preparing for, for many years now. I AM ready now, as is Donald [*to take the fight to the Illuminati, and ensure their downfall*].

3SG2: I never claimed to know you.

DM: We are all on the same side [the populace against the Illuminati]. You have a good spirit 3SG1; your revenge against the Illuminati will be complete, as will be mine. *As a REM driven clone version of herself at the cloning center* Queen Elizabeth II has said to me *as a REM driven clone version of myself,* that she and members of her family have cyanide capsules ready... [They have cyanide capsules ready for when the populace rises and demands answers about the Illuminati's *REM driven human* cloning subculture, as well as, Queen Elizabeth II's ownership of the above ground cloning center in western Canada, among many other questions... Queen Elizabeth II and other members of her family involved with the Illuminati's *REM driven human* cloning subculture plan on killing themselves with the cyanide capsules which they have close to hand before the public decides which cause of action to take against them for their involvement in *REM driven* human cloning].

However, with that said, I would prefer it if Queen Elizabeth II rotted alone in a six feet high by nine feet wide prison cell, with nothing and nobody to console for the rest of Queen Elizabeth II's wretched life. I also want the right to visit Queen Elizabeth II in her prison cell, when she is thrown in for her atrocities against mankind. I know the prison officials will not permit me spitting paper balls from a straw at Queen Elizabeth II as she sits in solitude rotting in her prison cell... although I would love it if I could spit paper balls through a straw at her when Queen Elizabeth II is imprisoned... However, I will settle for just staring at Queen Elizabeth II as she sits sombre in her prison cell, and I would like our eyes to meet, and when Queen Elizabeth II's gaze meets mine, I will smile. **May 24, 2012 at 10:20pm**

3SG1: Now you understand Donald. You now understand why I support this international investigation. This international investigation is personal for me too, and my bloodline. Moreover, 3SG2, mankind will have to save itself. Mankind makes its own decisions. However, children do not have the luxury of making their own decisions, and it is the children I am fighting for. If you all wish to be saved, then do it yourselves. I am too busy going after the boogieman [the Illuminati].

3SG1: Moreover, the Illuminati made a movie about my tormented childhood; you should watch it [to give yourself an idea of the horrors I experienced], it is called "The People Under the Stairs" (1991) directed by Wes Craven. Watch what happens to the daughter in the movie when they put her in a scalding hot bathtub and scrubbed her while she was screaming in pain with a rough edged brush... that is my childhood, and now how was yours? Furthermore, because I did not have an adult to save me from such torment, when I was a little boy, I now take on these kinds of monsters wherever they may be... or whoever they may be.

DM: That is very noble of you 3SG1. In the very end, we will win. The Illuminati are waiting... they have told *me as a REM driven clone version of ourselves at the cloning center* that "We [the populace] have already won"... Even if I was to die [*in an unfortunate event at the hands of the Illuminati*] we [the populace] will win faster... The Illuminati want me alive, so that when we reach a stage where their *REM driven* cloning subculture is fully exposed and worldly known and the public is calling for their deaths, the Illuminati would like me to ask the public for leniency on the Illuminati's behalf... I will **NOT** ask the public for leniency, against the Illuminati members once their *REM driven* cloning subculture is fully exposed and worldly known! I just want Queen Elizabeth II kept alive [*once the world learns about the Illuminati's REM driven human cloning subculture*] and put into a prison cell, whereby I have opportunities to visit Queen Elizabeth II in prison.

Once the Illuminati's *REM driven human* cloning subculture is worldly known, the populace will most likely demand the execution of Queen Elizabeth II. In actuality, once the populace realises everything that Queen Elizabeth II has done with *REM driven* cloning technology, *and as a REM driven clone version of herself,* what Queen Elizabeth II has done to other *REM driven* clone versions of original people at the cloning center, AND what Queen Elizabeth II *as a REM driven clone version of herself* has done to REAL people (who were kidnapped and brought to the cloning center, as original people, and not as clone versions of themselves) the populace will **DEFINITELY** demand the execution of Queen Elizabeth II. I do not mind if that is the line of action the populace wishes to take against Queen Elizabeth II, as long as I get a front row seat... I want to watch it [Queen Elizabeth II] die at least.

After the execution of Queen Elizabeth II, I will reside in a bomb shelter, where I will live out the rest of my days. People will swarm me... all the time! I will not even be able to buy groceries in public... You will see how much [little] attention I want [when the time comes] in comparison to the attention I shall receive...

All I want is freedom for myself, and freedom for others, as well as to help save the lives of other human beings that the Illuminati plans to sacrifice [kill / murder] in the future. I want vengeance against the Illuminati members of course, as well as, the peace of mind that I can sleep soundly at night and never be [unwillingly] activated as a *REM driven* clone version of myself, trapped temporarily as a *REM driven* clone version of myself at remote locations (cloning centers) around world, while my original body lays at home in REM sleep. Most importantly: I also want my conscience to be clear, because I did not turn a blind eye out of fear, and did my duty to warn the world about the real evil deeds of the Illuminati, and what the Illuminati did in actuality with their highly advanced technologies: REM driven human cloning and more. People can love pictures of me if they so choose.

DM: However, once the Illuminati's *REM driven human* cloning subculture is fully exposed and worldly known, I want solitude, silence, and absence of light to clear my head of the evil I have seen and the experiences I have had to live. I have seen too much evil... an **EXCEEDINGLY** amount of evil in my short life on earth... Tila Tequila has also seen an extreme amount of evil (*as a REM driven clone version of herself*)... Britney Spears has also seen an extraordinary amount of evil... many of the world's public figures, such as celebrities, the wealthy, politicians and royalty etc. and more have witnessed extreme levels of evil in this world, *as REM driven cloned versions of themselves*. However, most of the world's public figures such as Tila Tequila, Britney Spears etc. were not forced to watch **EVERY** act of evil committed [by the Illuminati and others] *whenever they were activated as REM driven clone versions of themselves.*

As a REM driven clone version of myself, unwilling activated via the process of consciousness transfer to my duplicate REM driven clone at the cloning center whenever my original body entered REM sleep, Queen Elizabeth II *as a REM driven clone version of herself,* FORCED me to watch **EVERY** act of evil committed [by the Illuminati] at the cloning center(s) whenever I was unwillingly activated as a *REM driven* clone. *As a REM driven clone version of herself at the cloning center,* Queen Elizabeth II, would tell me (*also a REM driven clone version of myself*) that "I was too soft, and I must bear witness to the evils that men [mankind] do". I believe *as a REM driven clone version of herself,* Queen Elizabeth II meant I must also bear witness to the evil women do in this world too.

Psychological torment Donald Marshall MAY face once the Illuminati is exposed

Revelations from Donald Marshall's MK Ultra PROBABLE simulations

DM: Nevertheless, when the Illuminati's *REM driven human* cloning subculture is fully exposed and worldly known, I am still in trouble. I will be in trouble **psychologically** (as well as, mentally and emotionally).

Through the advent of [the Illuminati's] MK Ultra technology, it is possible to immerse the conscious mind in a 3D generated virtual reality simulation of any kind, whereby the person under the Illuminati's MK Ultra technology, 3D generated virtual reality simulation for the conscious mind, perceives the surrounding environment, and the scenario with their conscious mind as "real as real" to the point where the person's five senses (sight, taste, touch, smell, hearing) are active in this 3D generated virtual reality simulation while under the Illuminati's MK Ultra technology, convincing the person to believe the environment and conditions which the person finds themselves under is reality and not a simulation. The Illuminati also have the option of viewing everything the person experiences while under MK Ultra technology on a visual display terminal such as a computer monitor. Being put under the Illuminati's MK Ultra technology is similar to getting "plugged-in" and becoming connected to the neural-interactive virtual reality known as the "Matrix" as depicted in the movie "The Matrix" (1999); it is exactly like that, and the Illuminati can put *REM driven* clones under many different scenarios through the use of MK Ultra technology.

DM: *As a REM driven clone version of myself,* the Illuminati unwillingly activated me as a *REM driven* clone *version of myself* and put me through these MK Ultra "scenarios" (as the Illuminati calls them) and they warped my conscious mind with these MK Ultra visuals. The technology (MK Ultra) is extremely advanced and the 3D generated immersive virtual reality simulation has been perfected by the Illuminati and it is extremely realistic. The Illuminati KNOW THEY ARE DONE and they wanted to see the **probable** actions I may take once their *REM driven human* cloning subculture is fully exposed and worldly known, and so the Illuminati put my conscious mind under such a scenario through the use of their MK Ultra technology. The Illuminati wanted to see what I am likely to do once their *REM driven human* cloning subculture is fully exposed and worldly known, because it is very likely that the Illuminati members involved in *REM driven* human cloning will probably be dead or imprisoned once the world learns of their actions.

Therefore, through the virtual reality 3D simulation of MK Ultra technology, which my conscious mind was put under when I was unwillingly activated as a *REM driven* clone version of myself at the cloning center, the Illuminati made me believe it was all finally over, and that the Illuminati's *REM driven cloning* subculture was fully exposed and worldly known. In the scenarios I was put under (while under MK Ultra), I was made to believe the divulgement and exposure of the Illuminati's *REM driven human* cloning subculture met its conclusion perfectly. Moreover, while under MK Ultra as a *REM driven* clone *version of myself,* I was also made to believe I was in a bomb shelter; similar to the scenario where the Illuminati made Tila Tequila believe she was in her bedroom when three grey aliens came to her bedroom window, when in actuality she was a *REM driven* clone version of herself (*at the cloning center*), placed under an immersive 3D virtual reality simulation for Tila Tequila's conscious mind, through the use of MK Ultra technology.

Accordingly, because my conscious mind was under the effects of MK Ultra while I was activated as a *REM driven* clone *version of myself,* I believe I am in a bomb shelter, stocked with provisions and all my favourite things... Through the use of MK Ultra, the Illuminati *REM driven* clones, placed my conscious mind under this scenario **six different times**, while I was a *REM driven* clone *version of myself* at the cloning center, whereby I believe I am in a bomb shelter, stocked with my favourite things because the divulgement of the Illuminati's REM driven human cloning subculture had gone well, and their cult was fully exposed and worldly known. However, each time I was placed under this scenario through MK Ultra technology, I blew my own head off with a shotgun. I blew my head off with a shotgun **five different times** in each scenario, while my conscious mind was placed under an immersive 3D virtual reality simulation through MK Ultra technology. During the sixth MK Ultra simulation, the Illuminati *REM driven* clones stopped me from blowing my head off with a shotgun in the scenario (for my conscious mind), just as I was about to blow off my head with a shotgun for the sixth consecutive time while under the MK Ultra scenario for my conscious mind; I was stopped from doing so by the Illuminati *REM driven* clones... and I became extremely scared, *as a REM driven clone version of myself* when the Illuminati stopped me from blowing my head off with a shotgun while under MK Ultra simulations.

DM: On the onset, of being stopped from blowing my head off for the sixth time by the Illuminati *REM driven* clones, I was extremely panicked, because I did not know I was under MK Ultra simulations for my conscious mind, I thought the Illuminati had broken into my little fortress somehow, because I was made to believe I was in a bomb shelter, when in actuality I was just a *REM driven* clone *version of myself* under MK Ultra simulations. Eventually, I became conscious of the fact that I was placed under MK ultra simulations, and that I was a *REM driven* clone *version of myself at the cloning center*, and those scenarios were just simulations and not real... at the same time I was becoming conscious of the fact that I was placed under MK Ultra simulations for my conscious mind, the Illuminati *REM driven* clones tried to calm me down *as a REM driven clone version of myself* so that I would not be overly panicked by the scenarios I was placed under...the situation was very strange.

The Illuminati REALLY do not want me to have a heart attack or aneurysm in my original / real body, right now. Moreover, Tila Tequila is in the safest position she has ever been from the Illuminati. Tila Tequila is watched by the public now. If for any unforeseen or unfortunate reason Tila Tequila was to die from an aneurysm, the public will know exactly how Tila Tequila met such a fate, just like the public will know exactly what happened to me if for any unforeseen reason I was to die of a heart attack or aneurysm.

As I am thinking about the MK Ultra scenarios I was placed under while I was a *REM driven* clone version of myself at the cloning center, I cannot see how I will end up blasting myself, when the disclosure of the Illuminati's *REM driven human* cloning subculture meets its conclusion and the Illuminati's *REM driven human* cloning subculture is fully exposed and worldly known... taking my own life after the Illuminati is fully exposed does not seem possible [or rational] to me. However, the Illuminati, *as REM driven cloned versions of themselves*, have said that I will not be able to handle the flashbacks of all I have seen as a *REM driven* clone *version of myself* once this is over, and therefore I hope you can somewhat understand why I may be in trouble **psychologically**, (as well as mentally and emotionally) once the Illuminati's *REM driven human* cloning subculture meets its end.

I am sorry for the drama, but the Illuminati's *REM driven human* cloning subculture is all true. I have seen so much off the scale evil (*as a REM driven clone version of myself*), as well as absolutely retarded evil... What I have seen is beyond what the average person would classify as evil; it is **BEYOND** anything most people can conceive.

Bernie Mac's death MUST be avenged!

DM: Furthermore, **I MUST AVENGE** Bernie Mac! Bernie Mac died because as a *REM driven* clone *version of himself* Bernie Mac tried to save me from the Illuminati's *REM driven human* cloning subculture, and lost his life as a consequence. Public figures *as REM driven clone versions of themselves activated at the cloning center* did not dare speak up for the torment I suffer as a *REM driven* clone *version of myself whenever I am unwillingly activated as a REM driven clone version of myself* after the murder of Bernie Mac through *REM driven* cloning technology. It is only recently that the likes of Jay Z, Beyonce and Kanye West have spoken up for me *as REM driven clone versions of themselves at the cloning center...* and many celebrities included are also voicing that they wish to leave the Illuminati's *REM driven human* cloning subculture whenever they are activated as *REM driven* cloned versions at the cloning center... It is [almost] all over now... The Illuminati have stopped torturing me as a *REM driven* clone *version of myself* whenever they activate me unwillingly as a *REM driven* clone *version of myself at the cloning center*, thanks to all of you... Keep it up, and keep informing as many people as you can about the Illuminati's *REM driven human* cloning subculture. Now it is only a matter of time until the Illuminati are completely exposed and their *REM driven human* cloning subculture is brought to its end... and I want the Illuminati's *REM driven human* cloning subculture completely shutdown, as good as yesterday! **May 25, 2012 at 3:09am**

3SG3: I have told the Illuminati to "Come get me!" Maybe the Illuminati fear me too, ha-ha. Anyway, keep up the fight against the Illuminati Donald, and so should everyone else involved in this movement.

DM: Of course I will keep up the fight against the Illuminati. The divulgement of the Illuminati's *REM driven human* cloning subculture is progressing very well. **May 25, 2012 at 6:15am**

May 24th 2012

Inform more people about this disclosure. Tell your friends & family

Donald Marshall informs the public that he will be making a video disclosure

DM: I need more people to see this disclosure regarding the Illuminati's *REM driven human* cloning subculture... you guys [*on my Facebook friends list, as well as those reading and watching the disclosure from afar*] should tell your friends and family to add me on Facebook too [and read up on the information regarding the Illuminati's *REM driven human* cloning subculture, as well as, what the Illuminati does with *REM driven* cloning technology]. I need many, many eyes by the weekend... I will be making a cool video disclosure [which will divulge more information to the public about the Illuminati's *REM driven human* cloning subculture] and I need as many, many people to see the upcoming video disclosure as possible.

3SG1: Donald, it is cool that you are making a video, however, just consider that something [such as a document] which we can read is easier to spread around a lot faster than a video disclosure. A lot of people like me cannot even watch a video, which is why I am waiting for "Document 2". Remember, when there is a power-outage [*a period where service such as electricity is not available*], if your disclosures / testimonies are in a format which can be read [*such as a document*], it can be printed, and it can still be read, unlike a video disclosure which cannot be viewed during a power-outage.

DM: The statements you have made above, is true 3SG1, however, it will take a while to write out a document disclosure. It will also take some time to type Document 2 and I do not want to leave out any names [*of public figures which I have seen attend the above ground cloning center in western Canada when I have been unwillingly activated as a REM driven clone version of myself via the process of consciousness transfer to the above ground cloning center in western Canada*]. I would have thought Tila Tequila would have spoken up by now about the Illuminati's *REM driven human* cloning subculture to speed up this process... [Informing the public about the Illuminati's *REM driven human* cloning subculture, and edging ever so closer to a point where the Illuminati's *REM driven human* cloning subculture is fully exposed and worldly known]... **May 24, 2012 at 5:51am**

Tila Tequila continues to delay in exposing the Illuminati's human cloning subculture

3SG2: Tila Tequila blocked me from posting on her Facebook Timeline!

3SG3: I am slowly working on Tila Tequila [trying to influence Tila Tequila to talk more openly about the Illuminati's *REM driven human* cloning subculture]. I think Tila Tequila is more afraid of losing some fans [if she were to corroborate Donald Marshall on the Illuminati's *REM driven human* cloning subculture, by detailing her experiences as a *REM driven* clone at the cloning center] than anything else... [All Tila Tequila cares about is fame and money...]

DM: I'll check to see if the little alien [Tila Tequila] blocked me [*on her Facebook Timeline*] too. *Laughter*. I have just checked and Tila Tequila has not blocked me **May 24, 2012 at 6:14am**

3SG4: It is ironic that Tila Tequila chooses to block individuals who actually KNOW the REAL information about what the Illuminati does: which is *REM driven* human cloning.

DM: It is strange that I did not get blocked [*from Tila Tequila's Facebook Timeline*]... and I have detailed more information about the Illuminati's *REM driven human* cloning subculture on Tila Tequila's Facebook Timeline than 3SG2 did... I wonder what the little spider monkey [Tila Tequila] has in mind... **May 24, 2012 at 7:30am**

Document 2

3SG5: Donald, you have been mentioning Document 2 for a VERY LONG time now. Therefore until you have released Document 2 and verify what you have stated so far [in regards to the Illuminati's human cloning subculture and the list of names of public figures who have attended the cloning centers *as REM driven clone versions of themselves*, for which Donald Marshall has said he will detail in the upcoming Document 2] you will only be asking the public to go on blind faith alone [*in regards to the disclosure concerning the Illuminati's REM driven human cloning subculture*]. In my honest opinion you will be losing some supporters [*in regards to this cause, and exposing the Illuminati's REM driven human cloning subculture*] if you are asking the public to go on blind faith alone.

3SG6: [What you have said above 3SG5, is] true.

3SG5: Oh and do not worry Donald about leaving out some names [*when you write Document* 2]. I am sure there will be a Document 3, as well as an addendum [a thing to be added, to a book, document etc.]. Please contact me when Donald releases Document 2. Until Document 2 has been released, I do not think I will continue to share Document 1 [Donald Marshall's open letter to the public informing the public about the Illuminati's REM driven human cloning subculture] (Donald Marshall Proboards 2012a) until there is something more substantial to back up Donald Marshall's disclosures of the Illuminati's *REM driven human* cloning subculture. However, I will settle for Donald getting the exact location of the above ground cloning center in British Columbia, Canada.

3SG7: [I agree with some of the comments 3SG5 has mentioned above].This is what I mean Donald, you have got to come up with something which not only rattles the public [to the point where the public is shocked in terms of what the Illuminati members do as *REM driven* cloned versions] it also has to inspire the public to the point where the public wants to take action to see the exposure of the Illuminati's *REM driven* human cloning subculture reach its conclusion and meets its end. Donald, you will also have to come up with something that annoys and aggravates the public to their very core that such injustices are happening right underneath their very noses, that people will be more inclined to share and show your disclosures regarding the Illuminati's *REM driven human* cloning subculture, to many, many more people. As I have said before, in regards to the divulgement of the Illuminati's *REM driven human* cloning subculture: it HAS to go viral! You can do it Donald; we have got faith in you!

DM: Document 2 [which will contain the list of names of public figures who have attended the cloning centers as *REM driven* clone versions of themselves] is not going to be very long. I wanted to make sure I had enough people looking and sharing the information regarding the Illuminati's REM driven human cloning subculture... because guess what will happen to me if I make Document 2, and nothing happens [in terms of people taking action, and ensuring that the information regarding the Illuminati's *REM driven human* cloning subculture is being shared widely, so that the true nature of the Illuminati continues to be exposed]?! The Illuminati members will grow confident once more, that nothing can be done, or will be done to expose their *REM driven human* cloning subculture, and this will mean that I will be activated via the process of consciousness transfer to my *REM driven* duplicate clone (*whenever my original body sleeps and reaches REM sleep*) to be tortured constantly as a *REM driven* clone version of myself (for revealing Illuminati secrets)... I **NEED** to know people will take action...

If ANY of you were at the cloning center(s) as *REM driven* clone versions of yourselves, and you were getting tortured as a *REM driven* clone, on a stainless steel rack, as your *REM driven* clone body is strapped down, so that you are restricted and unable to escape... you would understand [**my desperation**]... because as difficult as it is to believe Document 1 (Donald Marshall Proboards 2012a) and the fact that the Illuminati really does have such high advances in science, medicine and technology [which in comparison dwarfs the technological advancements currently available to the public by **thousands of years**; not hundreds of years, **thousands of years**, and that it really is a factual reality, **present today**, that a person can go to sleep, and 'wake up' by having the very essence which contains their sensations, experiences, memories, thoughts etc. (their consciousness) **TRANSFERRED** into a different substrate body, and walk around the SAME earth, while their original body sleeps, and that such a technology was not just recently developed, but has existed and been perfected since 1945... well... such information which has not been researched extensively, or will be researched extensively by others... is just filed under 'nonsense' or 'science fiction' to the average person...]...

Document 2 will contain so many names of public figures which I have seen as *REM driven* clone versions of themselves, when I was activated as a *REM driven* clone *version of myself* at the cloning center. Document 2 will also contain many song titles which I have composed *as a REM driven clone version of myself from the cloning center(s)* that musicians have later performed; if the general public dismisses Document 2 as 'nonsense' or 'craziness'... I am **DOOMED (in real life)**! You 3SG5 and 3SG6 will continue with your lives... life will go on for you... I on the other hand, will be activated as a *REM driven* clone version of myself nightly (*whenever I sleep*) to suffer the worst fate as a *REM driven* clone *version of myself*, until I suffer a heart attack in my original body (*because consciousness is linked*). I will make Document 2 soon. In the mean time, bring me more eyes to read and spread the information regarding the Illuminati's *REM driven human* cloning subculture. **May 24, 2012 at 6:04pm**

3SG6: BUT WE WILL SPREAD DOCUMENT 2 FOR YOU DONALD! WE WILL PUT DOCUMENT 2 ON TILA TEQUILA'S FACEBOOK PAGE, WHICH HAS OVER 2 MILLION PEOPLE!

Difficulties in exposing of the Illuminati's REM driven human cloning subculture

3SG7: Well Donald… it is truly difficult to comprehend, conceive and imagine, what you are saying, in regards to the science and technology of REM driven cloning, as well as, what the Illuminati members do as *REM driven* cloned versions of themselves. Not many people have ever heard of such things, and unfortunately in these times the sheeple [-which is a derogatory noun to describe people compared to the animal "sheep" in terms of being docile, foolish or easily led] need unfiltered truth of proof (hard evidence), beyond just a document. Is it possible for you to get anyone else to corroborate your exposure of the Illuminati's *REM driven human* cloning subculture? Getting another person who attends the cloning centers as a *REM driven* clone version of themselves who retains the memories of their *REM driven* cloning experiences in their waking life would lend much more to help this cause in terms of exposing the Illuminati and their *REM driven human* cloning subculture. Honestly, I have been spreading your information and sharing your exposures, but I just get laughed at when I try to pass on your information or share your exposure to others. Nonetheless, I keep telling others about the Illuminati's *REM driven human* cloning subculture anyway.

3SG6: DONALD, YOU ALREADY HAVE 500 FRIENDS ON YOUR FACEBOOK FRIENDS LIST AND COUNTING! THERE ARE ALSO PEOPLE WHO JUST EMAIL YOU!

3SG5: Donald, people will act with proof (hard evidence) [*of the Illuminati's REM driven human cloning subculture*]. Hearsay does not even hold water in a court of law. How can we even act now without further details [about the Illuminati's *REM driven human* cloning subculture and the names of the people involved, and what they have done as *REM driven* clone versions of themselves at the cloning center(s)] as well as the EXACT location of the cloning center in British Columbia, Canada?

Oh and Donald, you may have thousands of 'eyes' [reading and sharing the disclosures about the Illuminati's *REM driven human* cloning subculture] but until anyone [significant] can do something for you [about disclosing the existence and reality of the Illuminati's *REM driven human* cloning subculture with hard evidence, in order that the general populace who have never heard of such topics will find it easier to believe you] and others [with "influence" can do something to help this cause] all these 'eyes' [reading and sharing the information about the Illuminati's *REM driven human* cloning subculture] are moot [of little or practical value]!

Discussions about the location of the cloning center & Talks of public protests

3SG6: Well… it is not possible for Donald to know the exact location of the above ground cloning center in British Columbia, Canada, because he has never been told by the Illuminati *REM driven* clones. Furthermore, Donald is activated as a *REM driven* clone version of himself, and he visits the cloning center *via the process of consciousness transfer whenever he sleeps and enters REM sleep*. Donald just 'opens his eyes' once his consciousness has been transferred *from his original body* to his *REM driven* clone duplicate, which is understandable. Donald has mentioned that other people who visit the above ground cloning center in British Columbia, Canada, know the exact location of the cloning center, and therefore we can demand the answer to the exact location of the cloning center from others.

3SG6: You are being so negative 3SG5! I understand we need Document 2 [as well as, more verifiable evidence to demonstrate the existence of the Illuminati's *REM driven human* cloning subculture] but we must also stay positive and have faith that the disclosure of the Illuminati's *REM driven human* cloning will meet its culmination and reach its end, and that this information about the Illuminati and their *REM driven human* cloning subculture will reach a point where it is fully exposed and worldly known. I cannot wait to read Document 2.

3SG5: [*Sarcastic comment which should not be taken seriously*] OK 3SG6 [if that is your reasoning], I will just ask [Former Canadian Prime minister] Stephen Harper where the exact location of the above ground cloning center is in British Columbia, Canada... I am sure Stephen Harper will tell me! *Laughter* Moreover, 3SG6 it is not negativity, it is logic!

3SG6: I did NOT mean YOU as one individual [demanding answers from public figures that attend the cloning center(s) and know where the exact location of the cloning center(s) is during their waking lives]! You are a 'NOBODY' [like I am]. However, I meant "WE", not "you" and "I" [as individuals] but many people, and all of "US", united as one, protesting about the Illuminati's *REM driven human* cloning subculture, and demanding the answers to the exact locations of the human cloning facilities. Or perhaps you 3SG5 believe this disclosure regarding the Illuminati's *REM driven human* cloning subculture is going to reach its end while we are all sitting at home behind our devices reading what Donald Marshall has to say in regards to the Illuminati and their *REM driven* cloning subculture... Oh please!

3SG5: 3SG6, you are going to protest, where? Moreover what will your sign say (?) "Stop human cloning and torture in an undisclosed location"?

3SG6: 3SG5, your logic does not work with me. I do not call what you are saying "logic". I call it "PLAIN IGNORANCE". How can you expect Donald to get you into the above ground cloning center of British Columbia, if Donald does NOT visit the cloning center(s) in his real body, and he does not walk to the location of the cloning center(s), take a bus to the location of the cloning center, or drive to the location of the cloning center(s)...? Furthermore, I did not say "I" [will be on the streets protesting about the abhorrent reality of the Illuminati's *REM driven human* cloning subculture]; I said "WE THE PEOPLE"... please read carefully.

3SG5: Well... then... [if that is your line of reasoning 3SG6,] how is ANYBODY going to get to the location of the cloning center(s) and stop the Illuminati's *REM driven human* cloning subculture? Duh!

["Duh" –is an interjection, which is used to express annoyance at banality, obviousness or stupidity]

The Illuminati's REM driven human cloning subculture WILL end!

3SG6: 3SG5 the Illuminati's _REM driven human_ cloning subculture WILL be stopped! It will be stopped when the general public "wake up" to this information, and realise that the science and technology behind Donald Marshall's disclosures is verifiable. Once a large percentage of the general populace starts discussing _REM driven_ clones, and the reality of the Illuminati's _REM driven_ cloning subculture, we will be well on our way to ending the Illuminati's _REM driven human_ cloning subculture. Remember it is not convenient for the Illuminati members to have the public discussing and informing many, many other individuals of the public about their _REM driven human_ cloning subculture, or convenient for the public to "wake up" and realise that many public figures in high positions of power are actually extremely decrepit and perverted people. Furthermore, it does not take one thousand people, or three thousand people to stop something as widespread and global as the Illuminati's _REM driven human_ cloning subculture... it takes hundreds of thousands of people to **millions and millions of people**, all on the same page, who KNOW and UNDERSTAND the reality of the Illuminati's _REM driven cloning_ subculture to meet its end, to the point where the Illuminati's _REM driven human_ cloning subculture is fully exposed and worldly known... it takes **millions and millions of people in unison** to achieve such a feat... THIS IS WHAT DONALD MARSHALL HAS BEEN TRYING TO TELL YOU [as well as, tell the world's populace]!

3SG7: Stop! There is no need for negativity needed here. Look, many of us here for this cause, believe Donald Marshall's testimonies about the Illuminati's _REM driven human_ cloning subculture; this has already been established. However, in order for us to draw many more people to this cause, to the point where they also feel compelled to spread Donald Marshall's disclosures regarding the Illuminati's _REM driven human_ cloning subculture, we need to be able to show irrefutable proof about the Illuminati's _REM driven human_ cloning subculture, to bring more people to this cause to ensure the Illuminati's _REM driven human_ cloning subculture meets its end, and it is fully exposed and worldly known. Nonetheless, it is apparently very difficult to demonstrate with irrefutable proof the Illuminati's _REM driven human_ cloning subculture, because it is a person's consciousness which gets transferred to their _REM driven_ clone duplicate, at a remote location (the cloning center(s)) whereby the victims are controlled in the Illuminati's environment (the cloning center(s)) and therefore the Illuminati have covered the possibility that individuals may leak the exact location of their cloning center(s) to the public, and therefore it seems we are at a bit of a standstill in this respect. Nevertheless, we need more names of public figures and what they have done as their _REM driven_ clone duplicate alternatives at the cloning centers, so that we can use this information to flood their personal emails (in real life), and bombard their Public Facebook pages with information about what they have done as _REM driven_ clone versions of themselves at the cloning center, and even in some cases, yes, attempt to be nice to the public figures which Donald will mention in Document 2 in order to create some form of communication with these people.

Discussions about movies imitating reality: "Eyes Wide Shut" & "Avatar"

3SG5: 'Convenient' 3SG6? Are you serious? Oh please! The movie "Eyes Wide Shut" (1999) is a true story referencing what the cabal [Illuminati] does in secrecy! Has that movie stopped any of it [the perverted actions of the Illuminati]?

3SG6: 3SG5 that is a STUPID comment! "Eyes Wide Shut" (1999) is a movie. A movie does not bring protestors, it brings FANS! I mean it is a movie, duh! Furthermore, I agree with 3SG7, there is no need for negativity [with this cause]. We should just let Donald Marshall expose and divulge the information regarding the Illuminati's _REM driven human_ cloning subculture in his way. After all, Donald is the one being tortured as a _REM driven_ clone version of himself when he goes to sleep (in his original body), nightly, and Donald knows what he is doing, so far as the exposure and divulgement of the Illuminati's _REM driven human_ cloning subculture is concerned.

Moreover, 3SG5, have a look at the movie "Avatar" (2009); that movie depicts "consciousness transfer" to a substrate body, to a remote location, whereby it is the same consciousness of the original person, which runs the substrate bodies (Avatars), at the remote location, just like Donald describes is going on today with the Illuminati's _REM driven human_ cloning subculture. HOWEVER, do people watch the movie "Avatar" (2009) and think, this is a reality or world governments and people in high positions of power and society, are doing such feats for real, and transferring their consciousnesses to substrate bodies?! No of course not! People go to a cinema house expecting to be entertained, and that is it, they do not think there MIGHT be real and practical implications to what they have just watched especially when such movies are titled as "Fantasy", "Sci-fi" and **not** "True-life Documentaries". Most people would laugh or dismiss it as nonsense even IF the movie Avatar (2009) was referenced as a "Documentary", because of the style and format in which it is presented. Therefore, and generally speaking, people look at a movie such as Avatar (2009), as just a movie, and consequently, such movies do generate fans and not protestors, and accordingly leads to the merchandise and sales of the products depicted in a movie such as Avatar (2009); which leads to people buying Avatar (2009) toys for their children, and not thinking there may be any REAL and PRACTICAL implications to such a movie.
Laughter

Discussions about: "Eyes Wide Shut"; Bryan Adams; "Avatar" & Hollywood

3SG5: Well I have done my part and shared Donald Marshall's letter (Donald Marshall Proboards 2012a) [on many different platforms and groups] to no avail. Therefore, until I have something more substantial regarding the Illuminati's _REM driven human_ cloning subculture, then... [I have done my part]... and I also happen to believe Donald's disclosures regarding the Illuminati's _REM driven_ cloning for the most part [despite how my above comments may come across]. Although, Donald claims to have written songs for Bryan Adams [_as a REM driven clone version of himself_] when he (Donald) was seven years old [it happened as _REM driven_ cloned versions of original people at the cloning center, and not as original people, experiencing life in their original bodies]. Bryan Adams and his guitarist [Keith Scott] claim they have never heard of Donald Marshall. I even asked Bryan Adams and his guitar player [Keith Scott] if they knew of Donald Marshall before and after I had sent Donald's letter (Donald Marshall Proboards 2012a) to each individual personally. Therefore, at this point, in terms of disclosure and exposing the Illuminati's _REM driven human_ cloning subculture... I only have Donald's word to go on.

3SG6: Do you know Bryan Adams 3SG5 [personally]?

3SG5: What on earth are you talking about 3SG6?! Avatar?! Have you (3SG6) seen the movie "Eyes Wide Shut" (1999)? It is about people that belong to a secret club where they have sex with masks on; and YES that kind of [perverted] thing DOES happen! The movie "Eyes Wide Shut" (1999) was not made to sell toys! Oh my goodness! What kind of people is Donald attracting to this cause, anyway?

3SG7: Yes it appears the 'wood of Holly' ["Hollywood", and the fact that magician's wands were made from the wood of holly trees] has cast a spell over the world, and desensitised many of us to the violence, rape, murder, torture, paedophiles, as well as, the possibilities and probabilities the directions of science, medicine and technology can and HAS advanced towards, to a point where many of us are docile, foolish, easily led, and deceived by the ruling elite who do not have one iota of our best interests at heart. However, when one's eyes are open, she or he is able to look around this world and see clearly what others cannot see... One begins to see more clearly, in regards to the violence, rape, murder, torture, paedophiles, and the possibilities and probabilities the directions of science, medicine and technology has advanced towards, more clearly than one could ever imagine [especially, in regards to the information concerning the Illuminati's _REM driven human_ cloning subculture].

3SG5: Yes 3SG6, I do know Bryan Adams personally. I actually grew up with Bryan Adams' guitar player [Keith Scott]. However, I have not been in touch much with his guitar player [Keith Scott] since I moved to Los Angeles, California [United States] twenty-five years ago. I also saw Bryan Adams and his band perform in Los Angeles approximately four years ago. I have Bryan Adams' guitar player [Keith Scott's] personal email address, and I wrote an email and sent it to Bryan Adams' guitar player [Keith Scott] asking him if he knew of Donald Marshall, and whether he [Keith Scott] knew if Bryan Adams knew of Donald Marshall; he [Keith Scott] did [not] and he [Keith Scott] replied to my email [in regards to whether either he or Bryan Adams knew of Donald Marshall].

3SG6: Do you even read 3SG5?! I said: People like the MOVIES and as a CONSEQUENCE of people liking movies such as Avatar (2009) so much, toys are made and sold as a by product to the movie. I did NOT say the toys were made PRIOR to the release of the movies... GEEZ!

3SG5: ^^^^ [I could say the same to you 3SG6: "Do you even read"?]

3SG6: Okay, so you know Bryan Adam's guitar player [Keith Scott], and you emailed him, what did he [Keith Scott] say when he replied?

3SG5: Anyway Donald, I do not care anymore to converse with some of the people you are attracting to this cause. Notify me when Document 2 is finished and released, and THEN we will see what happens [so far as the disclosure and exposure of the Illuminati's *REM driven human* cloning subculture is concerned].

DM: Oh my goodness [3SG5 (and 3SG6)]! Relax and calm down [3SG5 (and 3SG6)]! I am swamped with messages... I like the fact many people are messaging me in regards to the Illuminati's *REM driven* cloning subculture because it means the information is reaching more and more individuals of the general public... but I can only type so fast. **May 24, 2012 at 6:44pm**

3SG7: The movie "Eyes Wide Shut" (1999) was indeed a glimpse into the Illuminati. It is alleged that Stanley Kubrick [director of Eyes Wide shut (1999)] was given access, but Stanley Kubrick was greedy and filmed material which he should not have done. The alleged story goes that Stanley Kubrick was found dead with his eyes carved out of his head five days after the premier of "Eyes Wide Shut" (1999). I do not know if the above commentary regarding the death of Stanley Kubrick is true or not, but this is what the 'Hollywood' [also made in reference to the magician's wands which were made from the wood of the holly tree] spell does to humanity; it captivates us, however, it should never divide humanity, to the point where we fight over who is in the right or wrong.

DM: Wait... what?! I have to read this entire thread [above]? **May 24, 2012 at 6:45pm**

3SG6: ...What can I say [in regards to my comments made towards 3SG5]? *Laughter*. Donald, I have messaged you [privately, in Facebook messenger] with two important questions, please can you answer them. Thank you.

DM: OK [3SG6, I will]. **May 24, 2012 at 6:55pm**

Why it is difficult to express new information to others unaware of the information

3SG7: Anyway, enough of this bickering back and forth [in regards to what steps we can take to ensure the Illuminati's REM *driven human* cloning subculture is fully exposed sooner, and known about across the world sooner]! The bottom line is the same as always with anything you try to tell another person because, WHEN YOU TRY TO TELL SOMEONE ELSE ABOUT SOMETHING WHICH YOU KNOW TO BE TRUE BECAUSE YOU HAVE SPENT THE NECESSARY TIME AND DILIGENCE TO REACH THE CONCLUSION THAT WHAT YOU HAVE FOUND IS IN FACT TRUE, THE PEOPLE WHO DO NOT KNOW OF THE VERY THING YOU ARE TALKING ABOUT OR TRYING TO EXPLAIN TO THEM, WILL TRY AND DISCREDIT YOU IN ANYWAY THEY CAN SIMPLY BECAUSE THEY ARE NOT THE ONES WITH THE KNOWLEDGE [OF WHAT YOU ARE DISCUSSING], AND IT IS MUCH EASIER FOR THEM TO DISMISS WHAT YOU ARE SAYING, THAN TO ADMIT, THEY REALLY DID NOT KNOW WHAT YOU ARE TALKING ABOUT... So [3SG5 (and 3SG6) as well as everybody else] just relax, and let Donald Marshall release the next document regarding the Illuminati's *REM driven human* cloning subculture, and together we can go from there. Fighting amongst each other, when many of us here for this cause, are here for good intentions, and know Donald Marshall's exposures regarding the Illuminati's *REM driven human* cloning subculture to be true, because we have spent the necessary time, and through diligent research reached our own conclusions that there must be truth to what Donald is exposing, will only divide us if we continue to fight [over petty issues], we should all be coming together as one force, united to take down the Illuminati, and their *REM driven human* cloning subculture!

DM: Wow! [I have now read the entire thread, and I can't believe there is bickering amongst us, when we should be all united to take down our common enemy: the Illuminati, and their *REM driven human* cloning subculture]. **May 24, 2012 at 6:55pm**

"Eyes Wide Shut" & "Avatar" explained by Donald Marshall

DM: Yes, "Eyes Wide Shut" (1999) is a movie made by the Illuminati. The Illuminati do what is depicted in the movie "Eyes Wide Shut" (1999) (such as sex, torture, death sports and more) every single night of the year. However, with regards to the Illuminati, most of the events which is depicted in the movie "Eyes Wide Shut" (1999) which the Illuminati members do, they do as *REM driven* clone versions of themselves, which gives the Illuminati members the alibi of being at home (in their original bodies), although in actuality the Illuminati members commit crimes via the process of consciousness transfer to their *REM driven* clone duplicates, and it is the original person who controls the *REM driven* clone duplicate. Therefore, unlike the movie "Eyes Wide Shut" (1999), the Illuminati do not wear masks when they are activated as *REM driven* cloned versions of themselves at the cloning center(s); the Illuminati members wear jogging pants and sweat-shirts as *REM driven* clone versions of themselves at the cloning centers. Furthermore, sometimes the Illuminati bring REAL people (in their original bodies) to the cloning centers, and sometimes, the Illuminati members commit their crimes or perverse acts in their real bodies, in real life (and not as *REM driven* cloned versions of themselves)... However, the Illuminati members mostly meet to perform the actions depicted in "Eyes Wide Shut" (1999) as *REM driven human* clone alternatives (at the cloning centers). **May 24, 2012 at 6:56pm**

DM: Avatar (2009), on the other hand, is also a movie made by the Illuminati. The concept for the movie Avatar (2009) is based off from the reality of REM driven human cloning, for which REM driven human cloning has been a reality since 1945 and was perfected in complete secrecy by the Illuminati in 1945. **May 24, 2012 at 6:56pm**

Donald Marshall on: exposing the Illuminati & the danger he faces: "Megadeath"

DM: I know what I am doing in terms of exposing the Illuminati's *REM driven human* cloning subculture; I have been planning the exposure and divulgement of the Illuminati's *REM driven human* cloning subculture for many years. Furthermore, what will Document 2 do? Document 2 [*which will contain a long list of names of public Figures Donald Marshall has seen as REM driven clone alternatives, and what these public figures have done as REM driven clone alternatives at the cloning center(s), as well as, the list of songs Donald Marshall has composed as a REM driven clone version of himself from the cloning center(s)...*] is not proof (hard evidence) of the Illuminati's *REM driven human* cloning subculture either. Nonetheless I DO HAVE SOME PROOF about the Illuminati's *REM driven human* cloning subculture, however, [the small proof] it is a surprise [the surprise was Donald Marshall planned to have another person who had been cloned, and has *REM driven* clone experiences, appear on camera the following Saturday with Donald Marshall in order to corroborate Donald Marshall's disclosures about the Illuminati's *REM driven human* cloning subculture]... and moreover, if I released Document 2 now and everyone read it, and it achieved the same result as Document 1 (Donald Marshall Proboards 2012a), where the majority of the general public dismisses Document 2 and say it is not proof positive (hard evidence) of the Illuminati's *REM driven human* cloning subculture, then I am **DOOMED**! Your impatience 3SG5 does not mean anything to me. Your life is not in danger 3SG5. Furthermore, I am not only in danger of death, I am in danger of "**Megadeath**". **May 24, 2012 at 6:59pm**

["Megadeath" (spelled with an "a" in the word "death") is different from the American trash metal band of the same pronunciation "Megadeth" (spelled without an "a" in the word "death" –i.e. "deth"). Megadeath is where: after the body of an original person dies, the Illuminati clone the dead person from their dead remains, and transfer the dead person's consciousness into new cloned bodies (cloned from the dead person's remains), where the person whose original (natural born body has now died), suffers "death" multiple times, as cloned versions of themselves over and over again, from several hundred times, to **several thousand times**, by being killed and tortured, clone after clone, after clone –at the hands of the Illuminati, because the dead person's consciousness had not yet left this plane of existence.

A person is completely at the mercy of the Illuminati during megadeath (rituals), because a person's original body is now deceased, and therefore they can no longer wake up in their original body where their consciousness in their original body, overrides the capacity to allow the Illuminati to transfer their consciousness to (duplicate or new) cloned bodies; such as a person can wake up (from sleep) in their original body and avoid further torture suffered as a Mark 2 REM driven clone.

Donald Marshall is not theorising, when he says "He is not only in danger of death, he is in danger of "Megadeath"" because as a *REM driven* clone version of himself, Donald Marshall has seen through firsthand experience, other people, as well as, public figures, who have died (in their original bodies), and have been grown as cloned versions of themselves from their dead remains, only to have their consciousness transferred to their clones, where these people, as well as, public figures have been killed several hundred times as cloned versions of themselves after their original bodies have died, because their consciousnesses had not yet left this plane of existence. This is why Donald Marshall is **FRANTIC**, and chooses to divulge information regarding the Illuminati's *REM driven human* cloning subculture in phases, in order to guarantee his success, because there are worse fates than death, and one such example is: megadeath.

Public figures who Donald Marshall has seen megadeathed (die clone after clone, after clone, after their original bodies have died), when Donald Marshall has unwillingly been activated as a *REM driven* clone version of himself at the cloning center, at the hands of the Illuminati, will be discussed in upcoming documents].

DM: The Illuminati *as REM driven clone versions of themselves*, will make me suffer a worse fate than ever once they believe it is safe to carry on their perversity as *REM driven* cloned versions in complete secrecy, and once they believe they will never face repercussions for their actions as a result of their *REM driven human* cloning subculture; I will be **doomed** [if this were to happen]. I have to guarantee the success of this divulgement, regarding the full exposure of the Illuminati's *REM driven human* cloning subculture, and I must also (somehow) **COMPEL** the general public to the point where they know and understand that the Illuminati's *REM driven human* cloning subculture is indeed a reality and such an injustice on earth exists, which must end. I must do this correctly, to guarantee the success of this disclosure; I know those of you here [reading this information], know what I mean. I can understand everybody is excited, I know. Do you know why you are all excited? Because finally the populace has chance to confront and punish the Illuminati for the wrongs which the Illuminati has done, and continues to do... everyone is excited by this, and because they have a feeling that the information regarding the Illuminati's *REM driven human* cloning subculture is true, now, people want complete and absolute proof (hard evidence) about the Illuminati's *REM driven human* cloning subculture, so that they can confront the perpetrators in confidence and act now... Complete and absolute proof (hard evidence) regarding the Illuminati's *REM driven human* cloning subculture is not much farther. **May 24, 2012 at 7:01pm**

3SG5: Gee! How would I know if you have written Document 2 or not, yet? My life, and the lives of others MAY be in danger for sharing your letter (Donald Marshall Proboards 2012a) in regards to the Illuminati's *REM driven human* cloning subculture, have you EVER thought about that? Moreover, I am not 'excited', I just want this situation concerning the exposure of the Illuminati's *REM driven human* cloning subculture to escalate quickly, so that it can end quickly. Until then, the only attention I am seeing seems to be focus on you.

Donald Marshall does NOT want attention once the Illuminati is fully exposed

DM: I would have replied sooner 3SG5, but 3SG2 went a little strange and he has left. **May 24, 2012 at 7:02pm**

3SG6: 3SG2 LEFT?! HOW COME?

DM: 3SG5, I MUST STRESS: I do NOT want attention. I hate being on front of a (video) camera, because everything I have ever done (*as a REM driven clone version of myself at the cloning center*), since age 5, for **over thirty plus years** has been recorded at the cloning center. I really do **not** like being on camera. Moreover, and I am not sure when [or how exactly] this happened, but the Illuminati, inserted a càmera behind my right eyeball on the optical nerve [an image of the anatomy of the human eye, and where the "optic nerve" can be found is depicted below], and therefore, not only am I on camera constantly, whenever I am unwillingly activated as a *REM driven* clone version of myself at the cloning center, the Illuminati also **monitor EVERYTHING** I do in my real life, in my original body, every minute of the day, every second of the day, and have the option of playing events which happened in my everyday life on the big screen at the cloning center. Then of course there is the Global Positioning System (GPS), inserted in my right arm, in my original / real body, allowing the Illuminati to track my every movement on earth... not the mention the microchip implants inserted into my head... I do **NOT** like attention, and I do NOT want to be on camera... however, I must do this: I have to be the one to divulge information about the Illuminati's *REM driven human* cloning subculture, in the hope I can free myself and others from ever being activated unwillingly as *REM driven* clone versions of themselves, under the savagery of this dark and sinister international cult (the Illuminati).

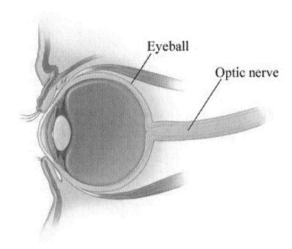

DM: Once the Illuminati's *REM driven human* cloning subculture is fully exposed, worldly known, and worldly exposure leads to the ban and practice of REM driven human cloning, as well as, the full and complete exposure of the Illuminati's *REM driven human* cloning subculture meets its end... I am not going to be on television... I will retreat into a bomb shelter with my Norwegian Princess, whereby I will live the rest of my life in seclusion. I will not be appearing on television; I will not be partaking in Skype video interviews / discussions... I will **not** want any interviews or discussions in terms of: "So Donny, you made all these songs"...

Furthermore, once the science and practice of *REM driven* human cloning is fully exposed, worldly known, and banned, as a science and practice, there will be no more torture of civilians unsuspectingly as *REM driven* clone versions of themselves, whenever their original body sleeps and enters REM sleep. Humans cannot be tortured as (REM driven) cloned versions of themselves, if (REM driven clones) cannot be grown (which will be a result of the Illuminati's *REM driven human* cloning subculture, becoming fully exposed and worldly known, leading to the ban and practice of *REM driven* human cloning).

The public is NOT in danger by sharing Donald Marshall's disclosures

DM: Moreover, the general public is not in danger from the Illuminati by sharing my disclosures regarding the Illuminati's *REM driven human* cloning subculture. People are not in danger now, because, I started to inform the public about the Illuminati's *REM driven human* cloning subculture, by first informing people in Middle Eastern countries; I did this because from my years spent as a *REM driven* clone at the cloning centers, the Illuminati *REM driven* clones expressed strong distaste for Muslims and therefore as a consequence, I figured 'they cannot be as terrible as the Illuminati *REM driven* clones were making them out to be'; as a matter of fact, Muslims are the Illuminati's **most** feared enemies. I have informed so many people many years ago about the Illuminati's *REM driven human* cloning subculture, to the point where the Illuminati would have to grow *REM driven* clones of **over a million** Arabs.

After sharing this information with many people in the Middle East, I began sharing information regarding the Illuminati's *REM driven human* cloning subculture disclosures to people in western countries, and since Anonymous (We Are Legion) discovered the information about the Illuminati's *REM driven human* cloning subculture, the information spread further, making it very difficult for the Illuminati to clone, or grow *REM driven* clones of, so many millions of individuals, in order for these individuals who are now informed about the Illuminati's *REM driven human* cloning subculture to face individual reprisals at the hands of the Illuminati.

DM: Therefore, you are not in danger now, and you can share these disclosures, and inform many members of the public with regards to the Illuminati's *REM driven human* cloning subculture, because there are too many people, many millions of people in fact, who are aware of the Illuminati's *REM driven human* cloning subculture, and therefore the Illuminati cannot clone all these millions upon millions of individuals who are now aware of the Illuminati's *REM driven human* cloning subculture, in order for these individuals to face danger or repercussions for learning the knowledge of REM driven cloning, at the hands of the Illuminati. There are too many people to clone now, or grow as *REM driven* clone duplicates, since Anonymous (We Are Legion) discovered the information regarding the Illuminati's REM *driven human cloning* subculture, whereby as a result of realising this information, Anonymous (We Are Legion) helped to distribute this information, to many more millions of the general public. You are not in danger now, continue to spread the word. **May 24, 2012 at 7:07pm**

3SG5: And I am sure you want the torture [*as a REM driven clone version of yourself, at the savagery of the Illuminati*] to end for you and for OTHERS!

3SG7: Donald, stay on your righteous path. Do not let ANY negativity stray you from your righteous path. In terms of your disclosure, regarding the Illuminati's *REM driven human* cloning subculture, if you had absolute proof (hard evidence) of REM driven cloning, then that would be the catalyst needed to truly reach the world.

3SG8: I agree with 3SG5, who can be described as anything else, other than ignorant on the subject of Illuminati or the Illuminati's *REM driven human* cloning subculture. 3SG5 is correct; what does it matter how many eyes are watching this information concerning the Illuminati's *REM driven human* cloning subculture; the truth is the truth; unless you seek something more [Donald].

DM: I **MUST** be successful, in my quest to expose the Illuminati's *REM driven human* cloning subculture! I MUST NOT fail! Vengeance [against the Illuminati perpetrators] is **FAR** too important to me... **May 24, 2012 at 7:25pm**

Why Document 2 will take a considerable amount of time to compile

3SG5: Donald was the one who brought up Document 2, and he has mentioned Document 2 a few times. At first, Donald said that Document 2 will take a while to write, and now he does not want to expose (this non written document) the individuals who have been *REM driven* clone versions of themselves at the cloning center, possibly for his safety? So what is it? Is Document 2 going to be written or not?

DM: Oh, I will write up Document 2 3SG5, and you [including everybody reading this information regarding the Illuminati's *REM driven human* cloning subculture] will get Document 2.

3SG9: 3SG5, I have personally been investigating this [the Illuminati / the occult] for many years. There are so many names involved in their shadowy cult; so many people involved in this sick cult [the Illuminati]; I understand it is going to take Donald a while to write up all the names of the original people, he has seen as *REM driven* cloned versions of themselves at the cloning center, and what they have done as *REM driven* cloned versions of themselves at the cloning center; it will take some time to write up. By the way, I have helped to solve over fifth-teen murders now; and I have also helped to find four to five missing people's bodies. I am a seer [a person with supposed supernatural insight, who has the ability to foretell events. Some "seers" also have the ability to "Remote view". Remote viewing is the practice of seeking impressions about a target or an unseen object by using extrasensory perceptions or "seeing with the mind"] and I am getting more, and more accurate with each passing day.

I believe Donald's claims about his experiences as a victim, in the Illuminati's *REM driven* cloning subculture [to be true], and I do agree that Donald must take steps in order to ensure his success, against the Illuminati. Furthermore, if it is the wish of everybody reading this thread, I will display results of some of my past investigations, with similar claims [such as the claims Donald Marshall has made against these high profile people mentioned in his open letter (Donald Marshall Proboards 2012a)] against these freaks [the Illuminati].

DM: So long as I get to see Queen Elizabeth II in a prison cell once the Illuminati's *REM driven human* cloning subculture has been fully exposed and worldly known [I'll be happy with that result]. Yes 3SG9, many people reading the information here concerning the Illuminati's *REM driven* cloning subculture, know [and feel] the information is true. Everybody just wants to get the Illuminati members for the crimes they have committed against humanity right now! I do too! However, "The best things come to those who wait" (Heinz Ketchup) (xlogold 2006; justking81 2008) –I stole that line [borrowed that slogan]; I thought it will sound cool [to use the Heinz Ketchup slogan]. **May 24, 2012 at 7:34pm**

The Illuminati culprits deserve to be lynched

3SG9: Six years ago, the truth [about the Illuminati / occult world] was revealed to the world. After such a revelation, people started buying alarms for their houses, and people started to REMOVE Lillibet's [Queen Elizabeth II's] pictures of the walls in their homes... Therefore, we know as a collective what is REALLY going on, and we KNOW who these people are, and we KNOW they "hide in plain sight" [to "hide in plain sight" is to appear **unnoticeable**, by staying **visible** in a setting that conceals a person's true identity]... so let's quit messing around, and ARREST these people! They [the Illuminati perpetrators] deserve lynching, Donald! If they [the Illuminati perpetrators] are evil people what does it matter [if humanity puts evil people to death]? I believe in the death penalty.

DM: Yes 3SG9, the Illuminati culprits do deserved to be lynched by the populace, however, I want Queen Elizabeth II kept alive for as long as possible. Once the Illuminati's _REM driven human_ cloning subculture is fully exposed and worldly known, I would like to see Queen Elizabeth II kept in a prison cell for as long as possible; in a prison cell without the pleasantries and luxuries she has become accustomed to, and the best part is: I want to be granted visiting rights. I have fantasised about the moment when I see the original (real) Queen Elizabeth II behind bars, in solitary confinement in a prison cell, since I was first activated as a _REM driven_ clone version of myself when I was a child, many times.

Moreover, Queen Elizabeth II will see what I just said about her above. The Illuminati members monitor my every post as _REM driven_ clone versions of themselves, from the cloning center. I told you I would get you [Queen Elizabeth II], you malevolent sinister hag! Who is laughing now [Queen Elizabeth II]? Well it is not you [who is the one laughing; is it Queen Elizabeth?!]...the last time I saw you [_as REM driven cloned versions of ourselves, at the cloning center_] you [Queen Elizabeth II, _as a REM driven clone version of yourself_] were crying! And what a disgusting sound too [to hear Queen Elizabeth II cry _as a REM driven clone version of herself_]! **May 24, 2012 at 7:52pm**

3SG5: 3SG9, which crimes have you solved? Where do you live in Vancouver?

Being monitored & the last six months endured as a REM driven clone

Monitoring

3SG10: Donald is the fact that the Illuminati are monitoring your every post, the reason why you write a little at a time, and in a short and concise manner?

DM: Yes [the Illuminati members monitor every single post of mine, and read my Facebook Timeline as _REM driven_ cloned versions of themselves, from the cloning center. The Illuminati also make disgruntled faces at me, as they read my Facebook posts from the cloning center when I am a _REM driven_ cloned version of myself, unwillingly activated at the cloning center, and sometimes they punish me for this. I also have to keep posts short and concise, because sometimes Facebook does not allow me to post (some) longer comments].

DM: All the celebrities, politicians, monarchies, and other Illuminati members of the world review my Facebook posts on a big screen at the cloning center, and all celebrities, politicians, monarchies and other Illuminati members are watching and reading my Facebook posts and waiting to see what happens so far as the exposure of the Illuminati's *REM driven human* cloning subculture is concerned. Furthermore, the Illuminati *REM driven* clones have interrogated me about what I have written on my Facebook wall when I have been unwillingly activated as a *REM driven human* clone version of myself in the past. The Illuminati *REM driven* clones, also tortured me as a *REM driven* clone *version of myself* at the cloning center for exposing their *REM driven human* cloning subculture via Facebook, in attempts to try and get me to stop posting about the Illuminati and about the Illuminati's *REM driven human* cloning subculture, once I wake up in my original body, and I am no longer a *REM driven* clone version of myself.

Donald Marshall on: REM driven clone torture during the previous six months

DM: I was almost close to a point where I was going to stop posting and divulging information about the Illuminati's *REM driven human* cloning subculture, when the Illuminati *REM driven* clones, started doing lumbar punctures (spinal taps), as well as, sucking the bone marrow out of my knees with a power-drill, whenever I was unwillingly activated as a *REM driven* clone version of myself, under the helm of the Illuminati's savagery. However, I have been waiting for this moment [where I can finally expose to the world the Illuminati's *REM driven human* cloning subculture, and have the good people of the world bring such a deplorable injustice to an end] and therefore, I preserved through the *REM driven* clone torture, whenever I would go to sleep in my original body and would be activated as a *REM driven* clone version of myself, by the Illuminati, who tortured me as a *REM driven* clone version of myself at the cloning center.

Moreover, I have been going to the library for a period of 2 - 4 hours a day, continuously for a period of six months now, to answer questions, and continue to expose the Illuminati's *REM driven human* cloning subculture. Through perseverance, the Illuminati have now stopped torturing me as a *REM driven* clone *version of myself*, and only activate me as a *REM driven* clone at the cloning center, in order to persuade me through conversation to stop exposing the Illuminati's *REM driven human* cloning subculture.

DM: These days whenever I am activated as a *REM driven* clone *version of myself*, it is not constant *REM driven* clone torture like it was in the past; I would have had an aneurysm in my original body if I had been constantly tortured as a *REM driven* clone version for many days on end... so [unfortunately] I have had to make more songs and give the Illuminati ideas, when I have been activated as a *REM driven* clone *version of myself* at the cloning center. Furthermore, the Illuminati *as REM driven clone versions of themselves*, have the vital signs of my original (real) body and the Illuminati *as REM driven clones*, monitor the extent to which *REM driven* clone torture is having on my real body... therefore as *REM driven* clone versions, the Illuminati *REM driven* clones put me to the edge of suffering a heart attack in my original body...and then they stop torturing me as a *REM driven* clone version of myself when the vital signals on their monitors begin to warn the Illuminati that I will have a heart attack or aneurysm in my original body if the Illuminati as *REM driven* clone versions continue with the torture of me as a *REM driven* clone. The Illuminati then transfer my consciousness from my original body to my *REM driven* clone the following evening, when I go to sleep and enter REM sleep, in further attempts to stop me exposing the Illuminati's *REM driven human* cloning subculture, in my waking life, when I am an original person, and no longer experiencing life, unwillingly activated as a *REM driven* clone at the savagery of the Illuminati.

The last six months has been more of an ordeal for me, than any of you will know, however, it will all be worth it when I finally get her [Queen Elizabeth II] and save many others from the Illuminati's *REM driven human* cloning subculture. Can you now appreciate how serious, and important this information is, and why it must be distributed to every corner of this earth and very speedily? I appreciate you guys so much [everyone helping to expose the Illuminati's *REM driven human* cloning subculture], I could not have done any of this without the good people of this world helping me to expose the Illuminati's *REM driven human* cloning subculture. **May 24, 2012 at 8:09pm**

3SG10: That's okay then. I understand [why you must type a little at a time, which is because the Illuminati monitor everything that you do]. As for me, I am going to help destroy the agendas of some of these Illuminati people, for the simple reason that these Illuminati people have polluted our God given land with their lies and deceptions, and therefore it does not matter who is watching or monitoring your posts to me. KILLUMINATI [kill (the) Illuminati]! I am so glad I have met a real friend on Facebook, who has valuable information which allows me to tell others the truth about what really goes on in this world! Oh YES, WE APPRECIATE YOU TOO DONNY!

DM: The practice of the Illuminati's *REM driven human* cloning subculture, is almost over... but I must ensure success. **May 24, 2012 at 8:10pm**

Computer generated scenarios of PROBABLE outcomes by exposing the Illuminati

DM: Moreover, the Illuminati as *REM driven* cloned versions of themselves, have shown me computer generated scenarios of what is likely to happen depending on how and what I say to the public concerning the Illuminati's *REM driven human* cloning subculture, when I have been a *REM driven* clone *version of myself, unwillingly activated* at the cloning center.

The Illuminati *REM driven* clones showed me (*as a REM driven clone version of myself*), probable scenarios on the big screen in the arena of the cloning center. The Illuminati also discussed with me, when we were *REM driven* cloned versions of ourselves at the cloning center, exactly **how and when** to disclose each level of information regarding the Illuminati's *REM driven* human cloning subculture, without widespread panic, without widespread rioting, without widespread violent protests, and without widespread lynching of government figureheads. In the computer generated probable scenarios which I was shown when I was a *REM driven* clone *version of myself* by the Illuminati *REM driven* clones, the army [of many nations] would even turn against them [the Illuminati].

Consequently, I do **NOT** want to be responsible for widespread death of the populace in the populace's attempts to rid the world of the Illuminati, whereby in retaliation, the Illuminati have drones [unmanned aircraft that can navigate autonomously, without human control, and beyond line of sight] deploy mini missiles on crowds of angry protestors [disgusted and seeking justice against the Illuminati's *REM driven human* cloning subculture].

In one computer generated probable scenario, which I was shown as a *REM driven* clone *version of myself, unwillingly activated as a REM driven clone version of myself* at the cloning center, an Asian country deployed a nuclear bomb [on their own people] in an attempt to save themselves [government heads and Illuminati members] from [getting lynched by] their own people. The computer generated probable scenarios which I saw as a *REM driven* clone *version of myself*, was reminiscent of talks discussing "The end of days" – [whereby world events, judgement and death, as well as the destiny of mankind reaches a climax].

Furthermore, in the computer generated probable scenario which I saw as a *REM driven* clone *version of myself* from the cloning center, after the Asian country deploys a nuclear bomb on their own people, World War III begins in Iran **(in the computer generated probable scenario which I was shown as a *REM driven* clone *version of myself*, from the cloning center).** Moreover, after World War III, Iran gets framed and known by nations worldwide, as the country which instigated World War III, although this is a total fabrication, as well as, lies and deceptions perpetrated by the Illuminati to frame Iran for World War III **(in the computer generated probable scenarios which I was shown as a *REM driven* clone version of myself from the cloning center). <u>May 24, 2012 at 7:38pm</u>**

3SG9: We [the populace] will win [against the overthrow of the Illuminati]. Even if the Illuminati try something such as deploying nuclear bombs on the populace and framing another country as the instigators of World War III, we [the populace] will still win [against the overthrow of the Illuminati] and the Illuminati know that.

The main concern RIGHT NOW to ensure the Illuminati is FULLY exposed!

DM: Oh we [the populace] have won [because the information regarding the Illuminati's *REM driven human* cloning subculture is now public, and known by groups of people in different countries across the world, and as a consequence, eventually the Illuminati perpetrators will be held accountable for their *REM driven human* cloning subculture as the years go by, and more and more of the populace learns of the Illuminati's heinous crimes], and now the main concern involves coming together as one force, in order to demand answers from the Illuminati perpetrators in masses and **millions upon millions** of numbers. The main concern right now, is to currently find many, many individuals who can look at this information **objectively**, get to point where many, many individuals realise the information concerning the Illuminati's *REM driven human* cloning subculture is **factual**, and feel **COMPELLED** to help bring the Illuminati's *REM driven human* cloning subculture to an end, by informing as many people as possible, in order to increase mass and public awareness in regards to the Illuminati's *REM driven human* cloning subculture, so that many millions can protest the abomination of the Illuminati's *REM driven human* cloning subculture physically, in mass numbers, and force the shutdown of the Illuminati's *REM driven human* cloning subculture, resulting in banning the science and practice of human cloning, as well as, REM driven human cloning. **May 24, 2012 at 7:38pm**

The LIES insisted by the Illuminati which Donald Marshall refused to tell the public

DM: Moreover, at the Illuminati's request, *which was a request the Illuminati made to me as REM driven clone versions of ourselves, when I was unwillingly activated as a REM driven clone version of myself through the process of consciousness transfer, is that,* the Illuminati would like me to say that "The cloning center [the one which I frequent *as a REM driven clone version of myself*] is just a "science playground"... and not much goes on there, just scientific silly nonsense, a silly place.

Furthermore, the Illuminati REM driven clones insisted that I inform the public that:

- "I was 17 years of age when the Illuminati first grew *REM driven* clone duplicates of me, and activated me as a REM driven clone *through the process of consciousness transfer as a REM driven clone version of myself*, and this did not happen when I was 5 years old" [although in actuality, the above did happen when I was 5 years old].

The Illuminati *as REM driven clone versions* further requested that I tell the public that:

- There are absolutely no *REM driven* clones of children, activated as *REM driven* clones of original children; real children are not kidnapped and brought to the cloning centers to be sacrificed; and children have never been brought to the cloning centers.

- There have never been any molestation of men, women and children as *REM driven* clone versions of original people; or molestation of original (real) people kidnapped and brought to the cloning centers in their original (real) bodies. [To "molest" means to assault or abuse a person sexually].

- There aren't any human sacrifices carried out in at the cloning centers as an honour to "Lucifer" "the light bringer"" for luck [money, fame, and fortune]; and that there aren't any human sacrifices to "Lucifer" "the light bringer"" in order to scare others [when people are activated as *REM driven* clone version of themselves at the cloning center(s)] to do what they are told and become complicit with the Illuminati's dogmas.

- There aren't any murder videos (such as the Robert Pickton (The Independent 2013; The Canadian Encyclopaedia 2016) murder videos) stored at the cloning center(s) or any alien abduction pornography videos stored at the cloning center(s).

- The Illuminati would also like me to reinstate to the public that I exaggerated about their *REM driven human* cloning subculture, (which is just laughable, because I have **NOT** exaggerated) and that I only ever received 'light' torture when the Illuminati activated me as a *REM driven* clone *version of myself*, and their reason for doing this was to scare me, ever so 'lightly' into producing songs for the Illuminati (which again is just laughable, because they have made me feel sick in my original (real) body as a result of torture of my *REM driven* clones many times, and the Illuminati, have also brought me to the brink of having a heart attack in my original body at times too), and;

- There are hardly any celebrities who are activated as *REM driven* clone versions of themselves and have to attend the cloning centers nightly as *REM driven* clones, whenever they sleep and entered REM sleep in exchange for fame and fortune [I suspect the Illuminati do not want the public to know this, because once such a reality is known, there will be masses of people who help to expose what happens to people who later became famous at the hands of the Illuminati, as well as the exchanges, forfeits and traps people fell into once they became famous, as well as, how certain famous individuals became puppets for the Illuminati].

DM: The above bullet points are what the Illuminati would like me to reinstate to the public, and it is what the Illuminati wanted me to do, when they asked me, *as REM driven clone versions of themselves, when I was unwillingly activated as a REM driven clone version of myself*, at the cloning center to "sugar-coat" the Illuminati's *REM driven human* cloning subculture. Nonetheless, I **CANNOT** and **WILL NOT** spread lies for the Illuminati! The Illuminati's plan was to destroy the above-ground cloning center [in order to destroy (hard) evidence] located in western Canada which I frequent unwillingly, as I am activated as a *REM driven* clone version of myself, at the savagery of the Illuminati, whenever I sleep and I enter REM sleep. Nevertheless, further details of the Illuminati's plan was to allow the other cloning centers to remain secret, and continue their *REM driven human* cloning subculture in secrecy once the above ground cloning center in western Canada is destroyed, and the populace is somewhat placated that a human cloning center has been nullified. **May 24, 2012 at 7:42pm**

DM: So... "And they say that a hero will save us, I'm not gonna stand here and waiiiiit" (Nickelback 2013) –and yes, I made the song as a *REM driven* clone version of myself from the cloning center, which Nickelback later performed. **May 24, 2012 at 7:44pm**

[Donald Marshall makes the above reference to the that line from the song "Hero" performed by Nickelback (Nickelback 2013), with respect to the fact that he, Donald Marshall, will continue to expose the Illuminati's *REM driven human* cloning subculture, (and this is a stance people who know the information regarding the Illuminati's *REM driven human* cloning subculture to be true, must also take, and therefore, help to also expose the Illuminati's *REM driven human* cloning subculture) and he will not wait for an outside force to 'save him', because by that time, it may be too late (and the Illuminati, will have achieved their aim of power and total world domination over the earth). Consequently, humans who know the information regarding the Illuminati's *REM driven* cloning subculture to be true, must also take a similar stance to Donald Marshall and start actively exposing the Illuminati's *REM driven human* cloning subculture, in order for the world not to fall at the demise of the Illuminati]

Donald Marshall explains why he must stay calm given the gravity of this situation

DM: "Why am I so calm?" [Given the gravity of the scale and seriousness of the situation concerning the Illuminati's *REM driven human* cloning subculture] –some people have asked me. It is because, I must remain calm [as best as possible] in order to win against the Illuminati and ensure the Illuminati's *REM driven human* cloning subculture is fully exposed and worldly known. If I start to go loopy [mad or silly] like Britney Spears [when she shaved her hair off so that she was completely bald and appeared in public, because watching many Robert Pickton murder videos as a *REM driven* clone *version of herself* drove Britney Spears to her limit in her waking life (All Spears 2016)] or Steven [Joseph Christopher] (also known as 'the Messiaaaaaah') *laughter* - I will be doomed! I will not just be a "dead man walking" [someone who is about to suffer an unavoidable loss] if I do not maintain composure and see to the end of the Illuminati's *REM driven human* cloning subculture, because as I have already mentioned, I am not just in danger of death, I am in danger of "megadeath" [which is explained on pp. 88 - 89 in this document]. Furthermore, if I do not maintain my composure and realise the end of the Illuminati's *REM driven human* cloning subculture, as Queen Elizabeth II has said *as a REM driven human clone version of herself* "I will be "irrevocably" doomed!" [because I will be re-animated as a clone after I die in my original body, and so long as my consciousness has not left this plane of existence, the Illuminati will trap my consciousness into multiple clone bodies, and kill me clone body, after clone body, after clone body, thousands of times, for divulging to the world: the Illuminati's *REM driven human* cloning subculture. This is what it means to be "megadeathed": –to die in one's original body, only to be reanimated as a clone, and have her or his consciousness trapped in multiple clone bodies, and killed as a "permanent clone" version of their original self, clone body, after clone body... multiple times]. **May 24, 2012 at 7:46pm**

DM: Wow I spelt that correctly too ["irrevocably"]. Someone please say something [on my Facebook Timeline]... The silence or lack of correspondence from people reading this information [on my Facebook Timeline] is unnerving. *Laughter* it is so quiet [on my Facebook Timeline] it is as if I am in an empty room and I can hear the echo, the EHCO [of my own voice]. Gee, I knew realising the truth about what the Illuminati really do, and how, why, and when the Illuminati do what they do is scary... but... I guess I have scared everyone away... That is okay, it appears everyone has become silent [on my Facebook Timeline] because people are in shock at this very moment, and are beginning to realise *REM driven* cloning is indeed reality; it is okay people usually react this way once they realise *REM driven* cloning is indeed a reality; the best thing to do is give yourself time, and let this information settle, in order to be understood without panic mentality; people also become braver and want to take the fight to the Illuminati once they realise that their silence is consent for this sickness to continue, and they **will NOT** and **CANNOT,** in their name, allow innocent children to continue to be kidnapped, molested, raped, tortured and sacrificed to "Lucifer" "the light bringer"" by a group of over-zealot individuals corrupted by greed and power [the Illuminati perpetrators].

Furthermore, people reading this exposure regarding the Illuminati's *REM driven human* cloning subculture can relax; they can relax, in respect to the fact that the continual exposure and widespread distribution of information [and documents] such as this **SIGNIFIES** that Illuminati's *REM driven human* cloning subculture will be fully exposed, worldly known, and ended soon. **May 24, 2012 at 7:49pm**

Tila Tequila MUST tell the TRUTH about the Illuminati's REM driven cloning

3SG10: Donald, I found you through Tila Tequila's Blogspot (Tila Tequila c. 2012) and posts.

DM: If Tila Tequila does not join this cause and help us to expose the Illuminati's *REM driven human* cloning subculture, I will have a LOT to tell everyone about "The Scorpion Demon". I know plenty about what Tila Tequila has done as a *REM driven* clone version *of herself*, at the cloning center, and this is why Tila Tequila has not blocked me from her Facebook Timeline. However, the fact the fact that Tila Tequila is aware that I know plenty of information about what she has done as a *REM driven* clone *version of herself*, at the cloning center, might be why she has not yet joined this cause to help us to expose the Illuminati's *REM driven human* cloning subculture; Tila Tequila may believe that I will betray her [if she were to join this cause], by revealing all she has done at the cloning center *as a REM driven clone version of herself.*

However, all that Tila Tequila needs to do is say "Yes, okay Donny, I have been cloned [by the Illuminati] too [and there are *REM driven duplicate* clones of me, go and follow Donald Marshall's Facebook page] everyone". Nonetheless despite what Tila Tequila may be thinking, I am nice, and I want freedom from the Illuminati's *REM driven human* cloning subculture. I mean does the name "The Scorpion Demon" sound like a nice name to you? *Laughter*. Tila Tequila also reads and watches my Facebook page in her waking life, on a Facebook account registered under: "Tila Nguyen" and not as 'Tila Tequila'. They are all [celebrities, politicians, royalty etc.] watching [my Facebook page]. **May 24, 2012 at 8:03pm**

3SG10: Oh my goodness, that many people are watching your Facebook wall and know what is going on? Well, I am not overly worried or overreacting about the Illuminati's *REM driven human* cloning subculture, and if people do know about the Illuminati's *REM driven human* cloning subculture, and choose to hide some truths or not speak up in regards to the Illuminati's *REM driven human* cloning subculture, then **SHAME** on them!

DM: OK, it is now your turn to type [directed at all reading Donald Marshall's Facebook page, who are watching behind their devices in silence]. Most people reading the information about the Illuminati's *REM driven human* cloning disclosure are now in a mild form of shock; it is okay people, you can relax. The shock stage will pass, it is common, it happens when people find out and realise the Illuminati's *REM driven human* cloning subculture is a reality. You guys are still so quiet; did you guys get aneurysms? *Laughter* ECHO! Hmm, perhaps I have bored them all away... that is okay though, I am my own best company. **May 24, 2012 at 8:13pm**

Document 2

May 23ʳᵈ 2012

The Purpose of Document 2

3SG1: I think the purpose of Document 2 is: if Donald [Marshall] names many high profile names [and Donald Marshall details the actions these high profile people have done as *REM driven* cloned versions of themselves at the cloning center], and in return the high profile people who have been named in Donald Marshall's Document 2 do not sue Donald Marshall (in real life) for: slander, libel, defamation etc...; then the lack of legal action, or silence, by the high profile figures mentioned in Document 2 will further confirm that Donald Marshall's exposure of the Illuminati's *REM driven human* cloning subculture as being true. Do you understand this? The lack of legal action from the high profile people which Donald Marshall mentions in his Document 2 will be more proof for people then [and that is the purpose Document 2 serves].

DM: [Yes 3SG1 that will be the purpose Document 2 serves. In other words Document 2 should raise alarm bells (**warn people of impending trouble and the need for action**) in people's heads if many high profile people are mentioned in Document 2, and these high profile people do not take legal action against Donald Marshall by suing him for: slander, libel, defamation etc....] Okay, [with the above said] I will be making a video disclosure this coming Saturday evening with a special guest [Donald Marshall's nephew who also remembers his *REM driven human* cloning experiences from the cloning center]. After the video disclosure [with my nephew] I will then complete Document 2. The amount of names, political leaders, and celebrities mentioned in Document 2 as people who have been *REM driven human* clone versions of themselves, and what these high profile people have done as *REM driven human* clone versions of themselves will be extremely long. The list of musicians who have also been *REM driven human* clone versions of themselves which I have interacted with as a *REM driven human* clone *version of myself* at the cloning center will also be long.

DM: Please remember I am not bragging or trying to be cool by listing the who is who that I have met as a *REM driven* clone *version of myself* at the cloning center, because after all I am an **unwilling participant** in the Illuminati's *REM driven human* cloning subculture. You must also understand that I have been having my consciousness transferred unwillingly from my original body to a *REM driven duplicate* clone body of me, located at the cloning center whenever I would sleep, nearly every singly night since the age of 5 years old. Now I must reiterate that I never made songs every single time I was unwillingly activated as a *REM driven* clone version of myself by the Illuminati at the cloning center, however, I did make songs on most nights when I went to sleep in my original body and I was unwillingly activated as a *REM driven human* clone version of myself. Furthermore, remember there are 365.25 days (*0.25 accounts for leap years*) in a year; 7 days in a week; where I was unwillingly activated by the Illuminati as a *REM driven human* clone *version of myself* nearly every night I went to sleep in my original body, whereby as a *REM driven human* clone *version of myself*, I had to produce songs or suffer *REM driven human* clone torture at the hands of the Illuminati *REM driven human* clones. On some nights when I was activated as a *REM driven* clone version of myself, I would compose as many as 5 songs in the evening *I was activated unwillingly as a REM driven human clone version of myself...* on other evenings I would only compose 1 song as a *REM driven human* clone *version of me...* it was usually just 1 song that I would have to compose as a *REM driven* clone *version of myself* at the cloning center (or suffer the consequences of *REM driven human* clone torture).

Nonetheless, even averaging 1 song per night over the course of 31 years, 365.25 days a year, is an absurd amount of songs to have composed from the cloning center, as a *REM driven human* clone version of myself. *As a REM driven clone version of myself, and an unwillingly participant in the Illuminati's REM driven human cloning subculture, activated unwillingly as a REM driven clone by the Illuminati,* I have made more songs than anyone on earth, ever! The songs which I composed from the cloning center, as a *REM driven* clone version of myself, include the biggest hits ever played on the radio and performed by other musicians. In actuality, plenty of songs which people have heard musicians perform [in the late 20th century to 21st century], are songs which I composed as a *REM driven human* clone version of myself from the cloning center. Moreover, most songs which I have composed as a *REM driven* clone version of myself from the cloning center, are songs which have been later given musicians to perform.

[The proclamation above is one of the hardest, harshest and most difficult realities for most people to accept in regards to how **false** the music industry is in actuality, and the reality that one man has composed thousands upon thousands of songs for others to perform].

DM: The fact that I have composed many, many songs as a *REM driven human* clone version of myself, whereby these songs became very popular is the reason the Illuminati, as well as others (celebrities, politicians, musicians, royalty etc.) who attend the cloning center(s) as *REM driven clone versions of themselves*, believe I have some kind of religious significance, which I do **NOT**, and neither do I endorse [I do **NOT** have a religious significance, and I just want freedom from the Illuminati's *REM driven human* cloning subculture]... Blah! The disclosure and exposure of the Illuminati's *REM driven human* cloning subculture would progress a lot easier with Tila Tequila's help! **May 25, 2012 at 6:34am**

[Donald Marshall is 36 years old here when he made the above statements. The important notes to take from his comments are that he is not bragging or trying to be cool; he is simply detailing fact, which happens to be based on the reality that because of the songs which he was **forced** to compose as a *REM driven human* clone *version of himself* since age 5, this is the main reason he was allowed to learn about the Illuminati's *REM driven human* cloning subculture, and in return (for composing songs) the Illuminati *REM driven* clones disclosed Illuminati secrets to Donald Marshall because the Illuminati *REM driven* clones were in awe of the songs Donald Marshall was composing.

Moreover, when Donald Marshall first had his consciousness transferred to his *REM driven* clone duplicate at age 5, Donald Marshall would think that he had been kidnapped... and he was experiencing life in his actual body, and not in a *REM driven* clone body. Furthermore, as a result of being afraid and finding himself suddenly in an unknown location, as a *REM driven* clone *version of himself*, Donald Marshall pleaded with the Illuminati *REM driven* clones, who in return turned to Donald Marshall asking "If he had any sort of use, and whether he could sing or dance?"; because Donald Marshall feared for his life during such an ordeal, this resulted in vasodilatation (a massive rush of blood to his head) (The Naked Scientists 2009), as well as, Donald Marshall producing large amounts of adrenaline (*in his REM driven clone body*), whereby as a result, Donald Marshall sang an original song freestyle, from start to finish, in the hopes that his capturers would let him free / spare him, as a child *REM driven* clone *version of himself* at age 5. Since that moment, Donald Marshall has been **forced** to compose songs as a *REM driven* clone version of himself, when he is unwillingly activated as a *REM driven* clone at the cloning center by the Illuminati *REM driven* clones, or suffer punishment and torture as a *REM driven human* clone version of himself.

Therefore, because Donald Marshall was **forced** as a *REM driven* clone to compose songs on behalf of the Illuminati, or suffer the consequences of *REM driven human* clone torture, which affects him in his original body (because consciousness is linked (Ehrsson 2013)), he means it when he says "He is not bragging or trying to be cool", and in actuality Donald Marshall is **embarrassed** that he has helped a group of contemptible, evil, greedy and power hungry individuals profit immensely through his talent.

Furthermore it must be stressed that when Donald Marshall says he composed an absurd amount of songs as a *REM driven* clone *version of himself* from the cloning center, he **MEANS** an absurd amount of songs! The simple reason is this: there are 365.25 days in a year (*0.25 accounts for leap years*), multiplied by 31 years (because Donald Marshall was 5 years old when he first started to compose songs *as a REM driven human clone version of himself*; 36 take away 5 = 31) equals 11322.75! Consequently, with the possibility that Donald Marshall averaged just 1 song a day, 365.25 days a year over the course of 31 years, this would mean Donald Marshall has composed as much as over 11,000 songs, over the course of 31 one years, whereby he was **forced** as a *REM driven human* clone version of himself to compose songs on behalf of the Illuminati, or be tortured as a *REM driven* clone version of himself!

It is very important to understand this, (or try as best as possible to understand) in terms of the magnitude of songs Donald Marshall has composed as a *REM driven* clone *version of himself* from the cloning center, because as outsiders, it allows us to better understand how Donald Marshall learned the information he did from the Illuminati *REM driven* clones; the Illuminati *REM driven* clones were in awe of Donald Marshall's ability to compose original songs. Understanding, or trying to comprehend the magnitude of the songs Donald Marshall composed as a *REM driven* clone version of himself, also allows us to further understand how Donald Marshall learned the information which he is presenting to the world, concerning the Illuminati's *REM driven human* cloning subculture; and the (supposed) reasons why the Illuminati have not killed him: because, through **force**, he provided a huge source of income for the Illuminati (**which he is embarrassed about**); and nobody kills a man who is going to make them a substantial amount of money. Therefore, understanding or trying to comprehend the magnitude of songs Donald Marshall has composed as a *REM driven human* clone, allows us to further understand other topics and rectify certain discrepancies so far as Donald Marshall's exposure of the Illuminati's *REM driven human* cloning subculture is concerned].

Donald Marshall's life purpose

May 19th 2012

Pollution, Wildlife Preservation, Sustainability & Donald Marshall's main priority

3SG1: [...] I was mentioning gem stones for pollution. Donald, you mentioned "How to deal with pollution" in one of the videos you made at home with those dudes [...]

DM: No. I currently have little interest in pollution. I WANT to ESCAPE the cloning station and never be activated as a *REM driven* clone again in my life. I also want to tell the world what the Illuminati / New World Order (NWO) do with REM driven cloning technology.

Escaping the cloning centers, and telling the world about what the Illuminati / NWO do with REM driven cloning technology is currently my only interest, and prime purpose in life. As I've already explained, REM driven cloning torture hurts, just as badly as it would do if such pain was exerted on a person's original body. *REM driven* clone torture also affects a person's original body, because consciousness is linked (Ehrsson 2013); *REM driven* clone pain, hurts just like pain hurts in real life. I have **no choice** but to tell the world exactly what the Illuminati do, as well as, tell the world about the **CURRENT** technologies which I have seen, and haven been proven to me with my very own eyes through the process of consciousness transfer and REM driven cloning technology, as **CURRENT** technologies which exist, presently. **May 20, 2012 at 4:58am**

3SG2: Don, what about wildlife preservation, and sustainability?

DM: Currently, those topics are not relevant to me. I am currently not concerned about whales or koala bears. I just **WANT TO ESCAPE** the cloning centers and the Illuminati's *REM driven* cloning technology... I want to ESCAPE *REM driven* cloning a LOT MORE than Tila Tequila does, trust me... **May 20, 2012 at 5:01am**

May 20th 2012

Donald Marshall expresses his views on his desire to have an ordinary life

3SG1: Donald, do you find your "normal" daily life, while you are not asleep and "engaged" [*as a REM driven clone version, at the cloning center*] mundane (?); or are you just more thankful [for a "normal" everyday life]? I mean [given everything you have disclosed regarding the Illuminati's *REM driven human* cloning subculture] I think I would be [more thankful for a "normal" everyday life].

DM: I love mundane. I do not want to be on television, or become famous... I only want to complete my primary objectives [which is escaping the cloning centers, exposing the Illuminati fully, and their *REM driven human* cloning subculture, and exposing all the evil the Illuminati have done and continue to do, so that it is worldly known, and their reign of terror is ended]. **October 28, 2012 at 1:38am**

3SG1: I think you have [completed your primary objectives –to some effect]. I mean, at this present moment in time, people who have decided to pay attention know [*about the Illuminati's REM driven human cloning subculture*] at the very least. However, I wish more people knew [*about the Illuminati's REM driven human cloning subculture*].

This is why it is imperative to share these disclosures so that more people do become aware of where a prominent source of evil is manifesting from in this world.

Illuminati Factions

May 23rd 2012

Illuminati Bloodlines: Papal Bloodlines

3SG1 posted the following comments (below) about bloodlines of the Illuminati

3SG1: Hi Donald, I am just curious about what you know regarding the following information:

"... [T]he true ruling elite bloodlines of the world are the Papal bloodlines: the Ptolemaic; these [bloodlines] being Farnese, Orsini, Breakspeare, Somaglia and Aldobrandini; they are Ancient bloodlines of Rome which practice to this day Zoroastrianism and Mithras."

["Zoroastrianism" is one of the world's oldest monotheistic religions. "Monotheism" is the belief in a single all-powerful god, as supposed to religions that believe in multiple gods. Judaism, Christianity, and Islam, are widely practiced forms of monotheism. Zoroastrianism was founded by the prophet Zoroaster in ancient Iran, approximately 3500 years ago (BBC Religions 2009; BBC Religions c. 2014).

"Mithraism" as an alternative religion, and also known as "Mythraic mysteries", was a mystery religion centred on the god "Mithras". Mithraism was practised in the Roman Empire from approximately the 1st to the 4th century A.D. (Encyclopaedia Britannica 2016a)]

"Hollywood is controlled by the Orsini (Maximus) Papal Bloodline of the shadow hierarchy of the Jesuit Order. Pepe Orsini "The Grey Pope" controls Hollywood. Take a look at the President of the Screen Actors Guild (SAG–AFTRA 2016).

[The Screen Actors Guild (SAG) was an American labour union that existed from 1933 – 2012. SAG represented over 100,000 actors, announcers, broadcast journalists, dancers, DJs, news writers, news editors, program hosts, puppeteers, recording artists, singers, stunt performers, voiceover artists and other media professionals. On March 2012, the leadership of the union decided to merge with The American Federation of Television and Radio Artists (AFTRA) to become SAG–AFTRA (SAG-AFTRA 2016)]

Who is it? It is a Rosenberg by the name of Alan [Alan Rosenberg]. Who are the Rosenbergs exactly? The Rosenbergs are an offshoot of the Orsini! Interesting isn't it how the latest and biggest vampire movie "Twilight" (2008) also had Melissa Rosenberg (Orsini) [American Screenwriter] [write the entire] screen play [for the movie "Twilight" (2008)]. Take note of the Twilight series of books and films, as Stephenie Meyer [American author of the "Twilight" series (Meyer 2005; 2006; 2007; 2008)] hints to the world about who is really in charge [of this world]. Through her writing, Stephenie Meyer, is subliminally giving the reader "Rome" [Stephenie Meyer is letting the world know that "Rome" is the epicentre of power in this world]. The reader should also note how Stephenie Myer is pushing Tuscany [city in Italy] where many powerful "Pontifex Maximus'" have come from!

[In ancient Rome "Pontifex Maximus" was the head of the principal college of priests. In the Roman Catholic Church, "Pontifex Maximus" is a title for the Pope]

My God these Papal Bloodlines have more money and knowledge than anyone can dream of. Whilst the Rothschild (Investopedia 2015) were pikers ["A "piker" is a person who does anything in a small or contemptibly small or cheap way"; "a stingy, tight-fisted person"], however, the Jesuit Pallavicini family was funding both sides [of the war] as usual.

[The Pallavicini family belongs to an Italian aristocracy and was first mentioned in the 12th century. The Pallavicini family descended from Marquis "Obertus Pallavicini" (Palais Pallavicini 2016); "Marquis" –is a title (in some European countries) for a nobleman ranking above a Count and below a Duke.

Moreover, The House of Pallavicini functions as a bridge between the West and the Middle-East. The House of Pallavicini has major control over Islam. Furthermore, The House of Pallavicini's financial power is matched by few. The Rothschilds (Investopedia 2015) would wish they had as much power as the Pallavicini family. The Rothschilds are subservient to the House of Pallavicini (One World Of Nations 2014)].

The Pallavicini family gave an astronomical amount of money to Queen Elizabeth I [of England] to fund her war with the Spanish (Anglo-Spanish War (1585-1604)) (BBC History 2011). This was [during the late 16th century] when such an amount of money given to Queen Elizabeth I by the Pallavicini family was truly astronomical; moreover, the funding of Queen Elizabeth I by the Pallavicini family happened before the Rothschilds were ever associated with the Cecil family (late 19th century to early 20th century (1845-1917) (One World Of Nations 2014)) for goodness sake!

The Papal Bloodlines invented [the profiteering] currency in the first place. We hear talk about the great Medici's (History 2009) all day long, and how the Medici's (History 2009) are the banking family of Europe; if the above statement is correct then tell me why the Medici's longed to breed into the Papal Bloodlines so that the Medici family could acquire great status? If people study which Bloodlines the Medici family bred into, they will finally start to make some real sense of the entire equation. It is not all as mysterious and difficult to see what is going on as one would expect.

All roads currently lead back to Pepe Orsini (Kirsch 1911), who right now is the richest man in Italy; however, did you know who Pepe Orsini is? Have you even seen a picture of Pepe Orsini? I bet not! The Romans laugh at individuals of the general populace who aim to expose the agendas of the Papal Bloodline's global conspiracy, because it is the Papal Bloodlines who direct and influence conspiracy enthusiasts to jump through Sci-Fi (such as the "Twilight" series (Meyer 2005; 2006; 2007; 2008; Twilight 2008)) and nonsense hoops (in order to gain a modicum of semblance about the real truth of the world, in which they live), like good performing little dogs. The Jesuits (Encyclopaedia Britannica 2015) own all the finance of the world, as well as, all the esoteric and occult (hidden) knowledge in the world.

Furthermore, the Casanova Family (who control Switzerland) are controlled by Pepe Orsini! "The Grey Pope" Pepe Orsini is protected and guarded by the Swiss Guard (Vatican c.2016), and this is symbolic and in truth about Pepe Orsini's power over Switzerland, for which Switzerland is incidentally the banking world headquarters (Bank for International Settlements 2016).

The Swiss Guard protection over "The Grey Pope" Pepe Orsini is merely symbolic, and this is why if "The Grey Pope" is ever really threatened, then what happens is the Swiss Guard is removed and replaced by "The Knights of Malta" (Moeller 1910; Zen Gardner 2013). "The Knights of Malta" were subordinated to the Jesuit Order in 1798.

Since 1798, "The Knights of Malta" have been loyal servants to the Jesuit Order and the Jesuit Papacy. "The Knights of Malta" control the military-industrial-pharmaceutical-Petrochemical complex (Zen Gardner 2013). King Juan Carlos I [of Spain, from 1975 - 2014] answers only to the Jesuit Order due to his stolen title off Emmanuel IV, the King of Jerusalem. King Juan Carlos I of Spain is the Roman Monarch who controls Southern Italy, including Sicily (which is a large Island in the Mediterranean Sea, off the 'boot' of Italy).

[It is possible the author is, perhaps referring to "Charles Emmanuel IV of Sardinia" – but this source could not be confirmed]

King Juan Carlos I of Spain controls the Mafiosi of the world, and the Mafiosi of the world are all subordinate to the Sicilian Mafiosi (Best of Sicily c. 2016). Juan Carlos I of Spain controls "The Black Pope's" illegal drug trade with the Island of Sicily, whereby Sicily is positioned as the Western Head Quarters, for illegal drug dealing, especially illegal drug trades of heroin.

[The current Black Pope is: Adolfo Nicolás, since 2008 (Society of Jesus c. 2016)].

This is the REAL 'Holy' Roman Empire, which is controlled by the Jesuit Order (Encyclopaedia Britannica 2015) and its shadowy Papal Bloodline hierarchy! This [the Papal Bloodlines] is the world's real Illuminati, which contains the shadowy hierarchy of the Jesuit Order (Encyclopaedia Britannica 2015); and the real Illuminati are the ones who practice Zoroastrianism (BBC Religions 2009; BBC Religions c. 2014) and Mithraism (Encyclopaedia Britannica 2016a). These Papal Bloodlines are the ones with increased lifespan through breatharianism [which is the belief that it is possible for a person to live without consuming food (How Stuff Works Science c. 2016)] and other techniques; and this is once again significant of the real Nephilim, the "Farnese family" (SGIRA c. 2016; Encyclopaedia Britannica 2016b; Villa Farnesina c. 2014).

This is the same Farnese family responsible for the construction of "Villa Farnese" (Rome Art Lover c. 2016a) or "Villa Caprarola" (Coffin 1988). "Villa Farnese" is situated in the town of Caprarola in the province of Viterbo, Northern Lazio, Italy, approximately 50 Kilometres north-west of Rome. The Villa Farnese is situated directly above the town of Caprarola and dominates its surroundings. The design of "Villa Farnese" (Vatican Assassins 2010a; One World of Nations 2014 [the reader should search for the image "Villa Farnese (the original Pentagon)" and compare that image to "The Pentagon"; the image "Villa Farnese (the original Pentagon)" is located nearer the bottom half of the article]; Rome Art Lover c. 2016b) is pentagonal in shape, and it is said to be the 'original pentagon' and prototype for the "Pentagon" based in the United States, Arlington County, Virginia, across the Potomac River from Washington D.C., for which the Pentagon in the United States is noted as a symbol of U.S. military strength. Incidentally, the Villa Farnese was also the original "war command center" in Italy for the hierarchy of the Jesuits orders, Counter-Reformation (Encyclopaedia Britannica 2014). The Pentagon building in the United States, in Arlington is based on the design of Villa Farnese in fact.

[The "Reformation" was a 16th Century movement for the reform of abuses in the Roman Church, ending in the establishment of the Reformed and Protestant Churches.

The "Counter-Reformation" was the reaction of the Roman Catholic Church to the Reformation which ended in the establishment of the Reformed and Protestant Churches. The chief aims of the Counter-Reformation was to increase faith among church members, eliminate some of the abuses to which the leaders of the Reformation objected, and affirm some of the principles rejected by the Protestant churches, such as the veneration [worship] of the saints and acceptance of the authority of the Pope. Many Jesuits were leaders of the Counter-Reformation].

Now the world is presently controlled by the 'war rooms' [a room at a military headquarters where maps showing the current status of troops in battle are maintained] within Borgo Santo Spirito [which is located on the vast territory between St Peter's, Castel S.Angelo and right bank of the river "Tiber", in Rome, Lazio, Italy (Rome Tour 2011; One World Of Nations 2014)]. Incidentally, the city within a city, Borgo Santo Spirito (One World Of Nations 2014) is missile protected. Borgo Santo Spirito is the headquarters for the ubiquitous Society of Jesus (Vatican Assassins 2010b), and it is the command center for the Black Pope. Furthermore, Borgo Santo Spirito houses the headquarters of the Jesuit Order, The Knights of Malta, and many, many more [Papal Bloodlines] including the "Teutonic Knights" (Crystalinks c. 2016; Imperial Teutonic Order c.2016). The Teutonic Knights are a Catholic religious order, originally founded as a German military order in the 12th Century (Crystalinks c. 2016; Imperial Teutonic Order c.2016), for which the headquarters of the Teutonic Knights is also based in Borgo Santo Spirito, Rome, Lazio, Italy. Wake up world!"

DM: 3SG1, what you have quoted about the Illuminati and their bloodlines is somewhat true. Soon you will know everything that I know about the Illuminati from firsthand experience, and what the Illuminati does with *REM driven* cloning technology and all that goes on and has gone in their *REM driven* human cloning subculture. **May 23, 2012 at 7:10pm**

Aliens in the Illuminati

May 23rd 2012

Phil Schneider; Grey Aliens; Outer-Space Aliens & Ancient Sumer & Babylonia

3SG1: Donald, do you have any information on Phil Schneider; was Phil Schneider a legitimate source, in regards to the information he provided to the public, or was Phil Schneider just another form of DISINFORMATION, and lying about the GREY [alien] ATTACKS?

DM: [I am not sure about] Phil Schneider [and his information currently, however as far as I am presently aware], must have been lying [to the public] because there are not any grey aliens [as far as I am currently aware]... Flying saucers on the other hand, are man-made technologies (the information on flying saucers has been detailed in Volume 1 of "Exposing the Illuminati's REM driven Human Cloning Subculture" (Marshall 2016b, pp. 104 -106)). Moreover, *as REM driven clone versions of themselves*, the Illuminati *REM driven* clones, told me everything [plenty of information], over the course of the years I was unwillingly activated as a *REM driven* clone at the hands of the Illuminati, and as a consequence the Illuminati *REM driven* clones shared plenty of information with me regarding flying saucers, as well as, information on aliens... and there are no greys [aliens]... so in that respect Phil Schneider is disinformation... However, there are a couple of [reptilian] scaly creatures, but that information is Phase Four information; and trust me, if people are feeling shocked and overwhelmed, by the reality of REM driven human cloning / the reality of the Illuminati's *REM driven* human cloning subculture, whereby original people go to sleep only to wake up as cloned versions of themselves, people are **not** going to want to know about the [reptilian] scaly creatures until there are at least 100,000 people informed about the Illuminati's *REM driven human* cloning subculture, and at least 100,000 people around us actively helping to expose the Illuminati's *REM driven human* cloning subculture, because people will feel much safer and confident once our numbers increase; and there is safety in numbers.

Furthermore, the [reptilian] scaly creatures are not from space; they are terrestrial creatures (of this planet). The Illuminati have never made contact with outer-space aliens [as far as I am aware]. The only things the Illuminati *REM driven* clones have told me in regards to outer-space aliens, *when I have been unwillingly activated as REM driven cloned version of myself, over the years*, at the cloning center, is that: the Illuminati knows that the Ancient Sumerians and Ancient Babylonians [claimed they] were visited by ancient aliens / gods from the sky in "Chariots of fire"... However the Illuminati have told me (*as a REM driven clone version of myself*) that they (the Illuminati) suspect that the leadership of the Ancient Sumerians and Ancient Babylonians fabricated the story of ancient aliens / gods from the skies in "Chariots of fire" in order to control the ignorant masses of the time period, and demonstrate to the ignorant masses who have always questioned the existence of god or gods, through the use of physical [fabricated] evidence, and representing physical beings (aliens) as god / gods in order to convince the masses there is god / gods and 'an afterlife' [in order to further use religions as a control mechanism].

DM: Furthermore, when the King of Ancient Sumer, or the King of Ancient Babylon says: "Hello my people. Last night my family, as well as, closest body guards were visited by gods in the evening who came by "Flaming chariot"" –the King of Ancient Sumer or the King of Ancient Babylon did not NEED any proof to placate the masses in regards to the King's statements... If you questioned the authenticity or proclamation of the King's statements... and you did not believe the King's assertions, you were killed... *Laughter* -it was as simple as that... and some religions present today, originated in this manner. **May 24, 2012 at 10:35pm**

Revised Statements based on Donald Marshall's REM driven clone experiences

Donald Marshall's perspective on the Illuminati in 2012

[The reader should note the above statements made by Donald Marshall, is Donald Marshall speaking in early 2012 in regards to the inside knowledge he had gained over 30 years where he was unwillingly activated as a *REM driven* clone version of himself in the Illuminati's *REM driven human* cloning subculture. The interesting aspect about Donald Marshall is that he only details what he knows from firsthand experience, and that which he is certain of, and that he has examined, checked, double checked and triple checked, to ensure it is not some trick by the Illuminati in order to deceive him into believing disinformation. Consequently, Donald Marshall only details information to the public that he has learned, from firsthand experience through the process of consciousness transfer from his original body to his *REM driven* clone body, where he continues to experience the SAME earth with his five senses, only this time as a *REM driven* clone, while his original body sleeps.]

Donald Marshall is sincere in his attempts to expose the Illuminati

[Furthermore, Donald Marshall is sincere in his disclosures and intentions to expose the Illuminati's *REM driven human* cloning subculture, in regards to the fact that Donald Marshall will apologise to people when he later learns through **HIS** firsthand experience, as a *REM driven* clone unwillingly activated at the cloning center, that he was initially wrong in his initial assertions. Moreover, in addition to apologising to others Donald Marshall will say "I don't know", when he is uncertain about particular information. Donald Marshall does not speculate or guess, in regards to the information he discloses about the Illuminati's *REM driven human* cloning subculture; he will only mention information he is absolutely certain of, in order **not** to distribute disinformation. This makes Donald Marshall credible in the sense that he is very sceptical, and will only detail verifiable information which he Donald Marshall has experienced firsthand with his five senses as a *REM driven human* clone version of himself.]

"Life" is a continual learning experience

[Therefore, like any personal narrative, nobody can ever know everything, or be perfect in their assertions, even if everything one describes is personal to their life experiences. There will always be new information which arises, which at times may contradict our previous life experiences, and therefore, if we are to continue to move towards a place a truth, and be true to ourselves and true to others; when the time comes and new information presents itself and contradicts our previous life experiences, if we have to say "Sorry" and make our apologies, then it is best to say "Sorry" and make our apologies; if we have to say "I was wrong" and what another said early about certain information is correct, then is best to say "I was wrong" and the information said earlier by another is indeed correct, if we are to continue to expand in our awareness' of what is indeed true, and continue to move towards a place of truth, and not live in ignorance when we are presented with new truths which contradict our previous life experiences.]

The downside of Donald Marshall's disclosures

[Donald Marshall has done the above, and has said many times that he is "sorry" or "wrong" about certain information which at an earlier time he believed to be incorrect. This is the downside of Donald Marshall disclosures regarding the Illuminati's *REM driven human* cloning subculture, in the respect that Donald Marshall continues to detail his firsthand experience which he is absolutely certain of, therefore in cases where Donald Marshall has not experienced something firsthand, he might say certain information is "disinformation" or "not true", when in actuality the information or disclosure which is being discussed is true.]

The upside of Donald Marshall's disclosures

[Thankfully, when Donald Marshall does have new experiences as a *REM driven* clone *version of himself*, which contradicts his previous experiences, he does apologise for his initial mistakes; he does say he is "Sorry" and he was "Wrong". Therefore it is best to keep in mind that Donald Marshall only details information regarding the Illuminati's *REM driven human* cloning subculture, which he is absolutely certain of, and if he is wrong in his initial assertions, he will later apologise, and tell the public his new findings based on his life experiences (*as a REM driven clone*), that he is now absolutely certain of.]

Donald Marshall's aim: with regards to FULLY exposing the Illuminati

[Donald Marshall's aim is to continue to present the world the truth (about the Illuminati's _REM driven human_ cloning subculture, through his eyewitness accounts), with the aim that the world will save him and others from there Illuminati's _REM driven_ cloning subculture. Consequently, Donald Marshall can only present to the world the truth about the Illuminati's _REM driven human_ cloning subculture from his perspective, and his experiences, and because Donald Marshall continues to detail only experiences as a _REM driven_ clone version of himself that he is certain of, this is why sometimes he is wrong in his assertions; however, because Donald Marshall will apologise, and recant on his initial statements, which he recants on the basis of new information and experiences which he has thoroughly examined as a _REM driven_ clone version of himself, this is also what makes Donald Marshall credible. Donald Marshall is presenting the world the truth about the Illuminati's _REM driven human_ cloning subculture based on his experience as a _REM driven_ clone that he is absolutely certain of.]

Statements which have been revised in later years by Donald Marshall

[With the above in mind, Donald Marshall was **incorrect** in 2012 in his assertions when he said there are not any grey aliens.
- There are grey aliens, and Donald Marshall meets grey aliens as a _REM driven_ clone version of himself later in his disclosures.
- Phil Schneider is **NOT** disinformation.
- The Illuminati have made contact with outer-space aliens.
- There is some truth to the narrative of the Ancient Sumerians and Ancient Babylonians.]

Donald Marshall and his experiences with grey aliens and outer-space aliens

[Donald Marshall met grey aliens and outer-space aliens when he was a child _REM driven_ human clone, activated at the cloning center by the Illuminati _REM driven_ clones. However, Donald Marshall did not like the look of aliens, as a child _REM driven_ clone, and therefore the Illuminati would remove the aliens from Donald Marshall's presence whenever Donald Marshall was activated as a child _REM driven_ clone version of himself at the cloning center.

Moreover, the Illuminati _REM driven_ clones would use sock puppets to help Donald Marshall get accustomed to the reality of aliens, however Donald Marshall had blocked out this memory... When Donald Marshall later reunites with the outer-space aliens during the 2014, as he continues to disclose his experiences as a _REM driven_ clone _version of himself_ unwillingly activated as a _REM driven_ clone in the Illuminati's _REM driven human_ cloning subculture, Donald Marshall realises and recalls that he had met many aliens as a child _REM driven_ clone at the cloning center, however he had blocked those memories (in order to help him cope), or thought the aliens were 'gene-spliced creatures', which is understandable, because the Illuminati likes to cross-breed and gene-splice animals in order to create new creatures / hybrids. Nonetheless, the species Donald Marshall saw at the cloning center were not hybrids or new gene-spliced creations, but rather aliens who claim to be from other galaxies...]

Phil Schneider's disclosures are legitimate WARNINGS to the public!

[Phil Schneider is **NOT** disinformation. Donald Marshall later corroborates Phil Schneider in Donald Marshall's video interviews, whereby Donald Marshall tells the audience "Phil Schneider was correct about the grey things [aliens]"... as well as the scaly [reptilian] creatures, although Phil Schneider called them something else [Phil Schneider called them "Long necked greys"]... Therefore Phil Schneider was legitimately trying his best to warn the public with his information...]

The Illuminati REM driven clones have made contact with outer-space aliens

[Moreover, the Illuminati have made contact and met with the outer-space aliens (as *REM driven* clone versions of themselves). In fact, we later learn, through Donald Marshall's disclosures of the Illuminati's *REM driven human* cloning subculture, that these outer-space aliens detailed by Donald Marshall have been living here on earth for thousands of years; however, these days the outer-space aliens stay out of sight, in the background, and frequent the cloning centers / live in underground cities, underneath the surface of the earth. That is one of the great deceptions: much of humanity has been exploring the skies, hoping to find aliens, when the outer-space aliens have been here all along, and have been living beneath their very feet, under the surface of the earth.]

The outer-space aliens are living underground right beneath your very feet!

[There is [some] truth to the narrative by the Ancient Sumerians and Ancient Babylonians, who claim to have been visited by 'gods in "Chariots of fire"'. According to Donald Marshall, as we learn more about his experiences as an unwilling participant, trapped as a *REM driven* clone *version of himself* in the Illuminati's *REM driven human* cloning subculture, we discover from Donald Marshall, from 2014 onwards (and this information will be detailed fully in future documents) that these so-called 'gods' of Ancient Sumer, and Ancient Babylon are nothing more than outer-space aliens, who are **extremely** advanced in their technological capabilities... The technological capabilities of the outer-space aliens dwarf the technological capabilities of humanity, as well as, the technological capabilities of the Illuminati **largely** in comparison. Therefore when the outer-space aliens came to earth, because of the ego-needs of the outer-space aliens, the outer-space aliens deceived primitive humans by claiming to be 'gods' worthy of worship, when in reality and practicality, the outer-space aliens have in their possessions, extremely highly advanced technologies, and the ownership of such **extremely** highly advanced technologies, afforded the outer-space aliens the capacity to convince primitive humans that they were gods... when in fact they are **not** gods, but rather, highly advanced technological aliens. Furthermore, most if not all of these outer-space aliens, currently here on earth, and living in underground cities, as well as, living in Deep Underground Military Bases (DUMBs), and frequenting the cloning centers are **decrepit and perverse** and are certainly not gods or indeed worthy of any worship.]

The Purpose of this Document

[Although the topic of aliens, and outer-space aliens, has been briefly discussed here in this document, the purpose of this document is to primarily focus on Donald Marshall's disclosures of the Illuminati's *REM driven human* cloning subculture at 2012, from the perspective of Donald Marshall's *REM driven human* cloning experiences in 2012. Topics such as grey aliens, aliens, outer-space aliens and more will be covered in upcoming documents and presented as, how and when Donald Marshall disclosed such information, as a result of his experiences as an unwillingly participant trapped in the Illuminati's *REM driven human* cloning subculture. The reader is more than welcome to read Donald Marshall's Proboards Forum or seek Donald Marshall's Facebook Timeline in order to learn more in regards to the information aliens and outer-space aliens.]

Donald Marshall's current views on the Illuminati has changed since 2012

[Furthermore, this information is included here, to lessen the shock once people who are unaware of such a reality, learn that there are indeed outer-space aliens present on this earth; the disclosure of aliens and outer-space aliens will be detailed fully in later documents. This information is also included here because Donald Marshall's experiences, and views in 2016 in regards to the Illuminati's *REM driven human* cloning subculture, is different from the experiences and views of Donald Marshall in 2012, which is based on the knowledge and firsthand experiences Donald Marshall has gained through being an unwilling participant activated as a *REM driven* clone version of himself by the Illuminati.

Moreover, this information adds to and corroborates others who have spent considerable time researching the concept and possibility of aliens and further demonstrates, it is in fact reality that there are aliens, and these aliens are with us right now on earth, and living beneath our very feet. The reality of aliens amongst us is confirmed because Donald Marshall has met these aliens, and outer-space aliens, firsthand, as a *REM driven* clone version of himself at the cloning center(s).]

The authenticity of aliens being part of humanity's reality

[Furthermore, because Donald Marshall is very sceptical, about many aspects in regards to the Illuminati's *REM driven human* cloning subculture, whereby as a result, Donald Marshall only discloses information he is certain of, for Donald Marshall to revise his statements concerning the Illuminati's *REM driven human* cloning subculture, and say that he was wrong, and yes there are grey aliens, and outer-space aliens, lends to the authenticity of aliens, and outer-space aliens being part of humanity's reality and here among us on earth, because Donald Marshall only ever discloses information he is absolutely certain of, which he has experienced firsthand, through the process of consciousness transfer from his original body to his *REM driven* clone, whereby Donald Marshall is still experiencing life on the **same earth**, only this time as a *REM driven* clone, while his original body sleeps. Donald Marshall is experiencing the **same earth** when he is activated as a *REM driven* clone version of himself, and because of this factor, Donald Marshall has met aliens, and outer-space aliens here on earth (*as a REM driven clone version of himself*), and he retains these memories, CLEAR as daylight].

Illuminati Symbolism

May 23rd 2012

Collage: German Chancellor Angela Merkel makes downward pyramid with hands

3SG1 posted the following collage of German Chancellor Angela Merkel (below) in regards to the many occurrences which Angela Merkel has held her hands together to form an upside pyramid which is synonymous of the pyramid symbolism used by the Illuminati.

DM: Yes, German Chancellor Angela Merkel occasionally makes the triangle symbol with her hands, which is synonymous to the Illuminati pyramid symbolism. German Chancellor Angela Merkel attends the cloning center as a *REM driven* clone version of herself, too. Angel Merkel and I have 'interacted' many times as REM driven clone duplicate versions of ourselves at the cloning center. 'Interacted' hmm, yes we'll use that word... *laughter and grimacing in disgust*. **May 24, 2012 at 10:41pm**

[In actuality, not only did Donald Marshall interact conversationally with German Chancellor Angela Merkel as *REM driven* clone versions, they had *REM driven* clone sex, and it is mostly likely Donald Marshall was forced into such positions with Angela Merkel (*as REM driven clone versions*) by the Illuminati REM driven clones and this why Donald Marshall insists on using the word 'interacted' and why he laughed and grimaced in disgust].

Individuals hindering Donald Marshall's Mission

May 20th 2012

Trolls; Government agents; Cointelpro; and disinformation agents

3SG1 posted the following video (below) regarding agents of disinformation who have the role of suppression information (HEREclickPlease 2011).

TROLLS ! Government disinfo! Cointelpro
Lucy Fir applies for a position working for the government as a troll. Trolls use various accounts to make it seem like they're agreeing with themselves...
YOUTUBE.COM

3SG1: Reading through some of today's posts it is obvious THEY [the Illuminati] have their troops of trolls [government agents] in an attempt to discredit [Donald] Marshall. ME THINKS THEY [agents of the Illuminati] DOTH PROTEST TOO MUCH... to be genuine... If your [Donald Marshall's] claims were as ridiculous as they [government agents] made out; they surely would not deem it so necessary to invest so much continued time and energy on ridiculous claims, and with their [government agents] continued investments and energies, it appears an ever more obvious and desperate attempt to debunk your [Donald Marshall's] claims.... Stay strong, Donald *smiling*

DM: I will... While in the public gardens, a friend and I had to check under this bridge for trolls... (Billy goats gruff) ((Fable)) *Laughter* **May 20, 2012 at 10:00pm**

May 21st 2012

Organisations hindering the progress of Donald Marshall's Mission

God Like Productions

3SG1 posted the following comment about how God Like Production (GLP) has banned and removed any content which mentions Donald Marshall's name or any content linked to Donald Marshall's disclosures. [In short: God Like Productions is Illuminati controlled, and this is a reason why Donald Marshall or content which is linked to Donald Marshall and his disclosures does **NOT** feature on God Like Productions].

3SG1: I first read about you [Donald Marshall and the situation regarding the Illuminati's *REM driven human* cloning subculture] on a "God Like Productions" (GLP) thread that I thought was interesting. However, after a few days passed, the thread which mentioned you [and the Illuminati's *REM driven human* cloning subculture] disappeared. As a result of this, I thought 'Hmm, let me experiment here' (not that I believe you or not, in regards to your situation and the Illuminati's *REM driven human* cloning subculture, however, I am tuned into your information), and I tried to start another thread with your open letter (Donald Marshall Proboards 2012a) to the world about the Illuminati's *REM driven human* cloning subculture, on God Like Productions; I had the words from your letter (Donald Marshall Proboards 2012a) copied from somewhere else and I pasted it to a new thread on God Like Productions.

The new thread I created containing your letter (Donald Marshall Proboards 2012a) was deleted within a few minutes after. I found this confusing, and as a result I started a few more threads asking why my original thread which contained Donald Marshall's open letter to the public (Donald Marshall Proboards 2012a) was deleted. These threads, where I was enquiring about why my threads are being deleted were also deleted. Shortly after all the content I had posted on God Like Productions was deleted, I was banned from the website God Like Productions. I then logged out of God Like Productions, and tried typing your name "Donald Marshall" in their search pane, and I realised everything containing your name was deleted too. It is as if God Like Productions has banned your name, and everything else related to you [Donald Marshall], and this added to my suspense. I wonder if another person reading Donald Marshall's information can go on the website God Like Productions and try and start a thread about Donald Marshall and see if a similar situation happens to them?

3SG2: God Like Productions is [Illuminati] controlled. This is why God Like Productions are continually banning IP addresses.

3SG1: I know God Like Productions is Illuminati controlled; however, do you know how many "nutter [crazy] stories" are posted on God Like Productions every day? There are even similar things posted on God Like Productions to what Don is disclosing [regarding the Illuminati's *REM driven human* cloning subculture]. I wonder if other people will get banned from God Like Productions for mentioning Donald's name on their website or have their threads deleted for posting anything which relates to the Illuminati's *REM driven human* cloning subculture.

3SG3: Do not let Steven Joseph Christopher deceive you! That Steven [Joseph Christopher] guy is [lying to people and] saying that I am "Satan"! *Shocked-face!*. It is not true [I am NOT Satan], I am just like anyone else. I am a proud father; I am me, and not Jesus! I am a free soul, and furthermore, God Like Productions are [Illuminati] controlled!

DM: There are some organisations, websites, people, industries, networks and other places which are aware of [human] cloning [*and REM driven human cloning*] too [such as God Like Productions, which intentionally suppress any information related to the Illuminati's *REM driven human* cloning subculture]. I am not going to be on "[The] Late Show with David Letterman" either, because David Letterman knows about the Illuminati's *REM driven human* cloning subculture, and I have spoken to David Letterman *as REM driven clone versions of ourselves activated via the process of consciousness transfer to our REM driven clones* at the cloning center. IF [and it is a massive "if"] hypothetically speaking, I am permitted to appear on David Letterman's television talk host show, I will ask David Letterman in the flesh (in real life) why he punched me in the face as a *REM driven* clone version of myself, when we were both active as *REM driven* clone versions of ourselves at the cloning center... I would also most likely end up smacking David Letterman on his Talk Show in real life, which would lead to the old guys in the band which feature on his show, as well as the camera crew, ganging up on me, and beating me up in order to defend David Letterman, and I do not need that hassle or such publicity. I would NOT do an interview with Oprah Winfrey either. The reasons I will NOT do an interview with Oprah Winfrey is similar to the reasons listed above for why I wouldn't appear on David Letterman's show. *Laughter* **May 21, 2012 at 11:44pm**

DM: Although there are some organisations, websites, people, industries, networks and working diligently against this cause, and are Illuminati controlled (organisations, websites, people, industries, networks), the Illuminati do not own everything though! The Illuminati *REM driven* clones have told me as a *REM driven* clone *version of myself* that the information regarding their *REM driven human* cloning subculture has spread too far for it to be stopped now! The Illuminati are waiting for the populace to demand answers from governments around the world, about REM driven human cloning.... the Illuminati have even stopped torturing me whenever I am unwillingly activated as a *REM driven* clone *version of myself* at the cloning center. The Illuminati *REM driven* clones are asking me to omit many details regarding the Illuminati's *REM driven human* cloning subculture. "Sugar-coat" is the word the Illuminati *REM driven* clones are using plenty of times whenever I am unwillingly activated as a *REM driven* clone version of myself by the Illuminati at the cloning center. **May 21, 2012 at 11:49pm**

3SG1: I knew Steven [Joseph Christopher] was bats**t crazy [certifiably nuts] [so you do not need to worry, and I will not be deceived by Steven Joseph Christopher, 3SG3]. Moreover, the information Don is disclosing regarding the Illuminati's *REM driven human* cloning subculture does not need more craziness in it [such as comments made by Stephen Joseph Christopher]. I just thought it is somewhat ironic that a website such as God Like Productions allow many different kinds of Illuminati junk and conspiracies on their website, so WHY didn't God Like Productions allow the information I put up about you [and the Illuminati's *REM driven human* cloning subculture] flow, with all the other crazy conspiracies on their website. The fact that they continually deleted any information related to "Donald Marshall" made me think.

3SG4: 3SG1, I had the same experience with God Like Productions (GLP). GLP deleted my threads about Donald too. I too kept creating threads and asking "Why did you delete my thread about Donald Marshall? Why did you delete my thread about Donald Marshall?" and then I got banned by GLP. I am still banned by GLP today, by the way *laughter*. I agree with you 3SG1, they have all sorts of articles on God Like Productions, such as: News; Dream Science; DARPA creating super bionic insects; Chinese Physicists teleporting photons over 100 kilometres, BUT any information regarding Donald Marshall, or relating to the Illuminati's *REM driven human* cloning subculture is quickly deleted and could result in a ban on God Like Productions website by the administrators. Have a look to see if you can read this thread on God Like Productions:
godlikeproductions.com/forum1/message1867334/pg1

[These types of websites and similar internet groups are "gate-keeping" websites / groups – they filter information, and "gate-keeping" is also one method of compartmentalising knowledge, so that truths such as the Illuminati's *REM driven* cloning subculture, are not known en masse].

3SG1: I am still banned, even when I visit God Like Productions (GLP) as an "anonymous" user. I had to hand GLP $10 so that I could log back into my original account I had with them; however, I still cannot post about Donald Marshall, nor do I see any posts related to Donald Marshall on GLP's website. Silly me! GLP have angered me! GLP can take my $10 and shove it up their backsides! *Laughter*

3SG3: Yes 3SG1 and 3SG4, people should question everything: why, why, why? Question everything always, and be your own judge [realise your own conclusions]!

3SG4: Agreed. Anything which touches on "truth" on GLP is instantly deleted.

3SG3: Ha-ha 3SG1! Stick with Donald's disclosures regarding the Illuminati's *REM driven human* cloning subculture. Through Donald, one of the world's major and prominent conspiracies has been exposed, and as a result: this dark and occult group are now forever exposed in text, thanks to Donald's bravery. Moreover, it is easy to discern my thoughts and feelings regarding everyday general life. I have nothing to hide, and you are welcome to ask me anything and I will answer to the best of my knowledge, I sincerely guarantee. I am not here for fame or money. I am here for Donald, and to help Donald expose the Illuminati.

3SG5: For Donald, or whoever did not know about Donald Marshall's back-story [click the image below to be directed to the article (CBSNews 2009)]

Man Accused Of Threatening To Kill Obama
Steven Joseph Christopher Reportedly Plotted Assassination For "The Country's Own Good"
CBSNEWS.COM

3SG3: OH MY GOODNESS! [The article above which details Steven Joseph Christopher's alleged plans and actions to kill President Obama, demonstrates the "extreme" nature of Steven Joseph Christopher (CBSNews 2009)]. Please! Do NOT include him [Steven Joseph Christopher] in ANY of our activity regarding the exposure and divulgement of the Illuminati's *REM driven human* cloning subculture. The ploys and actions of Steven Joseph Christopher are NOT related to Donald Marshall, NOR should anything related to Steven Joseph Christopher be mentioned alongside Donald Marshall or the exposure and disclosure of the Illuminati's *REM driven human* cloning subculture.

3SG5: I agree.

3SG3: Steven Joseph Christopher is NOT affiliated with Donald Marshall whatsoever! Thank you for posting an article regarding Steven Joseph Christopher's recent actions (CBSNews 2009), but please be aware of this matter! Thank you for your cooperation.

3SG5: I do hope Donald recovers [from *REM driven* cloning (tortures)] and he feels much better [in his original body]... also, I am personally looking forward to Document 2, with the list of various names who have been *REM driven* clone versions of themselves at the cloning center.

3SG3: Yes, Document 2 [containing the list of names of public figures that have been *REM driven* clone versions of themselves at the cloning center] will be released soon. There will be a video uploaded soon which demonstrates Donald Marshall can rap [even though he does not listen to rap music]. We are currently working on this video.

3SG5: 3SG1, here is the best information I have been able to find regarding the censorship on God Like Productions' website. It is for your reading pleasure [click the image below to be directed to the article (intheknow7 2010)]:

Godlike Productions (GLP) Controlled Opposition/Gatekeepers: BANS (SRI)...
INTHEKNOW7.WORDPRESS.COM

3SG3: Thank you 3SG1, for a valuable post informing others about how God Like Productions [GLP] is [Illuminati] controlled. The article is worth reading (intheknow7 2010). Moreover, Jason Lucas and Alex Shamash own GLP and both Jason Lucas and Alex Shamash are data mining gurus for the Department of Defense (DoD) (the military services). Jason Lucas and Alex Shamash, owners of the website God Like Productions, run their website just to collect information on anyone who is misinformed and readily believes the disinformation propaganda posted to their website.

DM: We do not need GLP to help us inform the world about the Illuminati's *REM driven human* cloning subculture. God Like Productions are going to be perceived very badly by the public once the Illuminati's *REM driven human* cloning subculture is fully exposed publicly, and worldly known. **May 22, 2012 at 10:28pm**

3SG6: The administrators of GLP blocked me and a friend from viewing their website. However, my friend found a backdoor to view the website God Like Productions, and my friend soon realised that one of the owners is in the air force. I'm sure it is more complicated than that [more complicated than just the owner works in the air force].

3SG3: The owners of GLP work for the military!

3SG6: I posted a story I came across on GLP, which was a story about a man (age 66) who shot an off duty police officer (also age 66) at 5:55PM. I Google searched the shooter's name, and the headline of the first link, among the list of returned searches included the phrase "Set up". I was banned and I have never been allowed back on GLP. These psychopaths and their occult games... they love their numbers and anagrams.

[3SG6 is referring to how the Illuminati conspirators love "numerology", and how he, 3SG6, was blocked on GLP for referencing an article which had references to occult numerology; - (age) 66, (age) 66, (the time) 555, above].

3SG4: Another interesting thing which happened to me regarding GLP is when I Google searched for "Deleted threads on Donald Marshall", I could not find anything. However, when I used a different search engine "DuckDuckGo" (DuckDuckGo 2016), I found those threads which had been deleted on GLP; that is where [by using "DuckDuckGo" (2016) as a search engine] I copied and pasted the information regarding GLP deleting threads about Donald Marshall from. Ha-ha Google!

[It appears Google is also suppressing information regarding human cloning or anything which pertains to the Illuminati's *REM driven human* cloning subculture, **UNLESS**, the user specifically enters "Donald Marshall human cloning", the user will not find much in regards to the exposure of the Illuminati's *REM driven cloning* subculture or Donald Marshall's disclosures if the user just enters into Google's search engine "Human cloning"].

3SG7: I am waiting for Document 2, as well [3SG5]. Donald is so concerned that the Illuminati might kill him; but what good will Document 2 be if it only remains in Donald's head, and he does not share Document 2 [if unfortunately Donald was to meet a premature death at the hands of the Illuminati]? When Document 2 is FINALLY released, will someone contact me?

DM: *Laughter*. I am constantly replying to peoples' messages and concerns regarding the Illuminati's *REM driven human* cloning subculture. I need more people looking and sharing this information with others... I will have Wi-Fi internet connection by Wednesday, and I will have 24/7 internet connection then. We are almost in Phase Two, and Document 2 will be released soon. **May 23, 2012 at 5:03am**

Legitimacy

May 19th 2012

Are Donald Marshall's disclosures about the Illuminati fraudulent?

3SG1: You're a fraud.

DM: I am **NO** fraud...

ATTENTION EVERYONE! **See this and remember:** the New World Order (NWO) **WILL** send people like this in twos and threes at **EVERY** attempt to discredit or denounce me; things will get worse towards the very end when this disclosure about the Illuminati and their *REM driven* cloning subculture gains wider exposure; the Illuminati will even have celebrities appear on Saturday Night Live [American Sketch Comedy Television Show] (NBC 2016) who will start doing comedy sketches about cloning, human cloning, REM driven cloning and about "Donald Marshall" (me)... The Illuminati will go to great lengths to prevent the public from realising the reality of this situation and taking it seriously, and you will see this unfold before your very eyes... do **NOT** allow the Illuminati and their containment and distraction tactics, prevent or deter you from realising the truth about their *REM driven* human cloning subculture. **May 20, 2012 at 5:04am**

3SG2: We don't know [if the Illuminati's *REM driven human* cloning subculture] it is the truth yet. We haven't seen anything to prove it [*REM driven* human cloning]. All we've got is faith in your word.

3SG3: *Sarcastic comment* Faith and Easter baskets. Double-check. I am ready.

3SG3: *Sarcastic comment, which should not be taken seriously* Hey, I had faith when Bambi's mother was about to get shot. But faith didn't stop the bullet from slamming into her heart, exploding upon impact, shattering her hopes and dreams. Her blood made a nice psalm in Steven's [Joseph Christopher's] book though.

3SG4: My favourite part [of Donald Marshall's disclosure] is how he is some amazing song writer (and that's why he's the Illuminati's [*REM driven* clone] slave, don't you know), yet on Facebook, Donald can barely string a coherent sentence together.

3SG3: *Smug comment* Poets don't even know it. *smiling*

3SG4: I've been called a "shill" and told by others that: the government are paying me to do so [troll this page] when I've tried to debunk conspiracy B/S [inconsistencies] on here [Donald Marshall's Facebook page]. I mean, how do you argue with unrealistic nonsense and with people who are willing to believe it? All logic and reason flies out the window. It seems to be a case of "believe everything until proven false" here, and even then...sometimes the truth seems an irrelevant inconvenience.

Where is the "hard evidence" for the Illuminati's REM driven cloning subculture?

3SG2: Eh, listen mate! David Icke can prove what he says, but this guy [Donald Marshall] is just saying things and Donald has absolutely nothing to back up what he says. That's what conmen do. Conmen keep you hanging on for false promises. The banking collapse really did happen and [David] Icke explains how. I've heard that Donald Marshall has written songs but Donald has never detailed which songs he has written; and apparently, [Queen] Elizabeth [II] is nearly always at the cloning center. She can't be f*****g everywhere at the same time, can she? Or is she cloned too?

3SG5: *Incredulous comment* David Icke can prove the reptilians? Yeah right.

[David Icke has not unequivocally proven the reptilian conspiracy; is the point the above commenter makes. However, David Icke has established that there is indeed the reality of a reptilian conspiracy (on earth). Nonetheless, the reality pertaining to the reptilian conspiracy is much different than David Icke details. The reality of reptiles will be detailed in upcoming documents]

3SG4: David Icke can prove that if you write with enough conviction, you can be as outlandish as you like (probably the more outlandish, the better) and people will buy books about it. That's it. *Ching; ching; ching* [The sound of cash]. David [Icke] is probably trolling us something awesome, making a career out of our gullibility and then jacking off [masturbating] into massive piles of cash.

3SG2: I'm not talking about reptilians. Reptilians are just a very brief side note in David Icke's books. David [Icke] talks about plenty of other things too. The Illuminati is real and so is Freemasonry. As for that Steve[n] [Joseph Christopher] guy, Steven is just f*****g nuts.

3SG2: 3SG4, you should actually try reading one of David Icke's books instead of dismissing him and resorting to insults. That just makes you look thick [stupid].

3SG3: *Jokey comment, not to be taken seriously* Hey, thick girls need loving, too.

3SG4: I have [read David Icke's books]. I have read "And The Truth Shall Set You Free" (Icke 2004) and "Children of the Matrix" (Icke 2001), as well as, books by Erich von Däniken and others. I also have undergraduate degrees in "Physics" and "Biology", as well as a masters' degree in "Physics". I know weirder things happen in Science and Nature than could ever come from the mind of some loon on FB [Facebook]. I also know a great deal about genetics, cloning, neuroscience, and other related things. See, that's what you do, 3SG2: you make assumptions based on nothing.

3SG2: 3SG4, I haven't made any assumptions based on nothing. Give me an example of an assumption that I have made that was based upon nothing.

3SG4: I'm sure they do 3SG3; however, not being thick in either a mental nor physical sense, the needs of thick girls is not something I concern myself with.

3SG4: *Sarcastic comment* Well... Donald Marshall's profile is so high now it would be too dangerous for the Illuminati to do anything to Donald... with all Donald's... what (?), 300 Facebook friends knowing about it [the Illuminati's *REM driven human* cloning subculture]? Apparently, the Illuminati killed Old Dirty Bastard (ODB), Tupac Shakur and Michael Jackson, because nobody in the world has ever heard of them, right?

Video testimonies from others will help to corroborate REM driven human cloning

DM: Wow guys [that's how you are currently feeling?]...well if that is the case, I will have to have a few other people who have had *REM driven human* cloning experiences, and have been activated as *REM driven* clones at the cloning center in Canada, when they have gone to sleep in their original bodies, and had their consciousnesses transferred to their *REM driven* clones, appear on video (in their original bodies, of course) and have them explain their experiences and memories to you on video. **May 20, 2012 at 5:32am**

3SG2: David Icke can be believed, because he gives detailed factual evidence that can be verified. However, just giving a video testimony [of these claims about *REM driven* human cloning] will not stand up in a court. You need physical proof of whatever it is that you are claiming.

3SG4: Having people speak on video about *REM driven* cloning is not proof, it is just weirdos saying stuff on film. Proof, please [hard evidence, please].

[In other words, people like this, who make such comments want to see "hard evidence" – which would be: for example, a camera panned into the cloning center(s) for which Donald Marshall describes, for such people above, to accept the reality of human cloning and REM driven human cloning]

Phase One of Donald Marshall's disclosures: REM driven human cloning

DM: Discussing and detailing the reality of reptilians is in Phase 4 of my whistle-blowing disclosures. We're currently only in Phase 1 [exposing the reality of the Illuminati's *REM driven human* cloning subculture]. Have patience, ask me questions, and research the topic of "cloning" independently if you must, to further understand Phase 1 of my disclosure. **Human cloning, and REM driven human cloning is a major part of what the Illuminati does.** Furthermore, human cloning is a significant part of humanity's reality, and there are references to the reality of human cloning in so many areas of life, it really is worth devoting serious time to. **May 20, 2012 at 5:33am**

3SG4: *Snide comment* I also imagine one of these phases [of Donald Marshall's whistle blowing disclosures] involves donating a large cash sum.

DM: Well... if you feel I am being disingenuous, 3SG4, you could always block me, but then, you'll be missing out... **May 20, 2012 at 5:34am**

3SG4: That's exactly it, Donald. I'm curious as hell as to where this [your whistle-blowing disclosures] is going. I'm a sceptical, but I am open-minded. However, as with everything else, provide credible evidence and I will consider believing you.

3SG5: Donald Marshall, I won´t say you're a total lie, as I can't say I believe what you say 100%, because, as you wrote in your letter (Donald Marshall Proboards 2012a), you say things that are quite fantastic... all I can do for now is wait for proof... and keep researching... I have been thinking for a long time about how there must be human clones secretly created somewhere...

3SG4: What is Phase Two anyway? Step two? Step three: PROFIT!

3SG2: You are making serious allegations Donald. You do realise that, don't you? Yeah what are these phases all about?

3SG4: If the Illuminati really are doing these awful things to you and others, and you are able to talk about it (as you seem to be able to....) isn't it kind of your responsibility to get this stuff sorted as soon as possible instead of waiting around for more people to join your Facebook page? I mean, if the Illuminati were torturing MY [*REM driven*] clone, while I was in REM sleep, I would want to get that stuff sorted sooner, rather than later.

3SG4: Hurry it up man, I have to get ready for work.

3SG2: I think this is a road leading to nowhere, personally.

DM: OK. Right now, we are in Phase One: [discussing *REM driven* cloning, the Illuminati's *REM driven* cloning technology, and what the Illuminati does with their *REM driven* cloning technology as *REM driven* clone versions] which involves gathering as many eyes and ears to look at and understand the information of the Illuminati's *REM driven human* cloning subculture [it is important to get as many eyes and ears at this stage to guarantee my survival / life]. Phase Two is coming very soon and people paying attention will know what Phase Two entails **DURING** Phase Two, and not before we actually reach Phase Two...

Donald Marshall wants YOU to expose the Illuminati & does NOT need your money

DM: Allow me to assure you, and everyone else reading, I will **NOT** request money as it would be a detriment to my success. The only thing I care about is escaping the cloning center(s); exposing the Illuminati and informing the world about what the Illuminati does with *REM driven* cloning technology, as well as, informing the world about the true nature of the New World Order (NWO). I never want to be activated as *REM driven* clone again once this is known about publicly and dealt with, –that is my aim. **May 20, 2012 at 6:22am**

Disclosure must happen gradually to guarantee success

3SG4: How long until Phase Two, Donald? How many people do you need for that?

DM: Listen, as I have already mentioned, I must disclose things gradually to guarantee my success in exposing the Illuminati's _REM driven human_ cloning subculture, and eventually escaping being activated as a _REM driven_ clone version at the cloning center(s). The Illuminati _members as REM driven clone versions_ are currently discussing putting me (real me) in prison when I have been activated as a _REM driven_ clone version at the cloning centers recently. However, the Illuminati do NOT want me to go to court... I'll do a lot of talking that day in court and disclose all the nefarious deeds the Illuminati members do with REM driven cloning and more, and it will be public record and public knowledge then... the Illuminati do NOT want me to have my day in court...

The Illuminati would like to put me in prison for slandering names... *laughter*... however, it is not slander when one is speaking the truth... *smiling* **May 20, 2012 at 6:27am**

3SG3: [Sarcastic comment, which should not be taken seriously, about how Donald Marshall has chosen to disclose the Illuminati's REM driven cloning subculture in Phases] OK, so we know Donald has the capability to count from one to two, however; he has difficulty reaching three, but he knows a great deal about four. Intriguing...

Remember to be kind towards Donald Marshall, because he has suffered immensely

DM: Stay tuned and check my Facebook page regularly for more upcoming disclosures. Moreover, try to **remember** not to be too nasty to me; I have been through plenty of pain, torture, plagiarism, witnessed murders, blood and gore, and plenty of outlandish things, all through the process of the Illuminati's _REM driven_ cloning technology to bring the world the real truth about what the Illuminati members do and how they do it, all to the world for free. I have suffered a lot, and I continue to suffer today because I am still unwillingly activated as a _REM driven_ clone whenever I enter REM sleep. I have been through a lot, and in the future, people who made nasty, snide or sarcastic comments, when all I was trying to do was warn the world about the highly advanced technologies the Illuminati uses against the public unsuspectingly, will feel dumb for making such comments against me, especially given what I have had to endure and I am still going through. I do have proof about the Illuminati's _REM driven human_ cloning subculture... just wait for it... Furthermore, no, I do **NOT** want money or fame... asking for money will reduce my chances for success in getting the populace's help. Large numbers of the populace demanding answers about the Illuminati's _REM driven human_ cloning subculture is the only thing that will stop the Illuminati. I WANT TO ESCAPE REM driven human cloning, that's it! It is my only objective; I do not care about money or fame; all I WANT is to escape being activated as a _REM driven_ clone for the rest of my life, so **please, tell a friend, share, my Facebook Posts, share my documents**. Large numbers of the public demanding answers about the Illuminati's _REM driven_ cloning subculture is the only thing which will stop the Illuminati, and it is the only thing which will guarantee my success and ensure that I escape being activated as a _REM driven_ clone. That is all I want: to escape the cloning centers!

Polygraph tests will help to demonstrate the reality of REM driven human cloning

DM: Furthermore, polygraph tests, independent unbiased lie-detector tests, of low level Illuminati members who retain their *REM driven* cloning experiences when they wake up from sleep, will unequivocally prove to sceptics about the reality of the Illuminati's *REM driven human* cloning subculture. I will volunteer to be polygraph tested and after I have passed, I will point the way to members of my family, who have told me when we were activated as *REM driven* clones at the cloning center, that if they are ever confronted with a lie detector test regarding the Illuminati's *REM driven human* cloning subculture... they will decline the polygraph test and just say *"REM driven* human cloning is true". My family members do not want to dig themselves deeper by lying on a polygraph test. **May 20, 2012 at 5:48am ·**

3SG4: Polygraph tests have an approximate 60 - 90% accuracy rate. That is why polygraph tests are used on day time TV shows and not in courtrooms.

DM: No 3SG4. The accuracy of polygraph tests has improved in recent years and there is a much higher accuracy percentage, currently (Truth or Lie c. 2016). Research this 3SG4. **May 20, 2012 at 5:53am**

DM: Furthermore, 3SG4, in Canadian courts, polygraph tests are admissible when it involves the sexual exploitation of a child... research this statement and get back to me... *smiling* **May 20, 2012 at 5:55am**

[In general, polygraph evidence is NOT admissible in "Canadian Criminal Courts" (Mack's Criminal Law 2016). However, EXCEPTIONS where polygraph evidence is admissible occurs in "Canadian Civil Courts" (which is different from "Canadian Criminal Courts") whereby the admissibility of polygraph evidence varies from province to province in "Canadian Civil Courts" (Mack's Criminal Law 2016). In the family and child protection context, trial decisions on polygraph evidence are inconsistent. "Few appellate courts ['appeals courts' or 'courts of appeals'] have ruled directly on the use of polygraph evidence in family law cases. With this caveat in mind, generally, [Canadian] courts have been concluding that: evidence of willingness to take a polygraph test is relevant and admissible but no firm conclusions may be drawn from a refusal to take a polygraph." (Department of Justice Canada 2016) Furthermore, judges (in Canada), are more receptive to the receipt of polygraph evidence in family and child protection cases than in criminal cases (Department of Justice Canada 2016). The reader should seek the sources Mack's Criminal Law (2016) and Department of Justice Canada (2016) under section "9.10 Polygraph Evidence" for further details on the admissibility of polygraph evidence in Canadian courts. Moreover, with regards to Donald Marshall's above statements: yes, polygraph evidence is admissible in "Canadian Civil Courts" and in (some) family and child protection cases (depending on the context)]

3SG4: Since when Donald? Even a quick Wikipedia search shows this: "The accuracy of the polygraph has been contested almost since the introduction of the device. In 2003, the National Academy of Sciences (NAS) issued a report entitled "The Polygraph and Lie Detection". The NAS found that the majority of polygraph research was "Unreliable, Unscientific and Biased", concluding that 57 of the approximately 80 research studies that the APA [American Psychological Association] relies on to come to their conclusions were significantly flawed."

I know Wikipedia is hardly the most reliable of sources but I'm sure a quick Google search would bring up the original study. I would find it, and read it, but if I cannot be bothered to invest that much time and effort into your crazy [disclosures]. It is also 6am here.

3SG2: Actually, it is possible to learn techniques to beat a polygraph test. Techniques on how to beat polygraph tests are taught to Special Forces soldiers.

Use the BIGGEST & verifiable Illuminati secrets to save Donald Marshall & Others

DM: I am seriously telling you the **BIGGEST and verifiable** Illuminati secrets all for free. The disclosures regarding *REM driven* cloning (and more, which will be upcoming) involve the highest knowledge from Scientology and Freemasonry... for which the highest knowledge in Scientology and Freemasonry are the same thing.... For your information: REM driven human cloning is 32nd Degree Freemasonry knowledge... for which the initiate would have to pay thousands upon thousands of dollars, to move up the rank and achieve such knowledge... I'm giving the world all this knowledge for free, with the aim that the populace will save me [and others] from the Illuminati's *REM driven human* cloning subculture... **May 20, 2012 at 5:48am**

3SG4: OK Donald. I can't wait to be proven wrong; seriously.

3SG2: If you have some proof Donald, let's have it, because I'm getting tired of this. It's boring now.

DM: I'll save you at least 500,000 dollars with the information I am presenting to the world, because that is approximately how much it costs to buy such knowledge in Scientology, with regards to learning about REM driven human cloning and more. In the future you will look back on this moment and wish you had asked me more relevant questions... something good *smiling*... You are extremely fortunate to know such factual and verifiable knowledge, without having to join any weird cults –all for free. With time, patience and much diligence on your part, you will realise the information I am presenting to you is in fact true. You will soon see; stay tuned ladies and gents... you will not be disappointed... I must disclose information about the reality of the Illuminati, their *REM driven human* cloning subculture and more in gradual stages though. In time you will understand the need for my gradual disclosures, and in the future you will say 'Oh... Okay... That is why Donald disclosed information in phases and such'. I promise you will not be disappointed; stay tuned. **May 20, 2012 at 5:51am**

Conspiracies are a fact of life; they happen all the time

3SG2: Where do you work 3SG4, if you don't mind my asking?

3SG4: Although, I have mentioned what I do for a living to conspiracy weirdos before, they always seem to manage to tie my job into my involvement in the Illuminati... However, I would be far more credible in their eyes if I worked in customer services or something of a similar nature.

3SG2: Hey, if you are suggesting that I am a 'Conspiracy weirdo' [then] you aren't as intelligent as you think you are.

3SG4: I am not arguing with you here, 3SG2! I didn't say YOU were [a 'conspiracy weirdo']. You [3SG2] are not willing to accept Donald Marshall's claims of the Illuminati's _REM driven human_ cloning subculture without proof; however 3SG2, a surprising amount of people are willing to accept Donald Marshall's claims of the Illuminati's _REM driven human_ cloning subculture without proof [hard evidence]. These same people are also willing to accept plenty of other things they've read on the internet without proof... anyway.

3SG2: "Conspiracy weirdo" is just a label. If you are as educated as you say you are, then you have the ability to think analytically and critically. Conspiracies are a fact of life. They happen all the time. Labelling someone a "Conspiracy weirdo" is just stupid on the part of the person making such a comment because such a person has not bothered to investigate something and realistically, such a person does not have an argument.

Is Donald Marshall "Trolling" the public with his disclosures about the Illuminati?

3SG4: I hope one day Donald posts a video like "SURPRISE GUYS! I WAS TROLLING YOU ALL ALONG, DUMB PEOPLE!" Epic troll; that would be epic!

DM: That will never happen. I am a very sceptical person too... and everything I present is from first-hand witness accounts through the process of the Illuminati's _REM driven_ human cloning, science and technologies, as well as, "consciousness transfer". I am not guessing or speculating; I am detailing experiences I have witnessed with my five senses through the process of consciousness transfer, and _REM driven_ cloning technology, as a _REM driven_ clone version of myself. Yes, the science and technology are real. Moreover, the fact that I am a very sceptical person, the Illuminati _as REM driven clone versions of themselves_, had to PROVE many sciences and advances in technologies to me several times over, when I was activated by them as a _REM driven_ clone, for me to actually accept that they do in fact have such technologies capable of the functions they present. The information I present is true. Furthermore it is just (concealed) advances in science and technology, currently available, that I am disclosing to the world. **May 20, 2012 at 5:54am**

3SG3 *Sarcastic comment* Trolled softly, by "Donald"; performed (lip-synced) by Lady Tequila.

3SG4: Trollin' me softly with his song, trollin' me softly...with his song.

[Above comments are made in reference to the song performed by Lauryn Hill and the Fugees "Killing me softly" (TheFugeesVEVO 2011)]

DM: I enjoy your trolling. I did not know what "trolling" was, but soon learned...

[Troll: "Digital Technology. *Informal.*
To post inflammatory or inappropriate messages or comments on
(the Internet, especially a message board) for the purpose of
upsetting other users and provoking a response;
to upset or provoke (other users) by posting such messages or comments."]

YOUR duty as a human being: GET to the bottom of this information!

DM: Responding to you is only taking away time from getting more people in the know about the Illuminati's *REM driven human* cloning subculture... However, everyone should KNOW THIS!!! It **IS** your duty as a human being to get to the bottom of this information; blast through your own personal biases, cognitive dissonances and overcome personal fears and KNOW that this information about the Illuminati's *REM driven human* cloning subculture is indeed factual... this information about the Illuminati's *REM driven human* cloning subculture goes beyond Anonymous (We Are Legion); it goes beyond Al-Qaeda, it goes beyond me, or any one individual, **IT IS BIGGER THAN US**. Put simply: everyone can be cloned, and have *duplicate REM driven* clones stored by the Illuminati, and have their consciousness transferred to their *duplicate REM driven* clone body whenever they enter REM sleep in their original bodies. All it takes is a blood sample from the original to grow duplicate clones with the highly advanced technologies the Illuminati hold, and 5 months later the Illuminati have a duplicate clone of ANYONE ready to transfer the person's consciousness to, the next time that person reaches REM sleep. THINK about how many people have donated blood; have had a blood sample taken during their visit to hospital, AND have their blood records stored, and that only translates to mean many, many people can be cloned at the Illuminati's choosing, because many people have their DNA on file. Everyone can be cloned!

More reasons REM driven human cloning MUST GAIN WORLDWIDE EXPOSURE!

DM: Furthermore, once the Illuminati have a duplicate clone of a person, that person can be remotely killed undetectably, with *REM driven* cloning technology because consciousness is linked. Having one's consciousness transferred and being tortured as a *REM driven* clone version, causes side effects in the original person's body; prolonged *REM driven* clone torture causes the original to suffer from a heart attack or aneurysm in their original body during sleep. So YES! **Very serious, life threatening topic!** Then of course there is the slavery and torture. With REM driven cloning technology, the Illuminati have literally enslaved many individuals as *REM driven* clone slaves. Think about that! Being a slave, whenever you go to sleep, whereby you are activated as a *REM driven* clone, and you **MUST** do as the Illuminati say or else get tortured as a *REM driven* clone, which hurts just as badly as if you are being tortured for real, with the possibility of being mentally impaired, in your original body if the torture of your *REM driven* clones continues relentlessly... Yes! It's no fun to be a slave, especially during sleep! Sleep is also something we cannot avoid, because the body needs sleep, so eventually the Illuminati will get you when you have to sleep, and enter REM sleep. This is **EXTREMELY SERIOUS!** The torture spectacles, and what they do to innocent civilians when the Illuminati activate random civilians as *REM driven* clone versions is also something **not** to take lightly!

You cannot ignore this undesirable information or remain ignorant on this topic!

DM: This REALLY IS your duty as a human being to get to the bottom of this information! You CANNOT turn a blind eye to this [you CANNOT ignore this undesirable information] or remain ignorant on the topic of the "Illuminati's REM driven human cloning subculture". Human cloning, and REM driven human cloning involves everyone, and everyone's children. You couldn't fathom what I have seen, and continue to see whenever the Illuminati activate me UNWILLINGLY as a *REM driven* clone at the cloning centers... PLEASE BE SERIOUS... YES! It is LIKE THAT! THIS is how SERIOUS things are! **May 20, 2012 at 6:32am**

3SG2: I'm not a troll Donald. I just honestly don't know if any of this [your disclosures about the Illuminati's *REM driven human* cloning subculture] is true or not. I don't have anything to go on. If I saw a photo of Queen Elizabeth II sticking [stabbing] someone with an antique sabre, I would think: "Bloody hell, it is true". I don't believe in something until I have a good reason to, and someone saying something is true just isn't enough. I need something.

3SG2: I've never met you Donald. For all I know, you might be [crazy / completely lost in fairytales] in cloud Cuckoo land. I'm not trolling anyone. I'm just eager to know what the truth is. I know that plenty in this world is kept hidden from us [the general public] but I do not know what is hidden from us, until I see if for myself, otherwise how can I believe it is true? For all I know I might be [the one who is completely oblivious and naive] bat s**t crazy! I don't know what's going on in the flat next door to me unless I see for myself. No rational minded person should believe a story without some proof. You can't say that [questioning you about evidence relating to the Illuminati's *REM driven human* cloning subculture] is "trolling" because it isn't. I really do want to know if any of this stuff is true.

DM: I totally understand [where you are coming from], stay tuned. Assume [AND RESEARCH the topics pertaining to the disclosure about the Illuminati's *REM driven human* cloning subculture, and one will find many corroborations (in medicine, science and technological articles, movies, songs, literature, etc.) demonstrating the reality of the Illuminati's *REM driven human* cloning subculture concealed subtly right before their very eyes. It REALLY is your duty as a human being to get to the bottom of this information] it is true in the meantime, (it is) and share the information [regarding the Illuminati's *REM driven human cloning* subculture]; all in due time, you will realise these disclosures are in fact true. **May 20, 2012 at 7:40am**

It is rational to seek facts and evidence, than blindly believing something to be true

3SG6: Wow, such negativity 3SG4...What is it, with your [Facebook] cover photos... satanic-like pictures and rainbows?

3SG4: Some [Facebook cover photos] are a character from a computer game ("Pyramid Head -Silent Hill" (Giant Bomb 2016) –he is a super hotty [attractive]); some are art by "H.R. Giger" (painter) (HR Giger c. 2012). Some are [The] Simpsons (IMDb c. 1989) [Television Show] stills, and the other is a crab smoking a cigarette.

3SG4: 3SG2, I believe there is a lot more going on in our world and in government[s] than we [as the public] know about. I do not doubt that some of these things [which are concealed within our world and government] are horrible. You seem rational [3SG2], you ask for evidence and facts instead of blindly believing. My problem is with the people that don't require these things [evidence and facts], and there are plenty of them. It's unbelievable the amount of people on the internet that will post to a single blog, with no sources or references, and claim it as PROOF that there are reptilian humanoids; that Obama is the Anti Christ; or that this chap here [Donald Marshall, has *REM driven* clones, and every time he enters REM sleep, he] is being abused by the Queen of England [as a *REM driven* clone version of herself] for her own amusement. Such people cannot be reasoned with, it is infuriating. Try questioning such people and their main line of defence is: either that you are a Satanist or a shill sent by the government to debunk these theories.

Furthermore, for what it is worth: I do investigate claims before I dismiss them. If I can find ANY adequate evidence I will give it good consideration, but rarely that is the case [with claims and theories made online]. Anyway, I'm done with this [Donald Marshall's disclosures regarding the Illuminati's *REM driven human* cloning subculture]. Bye guys. It's been weird.

DM: Peace out [goodbye], 3SG4... I'll always love you. **May 20, 2012 at 9:36am**

3SG7: 3SG4, haven't you been kicked off the "Conspiracy Crazy" [Facebook] group for constant trolling and relentless insults towards everyone who posts to that [Facebook] group? You are also suspected to be one and the same person as the obnoxious troll "Rover", who was also kicked off [the same Facebook group]. Hmm you have made it your mission in life to suppress truth(s)...I wonder why [you have made it your mission in life to suppress truths]...? Actually, no I do not! 3SG4, you spend your entire life, online, insulting... how sad... how very, very sad.

"Condemnation without investigation is the height of ignorance"

3SG2: It's not rarely the case at all [that there isn't substantial evidence and facts to conspiracies put forward] 3SG4. The Devil is a very good deceiver but he is not a master deceiver, because a lie will always remain a lie, which means it becomes difficult to prove that what has been said or done is true, if the thing said or done was predicated on a lie and eventually the real truth pertaining to the lies will be uncovered in the very end.

There is one thing the Devil is afraid of, and that is the truth. There is plenty of evidence to prove that there is a conspiracy [in this world / in governments]; lots of it [evidence and facts], and it is all around us. Calling people "nut jobs" or "conspiracy weirdos" is resorting to condemnation and insults because you do not have a suitable argument and you are just dismissing it either because you are scared of the truth or because you are ignorant.

Albert Einstein said: "Condemnation without investigation is the height of ignorance". If Donald is telling the truth or the "Conspiracy theorists" are correct, that means that those who are trying to keep the truth hidden from the rest of us [the public] are in BIG trouble because the truth is coming out and there is nothing anyone can do to stop it. Those trying to keep the truth from us can kill me or they can kill Donald but they will never kill us all. There are too many of us. My advice to everyone is: seek the truth and tell the truth because if you do not tell the truth and we do have a soul, and if hell does exist, it's not a place you would want to spend eternity.

3SG2: I do not doubt that what you [Donald Marshall] say is the truth [regarding the Illuminati's _REM driven human_ cloning subculture] but at the same time I am reserving judgement until I see some solid proof [concerning the Illuminati's _REM driven human_ cloning subculture]. 3SG4 and Donald, including anyone else [on this crusade for justice and truth]: I suggest you all start getting truthful if you aren't already, because if you are not, judgement will come for you sooner if not later. Moreover, if Donald is telling the truth [about the Illuminati's _REM driven human_ cloning subculture] and you, 3SG4, are an agent of the criminals doing all these things, then watch out [3SG4]!

3SG2: Here's something for all of you. It's a poem by Rudyard Kipling called "IF" (Kipling Society c. 2012) http://www.kipling.org.uk/poems_if.htm

> Poems - If--
>
> If you can dream - and not make dreams your master; If you can think - and not make thoughts your aim; If you can meet with Triumph and Disaster And treat those two impostors just the same; If you can bear to hear the truth you've spoken Twisted by knaves to make a trap for fools, Or watch the...
>
> KIPLING.ORG.UK

There are two separate bodies in the narrative of REM driven human cloning

3SG7: Just to answer your question 3SG2, and it is a valid one [that no rational person should accept a story without some proof; and where is the proof regarding the Illuminati's *REM driven human* cloning subculture?]... Donald says that his tormentors at the cloning station are actual clones themselves...the bodies of the original people are asleep in bed at home while they carry out these things in their cloned bodies at the cloning station.

[Essentially, there are two bodies in this narrative. A person's original body and a person's *REM driven duplicate* clone body, which the person operates once she or he enters REM sleep, and have her or his consciousness transferred to the remote location (the cloning center). Donald Marshall is being tortured as a *REM driven* clone version of himself, by other *REM driven* clone versions of original people... for which his tormentors are people in high society, and in positions of power in this world, and the torture Marshall suffers as a *REM driven* clone version affects him in his original body because consciousness is linked (Ehrsson 2013). Keep in mind there are two bodies in this narrative; a *REM driven* clone duplicate, and a person's original body. Once you can keep in mind that there are two separate bodies in this narrative it becomes easier to follow the information Donald Marshall is disclosing. Moreover, once Donald Marshall wakes up from sleep in his original body, his *REM driven* clone at the cloning center drops limp noodle –as if dead. Crucially, there are only clones of original people at the cloning center, and not original people with their real bodies at the cloning center; the original people lie asleep in their beds, and carry out their deeds as *REM driven* clone versions of themselves. Accordingly, Marshall cannot take his cell phone and unequivocally prove with hard evidence the reality of the Illuminati's *REM driven human* cloning subculture / cloning centers via recorded video footage, because it is his consciousness which gets transferred, so his original body will still be asleep at home, and Marshall's cell phone will be by his side, at home in bed. Furthermore, when Marshall is a *REM driven* clone unwillingly activated at the cloning center, through the process of consciousness transfer, the Illuminati are **not** going to let Marshall as a *REM driven* clone version of himself, film the cloning center, and email it to himself from the cloning center, for him to retrieve once he wakes up from sleep. Marshall will have to go to the locations of these cloning centers in his original body, and obtain video footage that way... However, the cloning center is heavily guarded, and security is informed to "Shoot on site" if individuals do not have clearance to enter the surrounding area.

Nevertheless, Marshall has mentioned he does not know the exact location of the cloning center to his knowledge, but Former Canadian Prime Minister Stephen Harper knows the exact location of the above ground cloning center in Canada, and we should direct the question regarding the location of the cloning center to Stephen Harper. Moreover, as far as Marshall is aware: the above ground cloning center is within 5/6 hour drive radius of the Robert Pickton Farm in Port Coquitlam, British Columbia, Canada.]

DM: Exactly 3SG7... [The Illuminati have covered their tracks, making it very difficult to obtain video evidence (hard evidence) of their cloning centers] **May 20, 2012 at 9:43pm**

3SG2: O.K. Fair enough. I can understand that [there are two bodies in this narrative: a person's original body; and their *REM driven duplicate* clone]. This narrative can get confusing at times, and appear to be one of those "detective" movies where one cannot figure out who is who. Nevertheless, I am not on anyone's side here. I am giving Donald the benefit of the doubt here, but if I do see someone who I suspect to be a troll, I won't be polite to them!

May 23rd 2012

Does Donald Marshall have a hidden agenda with the aim of creating a "cult"?

Individuals convinced by the belief that Donald Marshall aims to start a "cult"

3SG1 posted the following comment (below)insinuating that Donald Marshall is trying to start a cult of some sort with his disclosures regarding the Illuminati's REM driven human cloning subculture, and that Donald Marshall's overall intentions may not be pure.

3SG1:
"Step I: Keep It Vague; Keep It Simple:

To create a cult you must first attract attention. This you should do not through actions, which are too clear and readable, but through words, which are hazy and deceptive. Your initial speeches, conversations, and interviews must include two elements: on the one hand the promise of something great and transformative and on the other a total vagueness. This combination will stimulate all kinds of hazy dreams in your listeners, who will make their own connections and see what they want to see.

To make your vagueness attractive, use words of great resonance but cloudy meaning, words full of heat and enthusiasm. Fancy titles for simple things are helpful, as are the use of numbers and the creation of new words for vague concepts. All of these create the impression of specialized knowledge, giving you a veneer of profundity. By the same token, try to make the subject of your cult new and fresh, so that few will understand it. Done right, the combination of vague promises, cloudy but alluring concepts, and fiery enthusiasm will stir people's souls and a group will form around you.

Talk too vaguely and you have no credibility. But it is more dangerous to be specific. If you explain in detail the benefits people will gain by following your cult, you will be expected to satisfy them.

As a corollary to its vagueness, your appeal should also be simple. Most people's problems have complex causes: deep-rooted neurosis, interconnected social factors, roots that go way back in time and are exceedingly hard to unravel. Few, however, have the patience to deal with this: most people want to hear that a simple solution will cure their problems.

The ability to offer this kind of solution will give you great power and build you a following; instead of the complicated explanations of real life, return to the primitive solutions of our ancestors, to good old country remedies, to mysterious panaceas [a remedy for diseases; a cure all].

Step 2: Emphasize the Visual and the Sensual over the Intellectual:

Once people have begun to gather around you, two dangers will present themselves: boredom and skepticism. Boredom will make people go elsewhere; skepticism will allow them the distance to think rationally about whatever it is you are offering, blowing away the mist you have artfully created and revealing your ideas for what they are. You need to amuse the bored, then, and ward off the cynics. The best way to do this is through theatre, or other devices of its kind. Surround yourself with luxury, dazzle your followers with visual splendour, fill their eyes with spectacle. Not only will this keep them from seeing the ridiculousness of your ideas, the holes in your belief system, it will also attract more attention, more followers."

3SG1: It's extremely eerie how similar this situation [regarding Donald Marshall's disclosures of the Illuminati's *REM driven* cloning subculture is to the methods outlined above on how to start a cult] is Donald, don't you think?

DM: Isn't what you quoted above, from a book? It sounds like it is written by the Illuminati about themselves. The Illuminati's is a long established cult though, spanning many decades... [The Illuminati as a cult was first established on 1st May 1776, over 240 years ago by Adam Weishaupt (Epperson 1990)]. **May 24, 2012 at 3:06am**

3SG1: No, what I quoted is not from a book. It is quoted from a website dedicated to inform people about the practices of "Scientology" (48 Laws of Power c. 2012), actually.

DM: So is my Facebook page. *Laughter*. My Facebook page is dedicated to inform the world about Scientology, the cloning centers, REM driven human cloning, among other subjects Illuminati related. My Facebook page is also dedicated to inform the world about the Freemasons / Freemasonry, The Vril Society, The Knights of Malta, [and other Papal Bloodlines] as well as, other Orders which are currently reformed as 'Religious Orders', although in actuality, groups such as the Freemasons, The Vril Society, The Knights of Malta etc. are all connected to the Illuminati; this includes Scientology too; Scientology is connected to the Illuminati.

REM driven human cloning is one of the highest level of knowledge which is learned at the highest degree of Freemasonry [and *REM driven* human cloning knowledge is only shared with a selected few]. Moreover, REM driven human cloning is reserved for the 32nd Degree of Freemasonry, and REM driven human cloning is the knowledge Scientologists pay to attain with each new level of knowledge the Scientologist initiate acquires, as she or he progress up the ranks in Scientology... REM driven human cloning knowledge is anything but cheap, and I am risking my life, and giving the world all this knowledge for free, saving each person at least, approximately 500,000 dollars to acquire such knowledge or join ANY strange cults in order to learn some practical truths regarding the world in which they live in.

DM: All I care about is that the public helps me escape the cloning centers, so that I am never activated as a *REM driven* human clone version of myself again. **May 24, 2012 at 3:15am**

3SG2: [3SG1] Have you read Donald's open letter to the public (Donald Marshall Proboards 2012a)? Donald's letter about the Illuminati's *REM driven human* cloning subculture, is anything, but vague!

Media

May 22nd 2012

Illuminati one-eyed symbolism referenced by a radio station in Winnipeg, Canada

3SG1: A radio station here in Winnipeg [city in Manitoba, Canada] posted this picture a few weeks ago.

3SG2: Winnipeg is under a major international investigation, so I am not surprised a radio station in Winnipeg has posted such a very telling picture. Winnipeg is a VERY evil town... which will soon be either freed or purged ["Purge" –an abrupt or violent removal of a group of people].

3SG1: What does the major international investigation concern?

3SG2: I cannot say yet... I AM being monitored. I will mention it soon, though...

3SG1: That is pretty scary because I am from Winnipeg.

3SG2: I know [it is scary]... All is well though. However, I cannot give away too much, but we cannot trust the local police or our governments and all this information will be made available to the world soon... I was in Winnipeg, approximately 10 months ago. When I went to Winnipeg, four killers ran out of that city. I know plenty of information about Winnipeg... and "they" [Illuminati members in Winnipeg] know who I AM too.

3SG1: That is crazy; I am scared now.

DM: "They" [the Illuminati] are scared now *smiling* **May 22, 2012 at 8:27pm**

3SG2: And they [the Illuminati] should be [scared], they have extremely angered some REALLY powerful forces.

DM: "They" [the Illuminati] have angered the populace. The Illuminati know they have angered some extremely powerful forces, and now they are scrambling *smiling*. Spreading the information about the Illuminati's *REM driven human* cloning subculture is working. **May 22, 2012 at 10:04pm**

Movies

May 18th 2012

Eyes Wide Shut (1999)

3SG1 posts a photo depicting the scene of the Occult Ritual, from the movie "Eyes Wide Shut" (1999)

3SG1: http://en.wikipedia.org/wiki/Eyes_Wide_Shut

Eyes Wide Shut - Wikipedia, the free encyclopedia

3SG1: http://en.wikipedia.org/wiki/Mentmore_Towers
"Mentmore Towers is a 19th century English country house in the village of Mentmore in Buckinghamshire. The house was designed by Joseph Paxton and his son-in-law, George Henry Stokes, [1] [2] in the composite English Renaissance revival style called Jacobethan, [3] [4] for the banker and collector of fine art, Baron Mayer de Rothschild as a country home, display case for his collection of fine art and as an assertion of status."

[Mentmore Towers, was one of the settings used in the movie "Eyes Wide Shut" (1999)]

3SG1: [Shares the following link about secret societies. However, the information is written in French] **http://www.eutraco.com/cristal/livre/le%20livre%20jaune%205.pdf** (Eutraco (no date))

DM: "Eyes Wide Shut" (1999) is an Illuminati made movie. **May 21, 2012 at 7:14am**

3SG2: Aren't most movies today, made by them [the Illuminati]?

DM: All the big blockbuster movies are made by the Illuminati... and even some low budget movies are also made by the Illuminati... **May 28, 2012 at 9:55am** ·

3SG3: That stuff is crazy!

3SG4: Where is this place?

3SG1: "Mentmore Towers [which was used as one of the settings in the movie "Eyes Wide Shut" (1999)] is a 19th-century English country house built for the Rothschild family in the village of Mentmore in Buckinghamshire. The house was designed by Joseph Paxton and his son-in-law, George Henry Stokes, in the 19th-century revival of late 16th and early 17th-century Elizabethan and Jacobean styles called Jacobethan for the banker and collector of fine art Baron Mayer de Rothschild as a country home, display case for his collection of fine art. The mansion has been described as one of the greatest houses of the Victorian era. In keeping with the contents intended to be displayed within, the interiors take their inspiration principally from the Italian Renaissance, although the house also contains drawing rooms and cabinets decorated in the gilded styles of late 18th-century France. Historically it was first known simply as 'Mentmore'. The design is closely based on that of Robert Smythson's Wollaton Hall. Mentmore Towers is a Grade I listed building, with its park and gardens listed Grade II*.""

May 19th 2012

Independence Day (1996)

3SG1: Donald, Have you ever watched "Independence Day" (1996), and did you notice the symbolism in the movie?

DM: Yes, I have seen "Independence Day" (1996). "Independence Day" (1996) is a movie made by the Illuminati, with Will Smith in it. **May 20, 2012 at 4:52am**

Religion

May 23rd 2012

School girl who was kidnapped and used for Vatican sex parties

3SG1 posts an article about the Vatican using a schoolgirl for sex parties (Business Insider 2012) *on Donald Marshall's Facebook Timeline.*

DM: This is why they [including the Illuminati] get away with things such as this mentioned in the article above... the Illuminati [including the Church] do outrageous things in secret that the public would just not believe if they heard it, unless they witnessed it in person themselves... when news such us this is leaked to the public, the public usually disregard it as "gossip" because on the surface it sounds so unbelievable to be true, and it is therefore disregarded by most as "gossip" when things such as this mentioned in the article are usually true... it is unfathomable that supposedly good and holy people would do these things to an animal, let alone a human being, but these people in high positions of power sometimes do such outrageous things as mentioned in the article. **May 23, 2012 at 3:25am**

May 23rd 2012

Is a dead school girl the victim of Vatican sex parties?

3SG1 posts a similar article to the one above about the Vatican using a schoolgirl for sex parties (David Icke 2012) *on Donald Marshall's Facebook Timeline.*

3SG2: That is disgusting! Those pigs!

DM: The Illuminati's *REM driven* human cloning subculture, and what the Illuminati members do in complete, complete secrecy, as *REM driven* clones, and as real people with their original bodies in complete, complete secrecy, is worse than you can picture... "Absolute power corrupts absolutely" –it is a motto of the Illuminati's. **May 23, 2012 at 7:29pm**

People sharing Donald Marshall's Open Letter

May 22nd 2012

3SG1 reposts Donald Marshall's original letter to the public about the Illuminati's REM driven human cloning subculture (Donald Marshall Proboards 2012a) *to Donald Marshall's Facebook Timeline.*

[Review the References section for a link to Donald Marshall's original letter to the public (Donald Marshall Proboards 2012a)].

3SG1: Check this out! It is very, very interesting [information]. Look for this guy; he is saying really interesting things. It is written in English.

3SG2: Is this a weak or sham argument which is easily refuted [in other words is it "Strawman"?]?

DM: No, the letter about the Illuminati's *REM driven cloning* subculture is not fallacious ("Strawman"). The information contained in the open letter to the public is all true. Feel lucky to know the information about the Illuminati's *REM driven human* cloning subculture; the information is beyond top secret (Donald Marshall Proboards 2012a). **May 22, 2012 at 11:42am**

3SG3: What on earth?!

3SG4: What is up with your dude, 3SG1?

DM: Read the open letter about the Illuminati's *REM driven* cloning subculture **attentively**. Research all which may initially seem like a contradiction, until you can wholeheartedly confirm whether the information contained in the open letter (Donald Marshall Proboards 2012a) is true or not with certainty. I guarantee the information contained in the open letter about the Illuminati's *REM driven* cloning subculture is all true. REM driven human cloning, is what the Illuminati do. **May 23, 2012 at 8:12am**

3SG4: Yes the Illuminati are either cloning people in secret or, you are a crazy fool.

DM: [With all I have witnessed as a *REM driven* clone version of myself] I should be [crazy] by now *smiling* **May 23, 2012 at 8:16am**

3SG4: Check this out. *3SG4 tags friends to notify them to read this post, containing Donald Marshall's open letter to the public* (Donald Marshall Proboards 2012a).

DM: Check it out, world! *Smiling* **May 23, 2012 at 8:49pm**

3SG5: *Said in disbelief, and NOT to be taken seriously* Ha-ha, I've seen this [Donald Marshall's open letter to the public regarding the Illuminati's *REM driven* cloning subculture]. He [Donald Marshall] is a cousin of a reptilian!

Personal life

May 20th 2012

Donald Marshall gives video tour of his hometown: Halifax, Nova Scotia, Canada

Donald Marshall added a new video: **Halifax. View. 1**

[Watch the video uploaded to Donald Marshall's Facebook Timeline by pressing "Ctrl" on the keyboard and using the left mouse button to "click" on "**Halifax. View. 1**" underlined and highlighted in bold above, OR, by using the same method outlined above and "clicking" the image below. The video is only 1 minute long. In the video, Donald Marshall tells the viewer that the video is unrelated to his disclosures regarding the Illuminati's *REM driven* cloning subculture, however, he wants to show the viewer where he grew up: Halifax, Nova Scotia, Canada]

3SG1: Nice [view].

3SG2: Welcome to the Jungle!

3SG3: Glad you're enjoying your day! Your weather couldn't be better! Happy for you!

May 20th 2012

Donald Marshall takes a picture of a flower during his walk in Halifax

DM: This is a solitary flower I saw [while walking in Halifax today]... It looked lonely so I had to take a picture of it... I believe it is some kind of tulip.

Video footage of Halifax Harborside shot by Donald Marshall

Donald Marshall added a new video: **Halifax Harborside... Sunset in my beautiful but corrupt city...**

[Watch the video uploaded to Donald Marshall's Facebook Timeline by pressing "Ctrl" on the keyboard and using the left mouse button to "click" on "**Halifax Harborside... Sunset in my beautiful but corrupt city...**" OR, by using the same method outlined above and "clicking" the image below]

May 20th 2012

Donald Marshall asks for opinions about having a new haircut

DM: Maybe I should get a haircut soon... What do you think?

3SG1: Aww sweet ^^

3SG2: I like it like that.

3SG3: Yeah I like your hair the way it is, but if you feel you want to try something new, do it for yourself.

3SG4: Um, maybe a little [haircut] *smiling*

3SG5: I love your hair! Uber cute!

3SG6: Never met a haircut I liked better than the longer hair before! Grow it!

3SG7: From what I learned the technique of cutting long hair was to decrease one's ability of enlightenment... after having read that, I quit cutting my hair three years ago. Why do all of the military have to have their head shaved (?), as well as, prisoners? Allegedly, cutting hair stunts the growth of consciousness... SO I HAVE READ >>> no facts.

3SG2: Yes, I have read something similar, and I have heard the Native American Indians kept their hair long for that particular reason you mentioned above [so that they do not stunt their consciousness]... So I have heard... Short hair looks good too on you though [Donald].

3SG8: I read an article which detailed that Native American Indians that were forced into war lost all their abilities on the battlefield after cutting their hair off. As a consequence [of losing their abilities through cutting their hair], the military let the Native American Indians keep their long hair, and then the military soon realised, long hair is an extension of our super human abilities to feel the energies around us.

3SG4: Honestly, I don't like the [short] hair.

DM: My hair is longer now; less maintenance. **October 26, 2012 at 9:19am**

3SG9: Wasn't Samson [ruler of the ancient Israelites mentioned in the Bible] told not to cut his hair? And yes 3SG7, I read the same article you are referring to. It was about the Navajo Wind-talkers, who lost their abilities of "awareness" once they had their hair cut short, I believe it was.

3SG10: In the military, hair is cut short because of long hair being a hindrance if another grabbed it. I used to have long hair; however, I have had short hair for many years now. These days, I have my hair a little bit longer because I do not have the 'fullness' of hair like I used to! Hairdressers loved my thick hair, but that was once upon a time. I used to look like Randy Rhoads [American heavy metal guitarist].

3SG11: I know a stylist! ME! You'll have a fresh look after a style [Donald]. *smiling*

DM: Yes. Glam shots only. **June 30, 2013 at 4:44am**

3SG12: No Donald, your hair is fine.

3SG13: Cool.

3SG14: The long fringe looks annoying, grow a ponytail instead, since you asked.

3SG15: No. Do not cut your hair yet, those [long hair] are your 'wings to heaven'.

3SG16: 3SG7 [and 3SG9], your comments about military studies of the Native American Indian abilities with and without hair is true. I saw that [article].

3SG17: *Posts an article regarding* "The Truth About Long Hair" (World Wide Hippies 2013).

The Truth About Long Hair
From United Truth Seekers This information about hair has been hidden from the public since the Viet Nam...
WORLDWIDEHIPPIES.COM

3SG18: Women dig the [long] hair... the ones that matter, anyway...

DM: My hair is very long now. **May 29, 2014 at 4:11pm**

3SG19: Oh wow, you're a cutie! No do not cut it!

3SG20: Yes [cut your hair].

DM: I won't lose my hair [cut it short], supposedly. **May 29, 2014 at 9:38pm**

3SG21: Shave the sides of your hair only, Mohican up!

3SG22: Your hair looks like my hair Donald; I need a haircut too...

DM: My hair is very long now... **May 30, 2014 at 8:01pm**

3SG23: No! [Don't cut it]. It is cute [your long hair]!

DM: My hair is long now, and all past my shoulders... my hair is all one length now... **May 30, 2014 at 8:14pm**

3SG23: Keep your hair long! You look like Jesus! *Laughter*

DM: Ha-ha! **May 30, 2014 at 8:17pm**

3SG24: Let your hair grow. Your hair is part of your nervous system.

Song Making

May 20th 2012

Did Donald Marshall compose the song "Personal Jesus"?

3SG1: My own "Personal Jesus"! (Warner Bros. Records 2009; MarilynMansonVEVO 2009) Did you write that song too?

DM: I cannot remember if I wrote that song ["Personal Jesus" (Warner Bros. Records 2009; MarilynMansonVEVO 2009)] *as a REM driven clone version of myself unwillingly activated at the cloning center* or not. **May 30, 2014 at 8:20pm**

May 21st 2012

"Heartless" made by Donald Marshall performed by Kanye West

DM:
In the night I hear em talk
coldest story ever told
somewhere far along this road
he lost his soul
to a woman so heartless
"Heartless" performed by Kanye West (KanyeWestVEVO 2009)
(Written by Donald Marshall)

3SG1: SUE HIM

DM: I plan to [sue him]. *Smiling* *When we were activated as REM driven clone versions of ourselves at the cloning center: as a REM driven clone:* Kanye West asked me for a gimmick... most celebrities I've interacted with as *REM driven* clones at the cloning center usually ask for gimmicks [to make themselves stand out]... but I do my best to tell them dumb stuff for them to incorporate as gimmicks [in their original bodies]... and these celebrities [usually] do it *laughter*. *As a REM driven clone version of myself,* I told *a REM driven clone version of* Kanye West at the cloning center to wear those nerdy sweaters as his gimmick *laughter*. I also told Chris Brown to wear a bowtie, when we interacted as *REM driven* clone versions of ourselves at the cloning center, and Chris Brown DID *LAUGHTER*. Chris Brown looked like Ronald McDonald's illegitimate child... a RED bowtie... *laughter* **May 22, 2012 at 10:24pm**

DM: KANYE! Can ye heea may [KANYE! Can you hear me?]? I know aw you scummy mudda f****s feya may [I know all of you scummy motherf*****s fear me!]! **May 22, 2012 at 10:25pm**

May 21st 2012

Video footage of Donald Marshall rapping the song "Good Feeling"

Donald Marshall added a new video: **Next... Soon 20 min one will take longer to upload...**

[Watch the video uploaded to Donald Marshall's Facebook Timeline by pressing "Ctrl" on the keyboard and using the left mouse button to "click" on "**Next... Soon 20 min one will take longer to upload...**" underlined and highlighted in bold above, OR, by using the same method outlined above and "clicking" the image above. The same video can also be found on YouTube by following the reference "Eric Hastey (2012)", which is listed in the "References" section of this document.

In the video, Donald Marshall raps the lyrics to the song "Good Feeling" (Flo Rida 2011) as he originally sang it when he was activated as a *REM driven* clone *version of himself* at the cloning center. Marshall raps, although he does not listen to rap music, and assures the audience he has not practiced the song he is about to rap, and he is not intending to "show off" but rather demonstrates to the many who question his song making ability, his ability in creating many different types of songs, for many different genres as a *REM driven* clone *version of himself* at the cloning center; because in this video, Marshall demonstrates he can rap, and rap very well although he does not actively listen to rap music.

Moreover, Marshall also explains which parts of the song were changed when Flo Rida performs "Good Feeling" (Flo Rida 2011) in comparison to how Marshall rapped "Good Feeling" (Flo Rida 2011) when he was unwillingly activated as a *REM driven* clone version at the cloning center. Marshall also explains the references to REM driven human cloning in the song "Good Feeling" (Flo Rida 2011) and Marshall's intense desire to expose the Illuminati's *REM human driven* cloning subculture, through this song, "Good Feeling" (Flo Rida 2011), for which Marshall created as a *REM driven* clone version of himself, at the cloning center. The lyrics to "Good Feeling" (Flo Rida 2011), as originally composed by Marshall can be found in "Exposing the Illuminati's REM Driven Human Cloning Subculture Volume 1" page 98 (Marshall 2016b)]

3SG1: That's insane man. Totally makes sense though [the explanations you give in relation to the song "Good Feeling" (Flo Rida 2011) –and REM driven human cloning].

3SG2: Oh my goodness! If you guys think this is amazing, you haven't seen anything yet, and thank God!

3SG3: Donald, are you ok? You seemed very "tense" in this video. It appears almost as if you wanted to cry at one point... maybe not... but my heart goes out to you.

May 22nd 2012

"Edge of Glory" made by Donald Marshall performed by Lady Gaga

DM: I'M ON THE EDGE OF GLORY... AND I'M HANGING ON A MOMENT OF TRUTH... (LadyGagaVEVO 2011) performed by Lady Gaga written by Donald Marshall [as a *REM driven* clone version of himself, at the cloning center]... **May 22, 2012 at 9:58pm**

May 23rd 2012

Donald Marshall on: the song "Hero" performed by Nickelback & Chad Kroeger

DM: *As a REM driven clone version of myself, unwillingly activated by the Illuminati, as a REM driven clone, via the process of consciousness transfer when I enter REM sleep in my original body*, I made the song "Hero" (Nickelback 2013) which Nickelback later performed. Furthermore, as a *REM driven* clone version of himself, when we interacted *as REM driven clone versions of ourselves* at the cloning center, I found Chad Kroeger to be extremely dislikeable, stupid, irritating, ridiculous and boring nerd, as a *REM driven* clone *version of himself*. Moreover, Chad Kroeger tries to imitate my hairstyle (in real life) too... **May 24, 2012 at 7:44pm**

May 24th 2012

"Decode" by Donald Marshall performed by Paramore: "Twilight" soundtrack

3SG1: Let me guess, you made the Twilight movies too?

DM: I made the song "Decode" (Fueled by Ramen 2008) from the cloning center as a *REM driven* clone version of myself, which the band Paramore performs, which was used for the movie "Twilight" (2008) as a soundtrack. **May 25, 2012 at 5:49am**

Donald Marshall on: the band Paramore & the meaning of the name "Paramore"

DM: *As REM driven clone versions of ourselves, activated by the Illuminati through the process of consciousness transfer to our REM driven clone duplicates*, Hailey Williams (lead singer of the band Paramore) and her band members as *REM driven* clone versions were mean to me as *REM driven* clone version of myself [in the past]. [Currently] Hailey Williams and her band members have left me alone whenever we are activated as *REM driven* clone versions at the cloning center... All the celebrities leave me alone now, whenever I am unwillingly activated as a *REM driven* clone version of myself at the cloning center. **May 25, 2012 at 5:49am**

DM: By the way, a "Paramore" is a person of religious significance (Vocabulary 2016; Online Etymology Dictionary 2016) which the Illuminati *REM driven* clones say that I am, and which in actuality is untrue and I do **NOT** endorse such claims. However, because a "Paramore" is a person of religious significance, this is why the Illuminati, named the band that: "Paramore"... Moreover, *as a REM driven clone version of myself, unwillingly activated as a REM driven clone, via the process of consciousness transfer*, I made nearly all the songs the band Paramore have sang, throughout the years I was unwillingly activated as a *REM driven* clone version of myself, from the cloning center. **May 26, 2012 at 8:01am**

["The noun "paramour" (same pronunciation as the band name "Paramore") evolved from the French phrase "par amour", meaning "passionately" or "with desire." If you break it down, you get par, meaning "by", and amour, the French word for "love". In the mid 14th Century (Dictionary 2016; Online Etymology Dictionary 2016), women used this word to describe Christ, and men would use it to refer to the Virgin Mary. But eventually, during the late 14th Century (Dictionary 2016; Online Etymology Dictionary 2016), paramour shed its religious connotations and came to mean "darling" or "sweetheart," and later "mistress" or "clandestine lover."" (Vocabulary 2016)]

May 24th 2012

Songs made by Donald Marshall performed by Cher

3SG1: I was wondering if Cher attends the cloning center as a *REM driven* clone version of herself? I was always a fan of Cher's but from what you describe about the actions of celebrities and how they got songs from you to sing as a *REM driven* clone version of yourself, I am thinking Cher may be one of the celebrities who harmed you too [and is complicit with the Illuminati]?

DM: Yes, Cher attends the cloning center *as a REM driven clone version of herself through the process of consciousness transfer to her REM driven clone duplicate*. I have made many songs as a *REM driven* clone version of myself from the cloning center for Cher, which Cher later performed, such as: **"Turn back time"** (CherTV 2012b); **"Believe"** (CherTV 2012a) ("Do you believe in life after love")... I made many songs from the cloning center, *as a REM driven clone version of myself*, for Cher to perform. Cher **never** harmed me as a *REM driven* clone *version of myself* unwillingly activated as a *REM driven* clone at the cloning center.

Moreover, Cher attended the cloning center *as a REM driven clone version of herself* when I was brought to the cloning center(s) *via the process of consciousness transfer from my original body to my REM driven clone duplicate body* since I was age 5. Cher has attended the cloning centers *as a REM driven clone version of herself* since I was age 5, when I was unwillingly activated as a *REM driven* clone *version of myself* at the cloning center(s) for the first time. Furthermore, Cher attended the cloning centers *as a REM driven clone version of herself* since I was age 5 all the way through the many years (over the 30 plus years) I was unwillingly activated as a *REM driven* clone *version of myself*, and forced as a *REM driven* clone to make songs for musicians to sing.

DM: *As REM driven clone versions of ourselves,* Cher sang the song "The Music's no good without you (baby)" (CherTV 2011) when we were both active as *REM driven* clone versions at the cloning center. Cher (*as a REM driven clone version of herself*) sang the song "The Music's no good without you (baby)" (CherTV 2011) to a *REM driven* clone version of me, in private, in a room off the concourse of the main arena in the 'diddle-dome' (the cloning center). **May 25, 2012 at 5:51am**

May 24th 2012

"Someone Like You" made by Donald Marshall performed by Adele

[The song **"Someone Like You"** (AdeleVEVO 2011) is a song Donald Marshall free-styled from start to finish *as a REM driven clone version of himself, activated unwillingly as a REM driven clone version of himself via the process of consciousness transfer from Donald Marshall's original body, to his REM driven clone, for which consciousness transference happens once an the original person sleeps and reaches REM sleep (REM sleep occurs 90-110 minutes after first falling asleep).* Donald Marshall made the song **"Someone Like You"** (AdeleVEVO 2011) at the above ground cloning center in western Canada, *when he was unwillingly activated by the Illuminati, as a REM driven clone version of himself.* Donald Marshall did **NOT** make the song **"Someone Like You"** (AdeleVEVO 2011) or any of the other songs listed for that matter, as a person experiencing the world in their original natural born body, but rather Donald Marshall composed many songs via the process of "consciousness transfer" to a **REM driven clone** version of himself, because it is SAME consciousness which experiences the SAME earth, whenever consciousness is transferred from a person's original body to a person's *REM driven* clone duplicate body, whereby *REM driven* clones are stored at a remote location by the Illuminati: the cloning center(s).

The song "Someone Like You" (AdeleVEVO 2011) was sang and free-styled by Donald Marshall as a *REM driven* clone version of himself, when Donald Marshall felt extremely saddened by the fact that as *REM driven* clone versions of themselves activated by the Illuminati as *REM driven* clones, the conspiracy theorists Lenny Bloom and Jane Steele, who host a TV radio talk show, decided to join the Illuminati in exchange for fame and fortune, rather than to help Donald Marshall expose the Illuminati's *REM driven human* cloning subculture, and as a result of their decision, Lenny Bloom and Jane Steele betrayed Donald Marshall and humanity. After conspiracy theorists Lenny Bloom and Jane Steele had betrayed Donald Marshall while each individual was experiencing life as *REM driven human* clone versions of themselves at the cloning center, Jane Steele as a *REM driven* clone version of herself tried consoling a *REM driven* clone version of Donald Marshall by insisting: "Donny, I wish NOTHING but the best for you..."

However, Donald Marshall *as a REM driven clone version of himself at the cloning center*, was extremely saddened and inconsolable for many minutes on end... and then out of nowhere... Donald Marshall *as a REM driven clone version responded to a REM driven clone version of* Jane Steele's above comment by declaring at the top of his lungs:

"NEVER MIND, I'LL FIND SOMEONE LIKE YOUUUUU, I WISH NOTHING BUT THE BEST FOR YOUUUUU, TOOOO, DONT FORGET ME I BEG, I'LL REMEMBER YOU SAID SOMETIMES IT LASTS IN LOVE, BUT SOMETIMES IT HURTS INSTEEAAAAD" (AdeleVEVO 2011).

-and this is how the song "Someone Like You" (AdeleVEVO 2011) originated... The song "Someone Like You" (AdeleVEVO 2011) later performed by the singer Adele, originated from the betrayal of Lenny Bloom and Jane Steele, as REM driven clone versions of themselves, towards a *REM driven* clone version of Donald Marshall at the cloning center, for which the song "Someone Like You" (AdeleVEVO 2011) was originally free-styled from start to finish by very solemn and grief-stricken Donald Marshall *as a REM driven* clone version of himself. Review "Experiences from the Cloning Center Volume 1" (Marshall 2016a, pp. 41 – 46) for further details regarding this experience of Donald Marshall's as a *REM driven* clone version of himself, as well as, for further information on how the song "Someone Like You" (AdeleVEVO 2011) came to fruition]

Technologies

May 20th 2012

Project Pegasus and the (CERN) Large Hadron Collider (LHC)

3SG1: Do you know of the "Pegasus" program?

DM: Do you know more than your saying about the Pegasus program? You just said something that caught my interest. **May 21, 2012 at 12:26am**

DM: Yes, I know about the time [manipulation] nonsense, which involves colliding protons [with the use of the Large Hadron Collider (LHC) at CERN]. Yes, yes, *as REM driven clone versions at the cloning center*, the Illuminati *REM driven clones* made me learn about some of the functions of the LHC... learning about the functionalities of the LHC [as well as time manipulation, as a *REM driven* clone, at the cloning center] was boring to me... I always just wanted to leave... **May 21, 2012 at 12:27am**

3SG1: What did I say that caught your interest?

DM: I'll talk about it later... You may not know what I thought you were hinting at... and I will discuss what you mentioned, which is the "Pegasus Program", which caught my interest in Phase Two of my assault. I have to stay on schedule. **May 21, 2012 at 12:29am**

3SG1: The Illuminati use the Pegasus Program to control outcomes in the future; weaving their web over decades; pulling strings; and the Illuminati have also learned how to collectively reincarnate their souls [or consciousnesses] into new bodies, while retaining all the memories that "Death" and "rebirth" would have blocked so that they would continue to exist as they see fit. They 'stack the deck' [to cheat or to fix something so a desired outcome is achieved], as it were, so that they are dealt whatever hand [favourable outcome] they please. It is similar to your [REM driven] cloning, but not quite. Your [REM driven] cloning process that you have been through is a new play on something very old. The Illuminati are trying to play God, and create soulless bodies. However, the Illuminati have not been able to surpass one very powerful law of purgatory yet ("purgatory" being the definite laws of the cosmos itself; an ever existing neutral power that cannot be trifled with, Correction: SHOULD not be trifled with).

Physical death releases you from your body, and your "human" mind. Rebirth "blocks" your old memories so that you can experience life to learn new lessons, and to spiritually grow. The Illuminati have no wish to grow as such, and only wish to have power on this earth.

DM: You are actually right [the Illuminati have been using concealed advances in medicine, science and technology for those aims to remain in power on this earth]... Are you on your "next go round" as the Illuminati call it? [In other words has your consciousness been – reanimated / brought back after death (?) and now your consciousness resides in a new (clone) body?] **May 21, 2012 at 1:32am**

3SG2: It is not just our second go around [second time our consciousness is experiencing this world], if that is what you are asking.

3SG1: I am not sure what you mean by what you just asked ["Is it my second go around?"]. Currently, my mind is a bit muddled by something else which has caught my interest. Please be a bit more verbose.

DM: OK. Send a message to my personal inbox. Tell me if you are talking about what I think you may be talking about... **May 21, 2012 at 1:36am**

May 23rd 2012

Siri Technology

Siri technology leaks Illuminati information

3SG1: Hello Siri.

DM: Siri? [Why did you mention Siri?] **May 25, 2012 at 5:24am**

3SG1: Siri, the technology they [the Illuminati] created is an epic fail [a failure of enormous proportions]. They [the Illuminati] are afraid Siri is leaking too much information [which the Illuminati do not want known].

DM: *Laughter* Yes, that is true, Siri leaks information which the Illuminati do not want known. 3SG1, you know about the Illuminati's *REM driven human* cloning subculture, REM driven cloning and you know about me [What I have done at the cloning center as a *REM driven human* clone version of myself]... Moreover, you are mentioning top secret information [about the Illuminati's *REM driven human* cloning subculture] which I have not yet mentioned... did they [the Illuminati] send you?

3SG1: No [I was not sent by the Illuminati]. I learned the true meaning of twinning [creating a twin of, which could include offspring (i.e. twins) in biology and agriculture; or twins of objects: towns, cities, roads, etc.] and I have a really high intelligent quotient (IQ). I wrote a new equation, but the idiots [the Illuminati] erased the equation. However, the new equation I wrote disproved all scientific theory and made time travel into what it really is: soul travel [or "consciousness travel"]. Basically, in earth time they [the Illuminati] would have to replicate me in less than one second, and before I ruined time travel, I changed some basic laws to what they really should have been in history.

158 | P a g e

[We will later realise that this person quoted here above as 3SG1, is also a victim of the Illuminati's *REM driven human* cloning subculture. 3SG1 has *REM driven* clones at the cloning center and Donald Marshall and 3SG1 have met as *REM driven human* clone versions of each other at the cloning center. Furthermore, speaking in 2012, 3SG1 was afraid to disclose knowledge gained or personal experiences in regards to Illuminati's *REM driven human* cloning subculture, and therefore this person spoke in hints and mannerisms which were not clear and concise for an outsider to comprehend or understand. However, the person above is a victim of the Illuminati's *REM driven human* cloning subculture who had their mind "warped" by the Illuminati as a result. The comments (and future comments) made by this person above, although they were mostly hints, (for which the hints made by this person are only understood as corroborations to Donald Marshall's disclosures, once a person examines the complete disclosures made my Donald Marshall regarding the Illuminati's *REM driven human* cloning subculture) added credence to the Donald Marshall's exposure of the Illuminati's *REM driven human* cloning subculture as being true, and a current reality; a current reality which must end!]

DM: Okay [3SG1] maybe you do not know [top secret information or what is actually true about the Illuminati's *REM driven human* cloning subculture]. *Laughter* there is no time travel yet... [as far as I am aware...] However, the Illuminati *REM driven* clones tell people who they have activated through the process of consciousness transfer to *REM driven* clone bodies... that it is 'time travel', a 'time stutter' or a 'different dimension'; some people who are activated by the Illuminati into *REM driven* clone bodies, and who do not know that they are simultaneously asleep at home in their beds in their original bodies, and have had their consciousness transferred to *REM driven* clone bodies, believe they are in their real bodies and are led to believe by the Illuminati *REM driven* clones that it is a 'time warp' or 'parallel dimension'... Moreover, the Illuminati *REM driven* clones told Tila Tequila, when she was activated by the Illuminati as a *REM driven* clone version of herself, that "It is the 5th dimension"... Tila Tequila now knows it is just consciousness transfer to a *REM driven* clone body, whereby Tila Tequila experiences the same earth at a remote location far from her home, which is the cloning center, as a *REM driven* clone version of herself. Tila Tequila knows it is just REM driven human cloning now; before she did not know... **May 25, 2012 at 11:49pm**

["**Siri** is a built-in a speech-recognition computer application technology, ("intelligent assistant") that enables users of "Apple iPhone 4S" and later and newer "iPad" and "iPod Touch" devices to speak natural language voice commands in order to operate the mobile device and its apps.

Siri also has both speech input and output, meaning you can speak to it, and it can speak back to you. You speak to Siri to ask it questions and give it commands, such as small tasks that you'd like it to complete. For example, ask Siri about the weather, and it will respond out loud with a short summary of the day's weather report and on-screen with a snapshot of the five-day forecast. (on devices such as the "Apple iPhone 4S", "iPod" and "iPad" etc.)" For further discussions about Siri technology review PC Mag (2011) "What is Siri?" –the link to the article is provided in the "References" section of this document]

159 | P a g e

Television Shows

May 21st 2012

I Cloned My Pet (2012)

[Press "Ctrl" on the keyboard and using the left mouse button to "click" on the image below to be directed to the first episode of "I Cloned My Pet" (Cassette Acme 2012), OR, simply click on the image below on your device.]

3SG1: There is now a television programme on TLC titled "I Cloned My Pet" (TLC c. 2012; Cassette Acme 2012) *blank face*

[TLC is a former abbreviation of "The Learning Channel". TLC is an American basic cable and satellite television network company]

3SG2: Thank you for this information, it is greatly appreciated!

DM: They [the Illuminati] are trying to warm the population into the idea of "cloning"... in their best attempts before I do [and the world realises the reality and extent of "cloning", "human cloning", "REM driven cloning" and everything else I must disclose regarding the topic of the Illuminati's *REM driven human* cloning subculture. With the continued spread of the letter (Donald Marshall Proboards 2012a) regarding the Illuminati's *REM driven human* cloning subculture and the soft disclosure of television shows such as "I Cloned My Pet" (TLC c. 2012; Cassette Acme 2012) which focuses on the topic of "cloning"... the Illuminati cannot kill me now, because too many of the world's populace know about the letter (Donald Marshall Proboards 2012a) which discusses the Illuminati's *REM driven human* cloning subculture.

DM: If the Illuminati were to kill me now, it would be an admission of guilt, demonstrating to any outsider that the Illuminati really does have *REM driven* cloning technology, and all the high advances in technology I have disclosed (the Illuminati really do have such technologies, existing today!). If the Illuminati were to kill me, this would prove to be an admission of guilt on their part to many people who known of my disclosure regarding the Illuminati's *REM driven human* cloning subculture. The Illuminati have also said to me, as *REM driven* clone versions of ourselves at the cloning center: "The letter I have written regarding their *REM driven human* cloning subculture will spread across the world even faster if I was to suddenly die of an aneurysm or heart attack". This is good news, so far as the disclosure and exposure of the Illuminati's *REM driven human* cloning subculture is concerned. **May 22, 2012 at 8:01am**

3SG3: Yes! We are waiting for Phase 2, and Document 2.

3SG4: Yes! "An admission of guilt" is correct [if the Illuminati were to kill Donald Marshall]

DM: Phase Two will come... I am currently very busy... I am typing all the time... do not worry... I do not like waiting in general either... and I do not want to string people along [to 'string someone along' is and idiom which means: to "maintain someone's interest or attention, possibly insincerely"] like Tila Tequila has done. If Tila Tequila was to start talking about the cloning centers, she would lie in terms of what she knows from firsthand experience regarding *REM driven* cloning and the cloning centers. I have to do this disclosure correctly... People will understand why I had to disclose information regarding the Illuminati's *REM driven human* cloning subculture slowly, and phase by phase, in the end once everything regarding the Illuminati's *REM driven human* cloning subculture is fully exposed, publicly and worldly known. However, people will know everything in regards to the Illuminati's *REM driven human* cloning subculture... the world will know. **May 22, 2012 at 10:13pm**

Contact Information

Facebook: https://www.facebook.com/donald.marshall.148

Press Ctrl+Click (hold "Ctrl" on your keyboard and left "Click" with your mouse, on each image to your right, to reach each source listed here).

My Facebook Timeline starts from March 2012. All posts are "Public" and therefore newcomers should start reading from March 2012, in order to fully understand the Illuminati's REM driven human cloning subculture and more. You may start reading my Facebook public Timeline from May 24th 2012, ONCE you have finished reading each document listed as "Volume 1" to "Volume 2" in the series.

Donald Marshall Proboards (Forum):
http://donaldmarshall.proboards.com/board/1/general-board
There is a "search" function on Proboards, and you can use this function to
search for and read all the disclosures I have made regarding REM driven clones, the people involved and more. I understand that it is human nature to want to know which people have been to the cloning centre as REM driven clones; therefore, use the "search" function to read about any public figure which I have already covered that you have an inkling about. You can also post anonymously on Proboards and Celine O'Carroll and other Administrators will transfer your question onto Facebook, which I'll answer.

Donald Marshall Revolution: http://donaldmarshallrevolution.com/
Donald Marshall Revolution details a brief overview of the Illuminati's
REM driven human cloning subculture; it also gives the viewer the most significant information relating to these disclosures in a small and easily understood style.

Instagram: https://www.instagram.com/donaldmarshallofficial/

Follow me on Instagram and help spread the information regarding

the Illuminati and their REM driven human cloning subculture.

Twitter: https://twitter.com/dmarshalltruth

Follow me on Twitter and help spread the information regarding the Illuminati and their REM driven human cloning subculture.

Email: donny865@hotmail.com
I currently have over 35,000 unread emails in my hotmail inbox and counting, at the address above. I cannot respond to all of these messages unfortunately, at this present stage of events. It is better to contact me through Facebook and private message me this way. You can also contact Celine O'Carroll on Facebook, or leave a message with Celine O'Carroll on the forum (Donald Marshall Proboards) and she will forward your message to me. I really appreciate everyone's efforts and well wishes.

Interviews

Readers can listen to the radio interviews I have done. Listen for consistency; particularly anything which you do not hear me, pronounce clearly for the first time; the best thing to do is to pause the recording at that particular point and replay it. You should also research the statements you do not understand. Sometimes reading helps comprehension a lot faster.

One of the main reasons you should pause and replay the recordings is because: the truth has been kept hidden for so long, that plenty of what I discuss in my interviews are beyond most people's current world view; so at some points I may speak too fast for you; my audio / microphone may not be so clear, so you may miss what I say etc. Others have also commented on the fact that they pretended 'as if': I was someone from the distant future sent back in time (I am **NOT**), to give important information to the world about highly advanced technologies, which currently exist, but are hidden and secret, and being used against the populace. Under such a premise, these people rationalised that they would not understand the information which was being presented to them straight away, and they would have to be patient in order to grasp certain concepts, technical speak, and the highly advanced technologies etc., BEFORE they can grasp the **SERIOUSNESS** of the information presented.

Furthermore, a friend has told me that when he first watched the Vinny Eastwood interview (Vincent Eastwood 2013); he did not hear me say the word "scars" (When Vinny asked: 'How do I know I'm the real me?') although he replayed that particular point in the video 8 times. Everything was just beyond his current comprehension, at the time. No matter how many times he replayed that part, he really could not hear me say the word "scars" –so he let that part go, and played the rest of the interview, pausing, and replaying points which he did not understand, especially to comprehend whether I was talking about my original body or my REM driven clone duplicate body. He also listened to all my interviews for consistency, to note any 'slip ups', or any parts of my testimonies which do not 'add up'. He would listen to all my interviews, pausing and replaying parts he did not understand, and he would reserve his judgements until he felt everything I was saying, was for example, as ordinary as: 'I woke up today, brushed my teeth, and took the dog for a walk'. He was also patient to realise the truth. After listening to my interviews, he would just let it 'sink in'. A week later he would come back and listen to the same interviews, to test whether his comprehension on the topics I discuss has improved, and whether he can understand what I am saying without having to pause and repeat at certain points in my interview; and soon enough he could now hear me say "scars" at that particular point of the Vinny Eastwood interview. He had reached the point where all topics I discuss sounded to him like I'm saying everyday common place stuff that people have heard, such as: 'I woke up today, brushed my teeth, and took the dog for a walk'. For anyone who may struggle to understand the topics I discuss: I strongly recommend you take the above approach as my friend did; soon enough, you too will realise the real truth of the world like he has: REM driven human cloning, kept secret and used for sinister purposes.

I cannot say the following is true for everybody, however, an unproductive venture a complete newcomer can do, is to listen to my interviews first time, all the way through, without pausing or replaying parts which he / she does not fully understand; if you do this, and if there is just a single part of my interviews which does not make sense to you; this will interfere with your understanding of the entire interview.

Remember, all I am discussing is technology, thousands of years advanced compared to what you currently use; available today, hidden and secret. If things start to get too complex for you, reduce it to its bare minimums: (advanced) science and technology. I hope that helps.

Another thing which I do in my interviews, that friends have picked up on, is:- because REM driven human cloning has been my reality for many years; I don't differentiate between my original body and my REM driven clone body. I just say: I did this, I did that, and (Queen) Elizabeth (II) did this and that, therefore it can become very confusing for newcomers. Please bear with me.

As I have explained in this document, the experience of REM driven human cloning is that a person LITERALLY goes to sleep in their original body, only to be activated by the Illuminati members as a REM driven clone, 90 - 110 minutes after first falling asleep, to experience the SAME earth the person left behind when he / she went to sleep in their original body, CLEAR as daylight. When the person wakes up from sleeping, their REM driven clone drops "limp noodle" –and a person goes from having an experience on the SAME earth CLEAR as daylight in a REM driven clone body, to waking up and experiencing the same world, now in their original body, CLEAR as daylight... –the **same** consciousness inhabits both bodies. Therefore and naturally, because I am experiencing the same world, with a CLARITY, in a body much similar to mine (a REM driven clone body), and because I am still "me", because it is my consciousness which resides in the REM driven clone body, and it is the same consciousness when I am experiencing the world in my original body, when I wake up from sleep; and because in each case, my consciousness includes the experiences, knowledge and memories which makes me, "me" in each body: REM driven clone body or my original body; I naturally do not differentiate between my REM driven clone version, and my original body, as an outsider discussing this topic and these concepts would. I understand it helps comprehension, and therefore I have painstakingly done this throughout this document. Consequently, please bear with me. Everything becomes easily understood once the reader gets over this hurdle.

I hope this helps; and I hope this helps to better understand the disclosure of the Illuminati's REM driven human cloning subculture, as well as, the interviews which I have done. On the following pages you can find 'Information for newcomers' which has been written with a checklist to help people with the topic of the Illuminati's REM driven human cloning subculture; followed by links to my interviews. You can copy and paste the links to your web browser or press Ctrl+Click – (hold "Ctrl" on your keyboard and left "Click" with your mouse, on the images below) to direct you to the interviews.

Information about Donald Marshall's Interviews for Newcomers

[Donald Marshall's interviews have been presented in this document, in an order, for the benefit of the reader who is a newcomer to the information of the Illuminati's _REM driven human_ cloning subculture.

It is **highly recommended** that a newcomer to the information of the Illuminati's _REM driven human_ cloning subculture focuses **solely and attentively** on Donald Marshall's interview with Vincent Eastwood (Vincent Eastwood 2013) before he or she proceeds to watch / listen to other interviews listed which features Donald Marshall. The reasons the newcomer should focus **solely and attentively** on Donald Marshall's interview with Vincent Eastwood before proceeding to watch and listen to other interviews featuring Donald Marshall are because (Vincent Eastwood 2013):

- In Vincent Eastwood's interview with Donald Marshall, the viewer can **SEE** Donald Marshall on video, shot from a "medium close up", "frontal", "eye level" perspective (UT Dallas, no date) and this allows the viewer to see the facial expressions, as well as, some body language gestures of the person being video recorded.

- Donald Marshall addresses the subject matter of the Illuminati's _REM driven human_ cloning subculture topic by topic, and this allows a person who is new to the information of the Illuminati's _REM driven human_ cloning subculture the opportunity to focus on one topic at a time, and dedicate **objective research** time towards one topic (such as REM driven human cloning) until the person reaches a point where that person can confirm with certainty, through **objective research**, that there is truth to _REM driven_ human cloning as detailed by Donald Marshall etc.

- Donald Marshall is allowed to speak for many minutes at a time uninterrupted, and this allows the viewer the opportunity to get into the flow of the topics being presented, with regards to the Illuminati's _REM driven cloning_ subculture. Moreover, there are two main topics mentioned in Donald Marshall's interview with Vincent Eastwood (in comparison to other interviews featuring Donald Marshall): REM driven human cloning, and the reptilian conspiracy. Although the soul-stone microchip and Nostradamus prophecy (as well as other prophecies), are main topics in their own right, and relevant to the disclosure of the Illuminati's _REM driven human_ cloning subculture, the relevance of Nostradamus prophecy and the soul-stone microchip, feature as subtopics in the Vincent Eastwood (Vincent Eastwood 2013) interview with Donald Marshall.

With the above in mind, remember Donald Marshall is revealing information which has been kept hidden and secret from the public for many decades to many thousands of years. The disclosure of REM driven human cloning, has been kept hidden from the majority of the world for over 70 plus years (since 1945). The true nature of the reptilian conspiracy which is indeed a reality, but takes **extensive research**, diligence and patience from the individual who truly wishes to realise the reality of the reptilian conspiracy, whereby the reptilian conspiracy involves a race of subterranean troglodytes known as "Vril", as presented by Donald Marshall, has been hidden form the majority of the world for thousands of years.

Therefore, keep in mind that as a newcomer you should NOT EXPECT to understand the topic of REM driven human cloning immediately. Furthermore, the reptilian conspiracy as presented by Donald Marshall which involves "Vrils" takes many week's worth of **independent research** before a newcomer to the information of the Illuminati's *REM driven human* cloning subculture can confirm with certainty that "Yes", the reptilian conspiracy involving Vrils as presented by Donald Marshall is in fact a reality.

With the above in mind: individuals should concentrate **solely and attentively** on the topic of REM driven human cloning as presented by Donald Marshall in his interview with Vincent Eastwood (2013), until the individual reaches a point whereby the individual **knows with certainty** and can explain the following clearly, concisely, and with confidence:

- REM driven human cloning (32nd Degree Freemasonry knowledge).
- Remote murder of an original person by *REM driven human* cloning technology.
- Give examples of, and describe the events relating to public figures that have died as a result of remote death by *REM driven human* cloning technology.
- Explain the differences between dying as a *REM driven* clone and dying as an original person.
- Memory suppression.
- Duplication cloning.
- Replication cloning.
- The different types of clones: Mark 1 to Mark 4 clones.
- Mark 2 *REM driven* clones.
- Consciousness transfer.
- Understand there are two separate bodies in the narrative of REM driven human cloning: a person's original body and a *REM driven* clone duplicate.
- Understand high profile people meet as *REM driven* human clone versions, via the process of consciousness transfer from their original bodies to their *REM driven* clone duplicates.
- Understand high profile people are experiencing life on the **same earth**, as *REM driven duplicate* clone versions when they meet at the cloning centers, and they are **NOT** meeting as original people the cloning centers, with their original (real) bodies.
- Understand *REM driven human* cloning experiences takes place at cloning centers, **here on earth**, when people **HAVE GONE TO SLEEP**, and have been activated as *REM driven human* clone versions of themselves.

166 | P a g e

- Understand as a result of *REM driven* human clone activation, the original (real) person's body is asleep while she or he is simultaneously 'awake' and active as a *REM driven human* clone version of themselves through the process of consciousness transfer from a person's original body to a *REM driven human* clone duplicate.
- Understand *REM driven human* cloning experiences **DOES NOT** take place in the 5th dimension, the astral realm etc.
- Understand *REM driven* human cloning inhibits a person's ability to have dreams or nightmares.
- Understand the experience of *REM driven* human cloning is **CLEAR as daylight**, and not similar to that of a dream or nightmare, (provided the person having a *REM driven* clone experience is not under memory suppression or the influence of drugs).
- Explain the history of *REM driven* human cloning: be sure to detail how *REM driven* cloning started with royalty and politicians, which then led to celebrities becoming involved in the Illuminati's *REM driven human* cloning subculture, which further led to random civilians being activated against their will as *REM driven* clone versions, and used by the Illuminati for the Illuminati's entertainment.
- Give examples of movies, songs, literature etc. which references *REM driven* human cloning, and explain what, why, when, how, where etc. the references to REM driven human cloning are made (in human culture).
- Give examples of events (e.g. death sports, *REM driven* clone sex etc.) which happen at the cloning centers with *REM driven* human clones of original people.
- Explain how fake Alien abductions are conducted through the use of *REM driven human* cloning technology.
- Explain the outcomes of intermittent *REM driven* clone torture, and the outcomes of constant unrelenting *REM driven* clone torture, as well as, the consequences, symptoms and side effects an original person is likely to experience as a result of intermittent *REM driven* clone torture, in comparison to constant unrelenting *REM driven* clone torture.
- Describe the environment of the cloning center in western Canada as detailed by Donald Marshall.
- Explain the real implications of 'selling one's soul' with regards to how 'selling one's soul' relates to Illuminati's *REM driven human* cloning subculture.
- Understand the reasons Donald Marshall was told Illuminati secrets as a *REM driven* clone version of himself.

The bullet points detailed above are the subtopics in relation to REM driven human cloning which Donald Marshall speaks about in his interview with Vincent Eastwood. There are 26 bullet points detailed above in relation to REM driven human cloning mentioned above. As you can see there are many subtopics one must familiarise themselves with before they can begin to understand the reality of REM driven human cloning in just Vincent Eastwood's interview with Donald Marshall alone.

This is why an individual who is new to the information of the Illuminati's *REM driven human cloning* subculture, **SHOULD** spend a considerable amount of time researching the subtopics in relation to REM driven human cloning presented in Vincent Eastwood's interview alone, because there are many subtopics one must understand clearly and concisely, before an individual who is new to this information can confirm: ""Yes" I understand the topic of REM driven human cloning with confidence." Nonetheless, once a newcomer has familiarised herself or himself through **objective research** with the bullet points mentioned above with confidence, whereby the individual can explain, understand, and give examples in relation to the topic of REM driven human cloning with regards to the Illuminati's *REM driven human* cloning subculture, this is when the individual will be able to make the distinction EASILY between when Donald Marshall is speaking about his original body, and his REM driven clone duplicate.

Furthermore, once a newcomer is capable of grasping the information in relation to REM driven human cloning, this is also when the individual will EASILY understand idiomatic (conversational) language used by Donald Marshall, such as 'they cloned me in'; whereby "they" refers to the Illuminati, and being "cloned in" refers to having one's consciousness transferred from their original body to their *REM driven* clone duplicate, while an original person sleeps, and is consequently activated as a *REM driven* human clone version of themselves experiencing life on the same earth at the cloning center etc.

This is the purpose this document, as well as, preceding documents serves: these documents allow individuals who are new to the topic of the Illuminati's *REM driven human* cloning subculture the opportunity to research Donald Marshall's statements objectively and reach a point whereby newcomers can realise the validity in Donald Marshall's statements at a faster rate.

These documents afford individuals the opportunity to watch Donald Marshall's interviews at their own pace, and at certain points whereby individuals cannot understand the exact implications of the information detailed by Donald Marshall, the newcomer can review this document (as well as preceding documents) and have their queries answered extensively. This is also why a "References" section is provided; most of the research in relation to the Illuminati's *REM driven human* cloning subculture, has been compiled allowing the newcomer the opportunity to easily find sources which corroborates Donald Marshall's exposure of the Illuminati's *REM driven human* cloning subculture.

Given all the reasons mentioned above, this is why it is recommended that the newcomer starts off by watching Donald Marshall's interview with Vincent Eastwood, because if the newcomer can focus on just one interview, and focus on just one topic: REM driven human cloning, and reach a point where that individual can realise truth in the topics mentioned as presented by Donald Marshall, then this alone will give the individual the momentum to research the corresponding topics and further investigate other topics such as the reptilian conspiracy etc. to a point where the individual realises the truth to other topics such as the reptilian conspiracy involving Vrils, as presented by Donald Marshall. Furthermore, by focusing on one interview and one main topic at a time, is a method recommended to the newcomer as a technique to lessen the overwhelming feeling and cognitive dissonances one experiences when she or he is first presented with the information pertaining to the Illuminati's REM driven human cloning subculture.

Remember, as a newcomer to this information, just concentrate on understanding the topic of REM driven human cloning, and once you are comfortable and understand the information as presented in Donald Marshall's interview with Vincent Eastwood (Vincent Eastwood 2013), you can then move on to watch the other interviews featuring Donald Marshall in the order presented in this document (although, of course you are welcomed to watch the interviews in whichever order preferred). After becoming familiar with the topic of REM driven human cloning, you can then move on to investigate the reptilian conspiracy, as well as, other topics as presented by Donald Marshall once you are sure you understand each main topic clearly, concisely and with confidence.

Without further introduction, the links to interviews featuring Donald Marshall are presented below]

Links to Donald Marshall Interviews

[The links to Donald Marshall's interviews are presented here. Copy and paste the links below to your web browser to be guided to Donald Marshall's interviews, OR, press Ctrl+Click on each image presented below, or simply "click" each image below (depending on your device), in order to be directed to each corresponding interview]

Vincent Eastwood (February 26th 2013) (Vincent Eastwood 2013)

Link: https://www.youtube.com/watch?v=M_1UiFeV5Jg
Running time: 73 minutes (1 hour, 13 minutes, 26 seconds)

Lisa Phillips (CFR) (April 11th 2013) (Astral 7ight 2014b)

Link: https://www.youtube.com/watch?v=bCD85L1yyIw
Running time: 119 minutes (1 hour, 59 minutes, 32 seconds)

Jeanice Barcelo (March 8th 2013) (Astral 7ight 2013b)

Link: https://www.youtube.com/watch?v=4TfioNHT19s
Running time: 73 minutes (1 hour, 13 minutes, 02 seconds)

Green Egg Radio Show **(March 21st 2013)** (Astral 7ight 2013a)

Link: https://www.youtube.com/watch?v=1ZmeLwyN2Gw
Running time: 46 minutes (46 minutes, 11 seconds)

Greg Carlwood (THC) **(February 26th 2016)** (mvoulgaropoulos 2016)

Link: https://www.youtube.com/watch?v=dOlsX5cj2tM
Running time: 134 minutes (2 hours, 14 minutes, 22 seconds)

Paranormal Central® **(March 6th 2016)** (Paranormal Central 2016a)

Link: https://www.youtube.com/watch?v=CaJBdfp4myQ
Running time: 130 minutes (2 hours, 10 minutes, 02 seconds)

Paranormal Central® **(May 29th 2016)** (Paranormal Central 2016b)

Link: https://www.youtube.com/watch?v=Yq5mXvKQctI
Running time: 79 minutes (1 hour, 19 minutes, 17 seconds)

[Donald Marshall is the first of three guests to appear on the show. Donald Marshall's interview ends at the 1 hour, 19 minutes, and 17 seconds mark of the video playback].

Brett Wayne Pachmeyer & Cole Johnson **(March 21st 2014)** (Astral 7ight 2014a)

Link: https://www.youtube.com/watch?v=X4Gvnr9Yq3M
Running time: 54 minutes (54 minutes, 09 seconds)

Donald Marshall's First Interview **(May 10th 2012)** (Astral 7ight 2015)

Link: https://www.youtube.com/watch?v=zh2u9x1E_To
Running time: 46 minutes (46 minutes, 40 seconds)

Radio Presenters –Contact Donald Marshall

Any Radio Presenters who sincerely want to contact Donald Marshall for radio interviews on their show is welcome to do this. Please contact Donald Marshall through Proboards by leaving a message for Donald Marshall to contact you.

Professionals who understand "Consciousness Transfer" –Contact Donald Marshall

Neuroscientists, engineers or professionals who understand how consciousness transfer works, and can provide Donald Marshall with a detailed methodology of how to block the consciousness transfer to Donald Marshall's REM driven clone; please leave a message for Donald Marshall on Proboards, and this will be greatly appreciated.

Other Sources Corroborating Donald Marshall

Press Ctrl+Click (on the images below to be directed to each source)

Astral 7ight Blogspot
http://astral7ight.blogspot.co.uk/

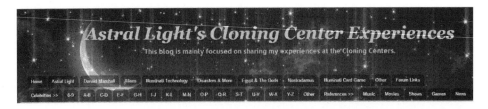

Astral 7ight has compiled Donald Marshall's disclosures regarding the Illuminati's *REM driven human* cloning subculture extensively. Astral 7ight also details his experiences as a victim of *REM driven* human cloning, and as a consequence, Astral 7ight corroborates Donald Marshall's exposure of the Illuminati's *REM driven human* cloning subculture as humanity's current reality.

Donald Marshall Books:
https://drive.google.com/folderview?id=0B6uNZqRUN8ceQnRRaGI1VEk2Nm8&usp=drive_web

The compilation guide to Donald Marshall's information, presented as short documents. Read, print, download and share.

Donald-Marshall.com
http://donaldmarshall.x10host.com/home.html

Donald-Marshall.com is a website dedicated to Donald Marshall's exposure of the Illuminati's *REM driven human* cloning subculture. This website is managed on behalf of Donald Marshall with the aim of informing the public about the Illuminati's *REM driven human* cloning subculture, as well as, to notify the public about the current state of the world in which we live in.

Donald Marshall Conspiratorium Room- Music Videos, Links, & News:
https://www.facebook.com/groups/Conspiratorium/

A place to learn; to privately post videos, links, and news related to the entertainment industry, cloning centers, Donald Marshall, and the Illuminati... Request to join.

Donald Marshall Public Figure Facebook Page:
https://www.facebook.com/donald.muktar.marshall

Donald Marshall's Public Figure page is run on his behalf, where posts from Donald Marshall's Facebook account are transferred to this page, to allow all to post, comment, read and share Donald Marshall's information.

***Rogue 1*:**
https://www.facebook.com/Rogue1DM/

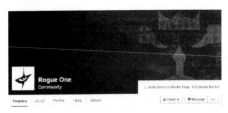

A Facebook group to learn more about Vril parasites; microchip bodysnatching; human cloning; especially REM phase human cloning which **must** be known and stopped.

***The Reference Palace*:**
https://www.facebook.com/TheReferencePalace

A Palace, where references [relating to the Illuminati's REM driven human cloning subculture and Donald Marshall's disclosures], are collected, catalogued, and collated for Donald Marshall.

***whoisdonaldmarshall Instagram*:**
https://www.instagram.com/whoisdonaldmarshall/

This Instagram account is run on behalf of Donald Marshall, where posts from Donald Marshall's Facebook account are transferred to Instagram in order to reach a wider audience and allow many more to comment, read and share Donald Marshall's information.

Petitions

Press Ctrl+Click (on the images below to be directed to each source).

Stop Human Cloning (Change Org 2016)
https://www.change.org/p/stop-human-cloning-by-sharisse-franklin

Sign this petition to help raise further awareness against the clandestine practice of human cloning, and REM driven human cloning. With your signature you will be helping to save many victims as a result of your stance against the covert practice of human cloning, and REM driven human cloning. By signing this petition you will also be voicing that you are AGAINST the kidnapping, rape, torture, molestation and sex slavery of innocent children by a clandestine group of individuals who refer to themselves as "The Illuminati", and with your signature you will raise further awareness for others to take a similar stance.

End Human Cloning. REM Driven Human Cloning. (The Petition Site 2016)
http://www.thepetitionsite.com/en-gb/952/622/178/end-human-cloning.-rem-driven-human-cloning./

Find Donald Marshall and learn more about human cloning and REM driven human cloning. On the petition website, you will be met with the first image above to your right (on this page); "click" anywhere on the image and you will be presented with Mr. Donald Marshall's interview with Vincent Eastwood (the second image displayed below here). Watch Mr. Donald Marshall's interview (if you haven't already done so) which discusses the widespread nature of (REM driven) human cloning, and how such highly advanced technologies are used against the populace unsuspectingly. You can sign this petition "anonymously", as well as, leave comments "anonymously". "Share", "Tweet" and "Email" this petition to others, in order to raise further public awareness about a clandestine **CURRENT** practice which affects all our livelihoods: The Illuminati's REM driven human cloning subculture.

177 | Page

Appendices

Appendix A: Steps YOU can take to help expose the Illuminati

Useful guidelines for understanding this disclosure

1) Know the information:

We are dealing with very complex topics involving advanced science and technology which is hidden from the majority of the world, underground, and in deep underground military bases. Without building a foundation and a thorough understanding with the regards to the topics relating to the Illuminati's *REM driven human* cloning subculture, you will not be able to help or understand what you are fully helping with so far as this cause is concerned, if you do not have a thorough understanding of the main topics in relation to the Illuminati's *REM driven human* cloning subculture. This is why, as a first step, it is fundamental to know and understand the information. Moreover your mind will need the time to adjust to the gravity of the situation humanity faces, which is counter to the conditioning, brainwashing and drip-feed disclosure information currently distributed publicly on a daily basis.

Listen to Donald Marshall's opening letter about the Illuminati

Listen to Donald Marshall's letter on YouTube (Astral 7ight 2014c) or read Donald Marshall's original and open letter to the public (Donald Marshall Proboards 2012a) if you have not done this.

Link: https://www.youtube.com/watch?v=td1Gc2Dv4xI (Astral 7ight 2014c)
Running time: 23 minutes (23 minutes, 21 seconds)

Watch George Green's interview

Watch George Green's interview and listen to George Green mention when governments first started to clone human beings.

George Green interview: Part 1 of 2

Link: https://www.youtube.com/watch?v=sSYXrWIA618 (Project Camelot 2008a)
Running time: 53 minutes (53 minutes, 31 seconds)

> **Project Camelot Interviews George Green - Part 1 of 2**
> George Green: Messages for the Ground Crew Part 1 of 2 Spokane, Washington, April 2008 http://projectcamelot.org/george_green.html George Green's career exte...
> YOUTUBE.COM

George Green interview: Part 2 of 2

Link: https://www.youtube.com/watch?v=6zSrg0IxHzI (Project Camelot 2008b)
Running time: 80 minutes (1 hour, 20 minutes, 14 seconds)

> **Project Camelot Interviews George Green - Part 2 of 2**
> George Green: Messages for the Ground Crew Part 2 of 2 Spokane, Washington, April 2008 http://projectcamelot.org/george_green.html
> YOUTUBE.COM

Phil Schneider's video lectures

Watch Phil Schneider's two lectures listed below; listen to Phil Schneider mention how **quickly** military technology advances in comparison to the technology the public uses.

Link: https://www.youtube.com/watch?v=Oljrjxnixtw&ab (Schneider 1995)
Running time: 72 minutes (1 hour, 12 minutes, 38 seconds)

Link: https://www.youtube.com/watch?v=Slgb5U-OqFM&ab (Schneider 1996)
Running time: 68 minutes (1 hour, 08 minutes, 44 seconds)

Read: "Information about Donald Marshall's interviews for newcomers"

The information is presented **on pages 165 - 169** in this document. Use the checkpoints / bullet points as learning outcomes one should aim to understand while watching Donald Marshall's interview with Vincent Eastwood (Vincent Eastwood 2013).

Watch Donald Marshall's interview with Vincent Eastwood

While watching Donald Marshall's interview with Vincent Eastwood (2013), simultaneously use the check points mentioned **on pages 166 – 167** in this document to review which points you may or may not have understood... with regards to the information about REM driven human cloning; go over the checkpoints and this particular interview with Vincent Eastwood (2013) until you understand it... Get to the bottom of the information (study this until you understand and discover the truth about this information).

Vincent Eastwood (February 26th 2013) (Vincent Eastwood 2013)

Link: https://www.youtube.com/watch?v=M_1UiFeV5Jg
Running time: 73 minutes (1 hour, 13 minutes, 26 seconds)

Read Donald Marshall's Proboards Forum (Donald Marshall Proboards 2012b)

Link: http://donaldmarshall.proboards.com/board/1/general-board

After following the above guidelines, whereby you have followed the above steps, and you have now reached the point where you have finished watching Donald Marshall's interview with Vincent Eastwood (2013); if you now have many unanswered questions about human cloning, REM driven human cloning, and you currently have an insatiable need to know which famous people have been to the cloning centers as _REM driven_ human clone versions of themselves and what Donald Marshall has seen famous people do at the cloning center (in western Canada) as _REM driven_ human clone versions, then seek Proboards (Donald Marshall Proboards 2012b).

It is only human nature to want to know about other human beings. Donald Marshall's Proboards Forum provides a "Search" function which allows you to find exactly what some of the world's most famous people have done as _REM driven_ human clone versions of themselves, at the cloning center. After searching for a specific person, use the keyboard function "Ctrl + F" (control and find); type the person's name into the search panel which will be displayed once you press "Ctrl + F"; –this will then highlight where the person's name is mentioned in the thread, you can use the "up" and "down" (or "previous" / "next") to navigate to the exact location the famous person's name is mentioned.

Watch the remaining Donald Marshall interviews listed in this document

After you are finished reading Donald Marshall's Proboards Forum (Donald Marshall Proboards 2012b), and you have researched all the questions you wanted answers to initially, and you have read about many of the famous people which primarily piqued your interest, as well as, what these famous people have done as _REM driven_ clone versions of themselves at the cloning center(s); it is now time to watch the remaining Donald Marshall interviews listed in this document **on pages 170 - 172**. Watch the other interviews at this stage for consistency with regards to the information being presented; also make note of any new information presented in further interviews.

2) Tell your close friends and family about this information

Once you have done all the above and have reached this stage; this is the stage whereby provided you have taken reasonable steps to avoid believing fallacies as truth, or falling into delusions, and your conclusions regarding the information concerning the Illuminati's _REM driven human_ cloning subculture, can be based on, and argued from a standpoint of **objectivity**, this is the point where most people are usually convinced there is some truth to the information of the Illuminati's _REM driven human_ cloning subculture as presented by Donald Marshall, because at this point, a person has found many, many corroborative evidence in favour of Donald Marshall's claims for the information concerning to Illuminati's _REM driven human_ cloning subculture to be substantiated beyond the point of 'mere coincidence'.

When you have reached this stage and you are somewhat convinced that there is some truth to narrative of the Illuminati's *REM driven human* cloning subculture as presented by Donald Marshall, you will still be at a stage where you do not know with completely certainty the extent to which Donald Marshall's information about the Illuminati's *REM driven human* cloning subculture is relevant in relation to the world you are currently living in; however, at this stage it is okay to have confidence in the fact that REM driven human cloning is a reality, and that governments are cloning human beings and have been cloning human beings for many decades.

This is the most critical stage that it is SUGGESTED that you inform ALL your close friends and family with regards to this information. There are several reasons why it is suggested you tell all your close friends and family members at this stage; the reasons are because:

Braveness: Naturally, the more people you tell on a one to one level, the braver you will become in terms of helping with the exposure of the Illuminati's *REM driven* cloning subculture. You will also learn the range of responses people give, when first being told about this information, when you inform many people on a one to one level. Moreover, you will become better at informing more people about this critical information as time and your experience regarding notifying others, about this critical information progresses.

Clear conscience:
Most people feel a sense of responsibility once they have some level of confidence that the information relating to the Illuminati's *REM driven human* cloning subculture has some truth to it, especially when people reach the stage when they have a level of confidence that REM driven human cloning is a reality. This is why it is important to tell your close friends and family at this stage because it will lessen any feelings of guilt you may feel from knowing this information is true, but staying silent. Remember: "silence" translates to "consent", and once most people realise their silence equals their consent for this deplorable action against humanity to continue, people tend to feel braver and as a result gain a clearer conscience from voicing their disapproval of the Illuminati's *REM driven* cloning subculture.

Comfort zone: Your comfort zone in terms of helping with the exposure of the Illuminati's *REM driven* cloning subculture will grow when you take more positive actions to help with the disclosure of this information. Furthermore, with each new action you take, you will feel discomfort; you will even feel discomfort with something as simple as clicking "Like" on one Donald Marshall's Facebook post, the **first time** you decide to do this. The discomfort which happens, results from going against the current trend of what has been socially acceptable for decades; you will be confirming that yes, human cloning is reality, with each new action you take in terms of helping with this disclosure, and that is what part of the discomfort is about.
However, taking positive actions and steps with helping to expose the Illuminati causes you to become braver, and further expands your comfort zone with each action you take, and as time and your experience with helping this disclosure progresses, you become more comfortable in supporting this cause. **Remember:** you are supporting humanity; that is all you are doing.

Safety: You will feel much safer once you have the knowledge that ALL your close friends and family members are aware of the fact that you know about top government secret information involving the clandestine cloning of human beings.

Remember, at this stage once you have a certain level of confidence, and know that there is truth to the information of the Illuminati's *REM driven human* cloning subculture, this is the best point to tell your close friends and family; tell your close friends and family; **the FUNDAMENTAL action here is to tell them**... do not worry about being believed... **it is much more critical to tell your close friends and family than to be believed at this stage**.

Furthermore, at this stage, you will feel discomfort EACH and every time you decide to tell a close friend or family member about the reality of REM driven cloning and the Illuminati's REM driven human cloning subculture. This is natural. It does not matter how many years you have known a friend or family member, human cloning in general is just an uncomfortable subject for many people to discuss, and human cloning will be a difficult topic to discuss for some people when you present the topic as a reality which is currently widespread and hidden from the majority of the world.

Tell people about this information in person

Sometimes, a better approach is to tell people about this information in person, and tell them from your personal experience, how you got to learn that there is truth to the disclosure of the Illuminati's *REM driven* cloning subculture, and mention the reasons why you are telling your friends and family members about this scary, but at the same time relevant and critical information. In other words how did you stumble across this information?

You can also start off by saying "I have something very important to share with you..." and carry on from there, by informing your friends and family members about the reality of human cloning and *REM driven* human cloning, and sharing Donald Marshall's Summary Disclosure document (Marshall 2015a) for friends and family members to read. Think of things this way: hypothetically speaking: if a loved one is in impending danger, at the very least you would warn your loved one of whatever impending danger exists. Therefore, at the very least, tell your loved ones about the Illuminati's *REM driven human* cloning subculture.

Moreover, telling people about this disclosure in person seems to work wonderfully; sometimes you are more likely to get this critical information across to loved ones much better when you inform loved ones about this disclosure in person; loved ones may be more inclined to believe you, as a result of you telling them in person, and on a one to one level in person. Keep in mind you are likely to feel discomfort with each new person you inform with regards to this disclosure; it is natural, however, it is most important that you inform others.

Offer to answer any questions which others may have about this information

When you have reached a stage where you are sure you known the information regarding the main topics concerning the Illuminati's *REM driven human* cloning subculture, you can also explain to your loved ones that you will answer any questions that they may have.

Warning: Some people are terrified by this information and do not want to know anymore. When your loved ones object to this information: **LEAVE it**, and move onto a different conversation topic. **DO NOT force** this information on anybody; this information is scary. Nonetheless, the more curious among your loved ones will be inclined to know more about this information, and discover the truth pertaining to this information themselves. When informing a curious loved one who wishes to know more about this disclosure, make sure to answer all their questions and remember to show people who display an interest in this information how books, movies, songs, television programs, etc. relates to the world in which we live in, and how this further references the information concerning the Illuminati's *REM driven human* cloning subculture. Moreover, remember to reference the fact that many famous people now use the word "clone" etc. on their social media accounts (Twitter, Facebook, Instagram etc.) and are indirectly referencing this disclosure.

Information for your contacts who would like to know about this disclosure

Once you start informing loved ones about the Illuminati's *REM driven* human cloning subculture; with people who display interest in this information, it will also be helpful to show these people **pages 47 – 51** in this document. **Pages 47 – 51** in this document discusses **"The reality of human cloning"**, as well as, **"Initial factors which stifles peoples' ability to accept the reality of human cloning"**, by informing readers that the **current environment** which we live in makes it difficult to see the clandestine operation of human cloning; the **technological comparison** which is incredibly advanced in contrast to what the public uses is also a factor which initially makes it difficult to realise the clandestine operation of human cloning; and **personal biases** which will have to be put aside; whereby this information must be reviewed **objectively**; or else, it will difficult to realise the truth contained in this information; which in actuality, the truths to this information are directly in front of their very face, and as a result, individuals will continue to be brainwashed if they cannot set aside their personal biases to review this information **objectively**. Direct your loved ones who become interested in this information to **pages 47 - 51** in this document.

Share Donald Marshall's Summary Disclosure document with loved ones

Link: https://drive.google.com/file/d/0B6uNZqRUN8ceOW1XNjg2bTg2Nms/view

Copy and paste the link above to your web browser or simply "click" (press Ctrl+Click, on computer device) the image above to be guided to Donald Marshall's Summary Disclosure (Marshall 2015a). Donald Marshall's Summary Disclosure document (Marshall 2015a) concerning the Illuminati's *REM driven* cloning subculture is **only 11 pages**. The Summary Disclosure (Marshall 2015a) lets the reader know straight away that Donald Marshall is discussing REM driven human cloning, whereby people go to sleep and have their consciousness transferred to a substrate body; a duplicate clone body; Donald Marshall is NOT talking about human cloning from a baby stage upwards, and most importantly Donald Marshall is a natural born human. These aforementioned points are important, because people find confusion when first reading Donald Marshall's original letter to the public, and do not research further, given the very serious implications and accusations made in the opening letter (Donald Marshall Proboards 2012a). Therefore, share Donald Marshall's Summary Disclosure document (Marshall 2015a) with loved ones so that it will help to explain straight away: that in Donald Marshall's original letter (Donald Marshall Proboards 2012a), Donald Marshall is discussing topics such as "consciousness transfer", multiple duplicate clone bodies; and most importantly: that all these experiences happen when Donald Marshall goes to sleep (as a natural born human). These are important distinctions which must be known.

3) Read ALL of Donald Marshall's information: March 2012 to December 2015

Once you have completed points 1 and 2 mentioned above, which are to: "**Know the information**" to a point where you are confident there is truth to this disclosure, and you "**Tell your close family and friends about this information**", this is the stage whereby it is suggested you read and investigate the remainder of Donald Marshall's disclosures regarding the Illuminati's *REM driven human* cloning subculture. There is plenty of important information on Donald Marshall's Facebook Timeline, all of which have been detailed over the course of three and half years (approximately). You will need to read and research the rest of Donald Marshall's information on his Timeline up till December 2015, because ALL the most relevant information concerning the Illuminati's *REM driven human* cloning subculture is contained on his Timeline within those years. After reading everything, including the corroborative articles listed on Donald Marshall's Facebook Timeline till December 2015 on Donald Marshall's Facebook Timeline, this is WHEN you will truly see the relevance of Donald Marshall's disclosures, and how this information relates to the world you live in. Furthermore, you will THEN realise the terrible situation humanity is in, and you will understand why humanity must know this information and rectify this situation immediately.

Start by reading Donald Marshall's short documents

Link:
https://drive.google.com/folderview?id=0B6uNZqRUN8ceQnRRaGI1VEk2Nm8&usp=drive_web

Read Donald Marshall's documents, which are a compilation of Donald Marshall's Facebook Timeline. The short documents are written with the aim to help newcomers to this information, and the main premise is: it is *REM driven human* cloning technology which Donald Marshall is tormented by. After you have finished reading the documents, start to read Donald Marshall's Facebook Timeline from where the document finishes off in the series and you will learn the biggest secrets which are kept hidden from the rest of this world, which relates to the life you are currently living. Continue to read until December 2015 on Donald Marshall's Facebook Timeline. As you are reading Donald Marshall's Facebook Timeline, you still may not be completely convinced by the information being presented, however, you may begin seeing how more and more of the pieces are starting to fall into place as you continue to read Donald Marshall's Facebook Timeline up until December 2015. The most relevant information has been written by Donald Marshall until December 2015; this is why it is important to read everything contained on Marshall's Facebook Timeline up till that point. After December 2015, Donald Marshall has mostly posted "Greeting Posts" to let the public know that he is still alive. The most relevant, and important information is contained on Donald Marshall's Facebook Timeline from March 2012 to December 2015, and it really **IS** worth investing this time.

Get on a Laptop / Computer and start reading

Some people have mentioned that their devices such as their mobile, iPad, tablet etc. does not allow them to scroll all the way to the beginning of Donald Marshall's Facebook Timeline. Some solutions to this issue are to read Donald Marshall's Facebook Timeline on a laptop or PC. You can scroll all the way to the very beginning of Donald Marshall's disclosures on Facebook, on a laptop or PC, and therefore if you are having the following issues with your mobile, tablet, iPad etc. this is a good solution to rectify the problem. Furthermore, if you do not have a laptop or PC, then invest the time to go to a public library and use their computers for the allotted time, until you have the resources to afford a personal laptop. Invest the time to read the information contained on Donald Marshall's Facebook Timeline from March 2012 to December 2015; **in all seriousness**, Donald Marshall's information regarding the Illuminati's REM driven human cloning subculture IS **extremely important**, and it IS worth investing such time. Remember Donald Marshall, invested 2-4 hours a day, **every day, for six months,** whereby he was going to the library to use their public computers, and divulge the information about the Illuminati's *REM driven human* cloning subculture to the public online; all you have to do is read the information to know and understand the reality of the Illuminati, and how the Illuminati controls the world you live in. It is a small ask, and therefore invest this time, and read ALL the most important and relevant information on Donald Marshall's Facebook Timeline from March 2012 to December 2015.

4) Click "Like" on Donald Marshall's Facebook posts which you like

As you are reading Donald Marshall's Facebook Timeline and you are at the point that you have read many, many corroborative evidence relating to the information of the Illuminati's *REM driven human cloning* subculture, and for whatever reason you begin to realise that the information concerning the Illuminati's *REM driven human* cloning subculture is now starting to make more, and more sense to you, to the point where you now understand concepts and topics, and you can now see the correlations between this disclosure, and the world in which you live in; and you are now at the point where you can realise references to this disclosure: for which you will realise these references are in songs, movies, books, on television etc. which you previously did not grasp; this is the point where you should start clicking "Like" on each of Donald Marshall's disclosure posts which you truly like.

Now the above may sounds like a small ask, however, it actually goes a long way towards helping to expose the Illuminati's *REM driven human* cloning subculture. The simple reason is: it is because of psychology. We are social creatures, and therefore we look to each other for social cues regarding 'acceptable behaviour'. Therefore, it does not matter how awe inspiring, attention grabbing or any other superlatives one can think of to describe a disclosure post Donald Marshall makes on Facebook; if say for example, a post only receives 3 "Likes" from 3 people, when others review the same post, EVEN IF, internally, others like the post they have now seen, the fact that the post received so few likes will also cause more people to refrain from clicking "Like" on the same post.

Accordingly, when you have reached the stage whereby you are seeing the truth to Donald Marshall's disclosures more clearly than ever, and how this information relates to the world you live in, start clicking "Like", it will cause others to instinctively click "Like" too. Moreover, in general, people do not think about these things too consciously; however this is exactly what happens because of the psychological phenomenon of **"social proof"** (Cialdini 2007; Soules 2007; Hallen 2014). Consequently, click "Like" on Donald Marshall's Facebook posts to show your support for this disclosure. It is a very small step, however it goes a long way in terms of lessening your fears, increasing your bravery, and supporting the exposure of the Illuminati's *REM driven human* cloning subculture.

Click "Like" on Donald Marshall's Facebook 'Greeting Posts'

Most people know of the reason why Donald Marshall continues posts "Good Morning", "Good Afternoon" and "Good Evening" on his Facebook Timeline. The simple reason why Donald Marshall has daily 'Greeting posts' on Facebook is because: the Illuminati can kill Donald Marshall at any second through the advent of *REM driven* human cloning technology. Therefore, the "Good Morning", "Good Afternoon" and "Good Evening" Facebook posts are to let the public know that Donald Marshall is still alive despite the fact that Marshall still remains a prisoner and a victim of the Illuminati's *REM driven human* cloning subculture, and this needs to change soon. Consequently, by clicking "Like" on these 'Greeting posts' made by Donald Marshall, you will be showing your support for every passing day Donald Marshall is alive, and continues to expose the Illuminati's REM driven human cloning subculture.

5) Share Donald Marshall's Facebook posts on YOUR Facebook Timeline

Start slow, if you must. This is one of the phases towards feeling completely brave and comfortable in terms of helping to expose the Illuminati's *REM driven human* cloning subculture.

This stage, whereby you must share Donald Marshall's Facebook posts to YOUR Facebook Timeline, is where you will feel the most discomfort initially. Although at this stage you have told many of your close friends and family about the clandestine operation of the Illuminati and their *REM driven human* cloning subculture, it is understandable that you are not close to everyone on your Facebook friends list, and therefore, and naturally, you would not want acquaintances and people whom you have not spoken to for many years to think that you are 'weird', 'crazy', 'insane' etc. –and you will feel this discomfort again, whereby these thoughts of what others on your friends list will think of you will arise; this is again based on the psychological phenomenon of **"social proof"** (Cialdini 2007; Soules 2007; Hallen 2014).

Many people who are now actively and openly sharing Donald Marshall's information went through this phase, and it is likely you will also go through this phase whereby thousands upon thousands of excuses run through your head as to why you cannot share Donald Marshall's Facebook posts on YOUR Facebook Timeline, based on the psychological phenomenon of **"social proof"** (Cialdini 2007; Soules 2007; Hallen 2014), whereby you will feel discomfort because you are worried about what people on your friends list may think. Many people actively and openly helping to divulge Donald Marshall's information to the world have heard many of the above excuses given from others, as reasons as to why they cannot share Donald Marshall's Facebook posts. HOWEVER, **remember:** it is the world which we live in that has become crazy through the advent of highly advanced technology used by a clandestine group of individuals calling themselves "The Illuminati". This world is crazy –not you, and IF anything, you are smart for realising the craziness which is around you, at all times, and wanting to help humanity rectify this situation; keep this perspective.

Furthermore, keep the following in mind: by sharing posts about human cloning, REM driven cloning etc. whether you are fully aware of this or not, you are helping to raise awareness among your audience, i.e. people on your friends list and people connected to you, and in the long run, you are helping humanity reach a point whereby humanity can relief itself of this terrible situation. Every little helps.

Start by SLOWLY sharing Donald Marshall's Facebook posts on YOUR Timeline

Donald Marshall has posts which are inspirational quotes (from the internet etc.) on his Facebook Timeline which relate to this disclosure; HOWEVER, on the surface, these quotes / Facebook posts do not have anything to do with human cloning and the rest of Donald Marshall's disclosures about the Illuminati's *REM driven human* cloning subculture; they are just inspirational quotes such as "**Never Give Up!**" and the image below etc.

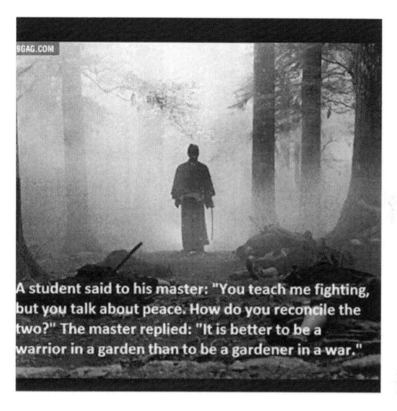

Share posts and information such as this. This way, at the very least, people on your Facebook friends list will see that you shared posts from Donald Marshall's Facebook page, and the more curious among your friends will review Donald Marshall's Facebook page by themselves; this is psychological, but it really does work. Furthermore, there are people who now openly and actively post Donald Marshall's information who found Donald Marshall's Facebook page and his information on the Illuminati because a friend of theirs either "Shared" or "Liked" a post from Donald Marshall's Facebook page.

Continue to read Donald Marshall's Facebook Timeline

Donald Marshall's disclosures regarding his experiences of the Illuminati's _REM driven human_ cloning subculture, becomes easier to understand for people at approximately March to May 2013 on Donald Marshall's Facebook Timeline. From having read from March 2012 to approximately May 2013 on Donald Marshall's Facebook Timeline, and reading and watching the corroborative articles and videos displayed on Donald Marshall's Facebook Timeline; at approximately March 2013 to May 2013 on Donald Marshall's Facebook Timeline is when people start to see the interconnectedness between Donald Marshall's disclosures and the world in which they live in. At this point, some people even have flashbacks form their childhood, whereby the life they experienced as a child, in terms of the cartoons, television shows, movies, books etc. which was experienced as a child, is now in their conscious forefront, and they can now remember television shows, books, movies, cartoons etc. which referenced human cloning, consciousness transfer to a substrate body etc, all of which are referenced in their favourite childhood memories. This is when people REALLY start to understand the significance of Donald Marshall's disclosures, and people begin to realise and KNOW with certainty that Donald Marshall is speaking real truths.

When you have reached the point where you now know with **certainty** that Donald Marshall is telling the truth with regards to his disclosures about the Illuminati's _REM driven human_ cloning subculture, this is where you are likely to feel an overwhelming sense of responsibility to do the right thing, and help this disclosure meet its full conclusion and reach a point whereby the Illuminati's _REM driven human_ cloning subculture is worldly known and fully exposed. At this point, when you know and understand this information with a much clearer level of certainty, and you have seen and experienced too many, many corroborations to this disclosure, for it to be mere happenstance or coincidence, this is the stage where you must share Donald Marshall's disclosures relating to the Illuminati's _REM driven human_ cloning subculture on YOUR Facebook Timeline.

Share Donald Marshall's posts to your Facebook Timeline

Understandably, some people cannot share Donald Marshall's Facebook posts on their Facebook page because it might jeopardise their employment [or *insert other reasons here*]. People such as this should join social networking activist groups which help with the exposure of the Illuminati's _REM driven human_ cloning subculture, and the information you share to these activist groups helping to expose the Illuminati's _REM driven human_ cloning subculture, will be appreciated and re-shared by many like-minded people. Some of these activist groups helping to expose the Illuminati's _REM driven human_ cloning subculture have been listed **on pages 174 - 176** of this document.

Share your FIRST Facebook post about REM driven human cloning

You will feel nervous and have discomfort sharing your very first post about human cloning / REM driven human cloning etc. on your Facebook Timeline. Many people who now actively and openly share Donald Marshall's Facebook posts have been through this stage, however, that feeling has long passed for people who currently openly and actively share Donald Marshall's Facebook posts to their Timeline, and it will not be surprising if when asked, they cannot remember the discomfort they felt when sharing their **first post** from Donald Marshall's Facebook Timeline to their Facebook Timeline. However, many people have felt like this and been through this stage. Moreover, when it comes to sharing your first post about human cloning, your mind might race, and you will think of many different scenarios, and excuses as to why you cannot share a post about human cloning on your Facebook Timeline, such as: excuses regarding what your friends might think; whether or not people on your social feed will remove you from their social networks because of what your post etc.

When your mind starts throwing these objections, take a breath and think about things this way: IF all you had to do to save the victims suffering from this clandestine torture through the use of highly advanced technology was to share one Facebook post about human cloning from Donald Marshall's Facebook page, could you do that? Could you be that brave? IF all that was required of you was to share ONE Facebook post to save countless lives, could you do that? If the answer is yes, then be brave and do it; then share a second post from Donald Marshall's Facebook Timeline about human cloning, and then share a third post about human cloning from Donald Marshall's Facebook Timeline etc. Keep sharing Donald Marshall's Facebook posts in relation to the exposure of the Illuminati's _REM driven human_ cloning subculture and you will become braver, and your comfort zone will increase as a result of you having taking steps to actively and openly help with the exposure of this information.

Expect some people on your social networking groups to remove you from their social networks. However, do not worry about this, it is not as many as you think it would be; it will be very few, and it will usually be people whom you have not spoken to in a very long time; who cannot fathom the reality of your Facebook posts, but instinctively know there is truth to it but overall they are afraid. Fear is one of the main reasons people will remove you from their social networking groups. Expect others to be confused by your Facebook posts, especially if you haven't spoken to these people personally, or informed them about the reality of the Illuminati's _REM driven human_ cloning subculture, as it is suggested above that you tell many of your close friends and family once you realise there is truth to this disclosure. Also expect to ATTRACT people, but just be wary of disinformation agents. People whom you have not spoken to in many years will also want to talk to you all of a sudden because of your Facebook posts exposing the Illuminati's _REM driven human_ cloning subculture, therefore, expect the following range of reactions, and more, from others in regards to helping with the exposure of this disclosure.

6) Join activist groups exposing the Illuminati's REM driven cloning subculture

These activist groups have been listed in this document **on pages 174 - 176** –and they are great for conversing and discussing this disclosure with like minded people. Share relevant information to these activist groups, and your information will be re-shared by the right audience.

__Invite like-minded people to join activist groups helping to expose this information__

This disclosure depends on the populace; therefore, invite more like-minded people to these activist groups and their contributions will help towards the overall exposure of the Illuminati's *REM driven human* cloning subculture.

7) Sign and share the petitions listed

Link: https://www.change.org/p/stop-human-cloning-by-sharisse-franklin
Link: http://www.thepetitionsite.com/en-gb/952/622/178/end-human-cloning.-rem-driven-human-cloning./

STOP HUMAN CLONING: by Sharisse Franklin

End Human Cloning. REM Driven Human Cloning.

Copy and paste each link above to your web browser or simply "click" (press Ctrl+Click, on computer device) each image above to be guided to each petition. By signing and sharing these petitions you will help to raise further awareness on the websites these petitions are listed on. You will also help to raise further awareness between your friends list on your social networks and any activist groups for which you are a member of, when you sign and share these petitions which help raise awareness about the Illuminati's *REM driven human* cloning subculture. Furthermore, it is possible to sign these petitions "Anonymously", as well as make "Anonymous" comments on the websites these petitions are listed on. Therefore, sign and share the two petitions listed here and this will count as one of the **BARE MINIMUM STEPS** you can take with helping to expose the Illuminati's *REM driven human* cloning subculture.

8) Share Donald Marshall's video / audio interviews on multiple online platforms

The links to Donald Marshall's interviews are listed **on pages 170 - 172** of this document. Share these interviews across multiple online platforms; such as for example: Facebook, Twitter, Instagram etc., and you will help raise further awareness concerning the disclosure of the Illuminati's *REM driven human* cloning subculture.

9) Share videos, audio, and other sources which corroborate this disclosure

Share videos, audio, and any other source which helps to reference and corroborate the disclosure of the Illuminati's *REM driven human* cloning subculture, and explain to the audience how, why, what, where, when, who, etc. in the videos, audios, and other sources you share across multiple platforms and multiple activist groups relates to the disclosure of the Illuminati's *REM driven human* cloning subculture.

10) Make your own videos about this disclosure

After you have read everything on Donald Marshall's Facebook Timeline, from March 2012 to December 2015 and you understand the information relating to the Illuminati's *REM driven human* cloning subculture wholeheartedly, and you can understand this disclosure to the point whereby you realise what is truly going on in this world, a great help will be to make videos which address each phase of Donald Marshall's disclosures in relation the exposure of the Illuminati's *REM driven human* cloning subculture. Upload these videos online, and this will be widely appreciated, shared, and re-shared by many like-minded people who are aware of this information but do not have the video editing skills to make short video clips directed at the exposure of the Illuminati's *REM driven human* cloning subculture.

11) Share Donald Marshall's document disclosures

Link:
https://drive.google.com/folderview?id=0B6uNZqRUN8ceQnRRaGI1VEk2Nm8&usp=drive_web

Donald Marshall Books

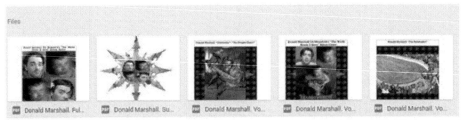

The purpose of these document disclosures which mirror Donald Marshall's Facebook Timeline is that they are written with the aim of helping newcomers to this information understand quickly, that it is REM driven human cloning technology that Donald Marshall and the populace are unsuspectingly tormented by, whereby Donald Marshall has been a victim of *REM driven human* cloning technology for over 30 plus years. Therefore, awareness about this topic must be raised extremely quickly, and awareness about the Illuminati's *REM driven human* cloning subculture must be quickly realised by the majority of the populace with regards to the clandestine operation of governments and their highly advanced technologies wielded against the populace unsuspectingly! Furthermore, these documents allow others to share much information, to multiple platforms: Twitter, Facebook, Instagram etc. The documents also allow people the opportunity to download this information to their devices; print hard copies of this information, and share hard copies of this information on a range of topics related to the Illuminati's *REM driven human* cloning subculture, instead of just sharing one post on online platforms, for which others may not understand straight away, or get confused by the post, if they are new to the information of the Illuminati's *REM driven human* cloning subculture.

Furthermore, these documents allow others to read a whole range of information, and research the information being presented, because there are multiple sources provided and this gives others the opportunity to form a better informed opinion concerning the topic of the Illuminati's *REM driven human* cloning subculture. These documents are also **FREE**, and provide a great introduction and explanation concerning the information of the Illuminati's *REM driven human* cloning subculture, and allows newcomers the opportunity to understand the relevance of the information being presented, whereby once a person finishes reading the information presented in each series of the short documents, the reader can resume by visiting Donald Marshall's Facebook Timeline, and continue to read this information, from the point the document series ends. Moreover, because these documents are **FREE**, feel free to share these documents and the links to these documents **EVERYWHERE** and among many people who are looking for this information, and are ready for this information. We are not all active on the same websites or online platforms, nor are we all active in the same activists groups; therefore, by sharing these disclosure documents on the online platforms, and activists groups which YOU frequent, you will ensure many, many more people learn about the information concerning the Illuminati's *REM driven human* cloning subculture, and the world in which we currently live in.

12) Form groups with like-minded individuals to help expose the Illuminati

A group should contain a minimum of 3 people and a maximum of 6 people (as a guideline). Groups containing more than 6 people usually tend to have one or two people who do nothing, or contain one or two people who do not contribute as much as other group members when groups exceed the guideline of 6 individuals. The term is called **"social loafing"** (Study 2015; Cherry 2016), which is the psychological phenomenon whereby a person exerts less effort to achieve a goal when they are working in a group than would have done, if that same person was working alone. Nonetheless, it is only a suggested as a guideline for people who wish to form groups to help with the exposure of the Illuminati's *REM driven human* cloning subculture, that they should ensure their immediate groups contain a minimum of 3 people and a maximum of 6 people.

When working in groups:

- Outline group goals
- Outline individual tasks which must be achieved by each individual
- Set agreed individual deadlines for each individual to meet
- Set agreed group deadlines to be achieved by the group
- Ensure harmony and cooperation between group members
- Work for the overall good to achieve group goals.

Working in groups, rather than individually helps to achieve goals faster because the burden and workload is shared among more individuals, and therefore if you can find others to work with, whereby group goals, individual tasks and deadlines can be agreed upon, then this is great. The implication of working in a group rather than individually means, the group will be helping to expose the Illuminati's *REM driven human* cloning subculture much more, than would be achieved individually.

Closing words: What we MUST do to help with this exposure

Remember these are only suggested guidelines for directions people can take to help with the exposure of the Illuminati's *REM driven human* cloning subculture. The suggestions mentioned in this appendix are NOT set guidelines and the only methods which we can do to help, and reach the point of the full exposure of the Illuminati's *REM driven human* cloning subculture. Nonetheless these suggested guidelines do provide you with steps to take if you are currently unsure about what you can do to help expose the Illuminati's *REM driven human* cloning subculture. We all have different talents and skills, and therefore, guidelines such as these listed in this appendix, may not be practical to you depending on your talents and skills. Therefore, as an example, if you are an artist, a musician, a part-time film producer etc., then by all means draw, paint, write lyrics and sing songs about the Illuminati's *REM driven human* cloning subculture. Remember to be as **DIRECT** as possibly when you are using your talents and skills to help with the exposure of this disclosure. Being as direct as possible will help others to understand the message you have to convey. There is no need for you to hint, or reveal this information concerning the Illuminati's *REM driven human* cloning subculture in veiled messages, as you currently see famous people do; be **direct**.

Furthermore, if you are a part-time film producer or the person who has great video production and video editing skills; then make short videos which address this topic, and your videos will be widely appreciated, shared and re-shared across many online platforms.

REMEMBER: every individual is unique and therefore whatever your individual talents are, use them in whatever way you feel is a positive helpful step towards the full exposure of the Illuminati's *REM driven* cloning subculture. The message paraphrased from "Conversations with Nostradamus Volume 3" (Cannon 1994, chapter 19) is very powerful, and therefore it is presented here as a closing message:

> It is extremely sad if we realise how terrible a situation is and we [as humanity] are not doing anything except feeling bad about the situation, the hopelessness that we feel about the situation is compounded [increased]. If we look at these things as too big for us to do anything about [such as looking at this information and thinking: 'what can "I" as one individual do to help expose the Illuminati's REM driven human cloning subculture? The problem is too big'] that means we have literally given up. Nothing is accomplished without individual human effort, which coalesces into group effort, and then action truly takes place. To give up is the worst thing that can happen to our world. It is essential while we are alive to **do whatever we feel is a positive helpful step**. To actually do it. Whatever it is!

Appendix B: Legislation

The references to the legislature listed below are reminders, that in the United Kingdom:

- The disclosures about the Illuminati's REM driven human cloning subculture qualifies under Public Interest Disclosure Act (1998) (PIDA) ('whistle-blowing disclosure act').
- Under the Enterprise and Regulatory Reform Act (ERRA) 2013 section 17 (*The new 'public interest' test)* is added for whistle blowing disclosures, amending section 43B of the Employment Rights Act (ERA) 1996 and therefore now reads as such (new words underlined): a 'qualifying disclosure' means any disclosure of information which, in the reasonable belief of the worker making the disclosure, *is made in the public interest and* tends to show one or more of the following-- [criminal offence, breach of legal obligation, etc]; the disclosures pertaining to the Illuminati's REM driven human cloning subculture meet the requirements set out in the 'public interest test', ERRA section 17, and are therefore made in the **public interest**.
- That it is a **serious crime** (Serious Crime Act 2015; Computer Misuse Act 1990), punishable by imprisonment, a fine, or both, to cite hatred or spread hoaxes by use of a computer which would cause mass hysteria or public dissension.

Nonetheless, despite Mr. Donald Marshall condemning many, many public figures, there has never been a single public figure named by Mr. Marshall who has issued a statement against Mr. Marshall for libel, slander, defamation etc., since 2011 when Mr. Marshall started to denounce public figures for their involvement in the Illuminati's *REM driven human* cloning subculture. Consequently, one should first look to the law in order to understand that Mr. Marshall IS providing accurate and detailed factual information relevant to the Illuminati's *REM driven human* cloning subculture, otherwise Mr. Marshall would have been fined or imprisoned many years ago for either: slandering names, (possibly) inciting a public panic and using a computer to do so. The references to the relevant legislature, is provided on the following page.

Computer Misuse Act (1990) Section 3A, *Making, supplying or obtaining articles for use in offence under section 1 or 3* [Online] Available from: http://www.legislation.gov.uk/ukpga/1990/18/section/3A [Accessed: May 8th 2015]

Enterprise and Regulatory Reform Act (2013) Section 17, *Disclosures not protected unless believed to be made in the public interest.* [Online] Available from: http://www.legislation.gov.uk/ukpga/2013/24/section/17/enacted [Accessed: May 8th 2015]

Employment Rights Act (1996) Section 43B, *Disclosures qualifying for protection.* [Online] Available from: http://www.legislation.gov.uk/ukpga/1996/18/section/43B [Accessed: May 8th 2015]

Public Interest Disclosure Act (1998) Section 43B, *Disclosures qualifying for protection.* [Online] Available from: http://www.legislation.gov.uk/ukpga/1998/23/section/1 [Accessed: May 8th 2015]

Serious Crime Act (2015) Section 41 3ZA, *Unauthorised acts causing, or creating risk of, serious damage.* [Online] Available from: http://www.legislation.gov.uk/ukpga/2015/9/section/41/enacted [Accessed: May 8th 2015]

All references in this document have been saved and backed-up; therefore if any link in this document, is ever deleted, modified etc. (online), let me know.

References

48 Laws of Power (c. 2012) The *48 Laws of Power: Law 27: Play on People's Need to Believe to Create a Cult like Following* [Online] Available from: http://48laws-of-power.blogspot.co.uk/2011/05/law-27-play-on-peoples-need-to-believe.html [Accessed: June 26th 2016]

AdeleVEVO (2011) *Adele –Someone Like You* [Online video] September 29th 2011. Available from: https://www.youtube.com/watch?v=hLQl3WQQoQ0 [Accessed: August 8th 2016]

All Spears (2016) *Britney Spears shaved head (complete video) (HQ). Mp4* [Online video]. May 23rd 2016. Available from: https://www.youtube.com/watch?v=wiNTBppukeU [Accessed: May 28th 2016]

Astral 7ight (2013a) *Donald Marshall Interview- Human Cloning, Hosts, Dead Chipheads & The Soulstone* [Online video] August 7th 2013. Available from: https://www.youtube.com/watch?v=1ZmeLwyN2Gw [Accessed: August 9th 2016]

Astral 7ight (2013b) *Donald Marshall Interview- MK Ultra, Clones, Drones & Vril Lizards* [Online video] August 8th 2013. Available from: https://www.youtube.com/watch?v=4TfioNHT19s [Accessed: August 9th 2016]

Astral 7ight (2014a) *Donald Marshall's 2014 Interview: Human Clones, Vril & MK Ultra* [Online video] April 5th 2014. Available from: https://www.youtube.com/watch?v=X4Gvnr9Yq3M [Accessed: August 11th 2016]

Astral 7ight (2014b) *Donald Marshall's UK Interview: Clones, Parasited Hosts & Vril* [Online video] April 5th 2014. Available from: https://www.youtube.com/watch?v=bCD85L1yyIw [Accessed: August 9th 2016]

Astral 7ight (2014c) *Shocking Letter from Illuminati Prisoner Donald Marshall* [Online video] May 16th 2014. Available from: https://www.youtube.com/watch?v=td1Gc2Dv4xI [Accessed: August 13th 2016]

Astral 7ight (2015) *Donald Marshall's First Interview* [Online video] April 29th 2015. Available from: https://www.youtube.com/watch?v=zh2u9x1E_To [Accessed: August 12th 2016]

Avatar (2009) Film. Directed by James Cameron. [DVD]. UK: 20th Century Fox

Bank for International Settlements (2016) *About the BIS – Overview* [Online] Available from: https://www.bis.org/about/index.htm?m=1%7C1 [Accessed: June 7th 2016]

BBC History (2011) *The Spanish Armada* [Online] Available from:
http://www.bbc.co.uk/history/british/tudors/adams_armada_01.shtml [Accessed: June 5th 2016]

BBC Religions (2009) *Zoroastrian worship and prayers* [Online] Available from:
http://www.bbc.co.uk/religion/religions/zoroastrian/worship/worship.shtml [Accessed: June 4th 2016]

BBC Religions (c. 2014) *Zoroastrianism* [Online] Available from:
http://www.bbc.co.uk/religion/religions/zoroastrian/ [Accessed: June 4th 2016]

Best of Sicily (c. 2016) *The Mafia* [Online] Available from:
http://www.bestofsicily.com/mafia.htm [Accessed: June 8th 2016]

Brandon Gaille (2014) *16 Exceptional Bystander Effect Statistics* [Online] Available from:
http://brandongaille.com/16-exceptional-bystander-effect-statistics/ [Accessed: May 20th 2016]

Business Insider (2012) *Catholic Priest Says A Schoolgirl Who Went Missing In 1983 Was Kidnapped For Vatican Sex Parties* [Online] Available from:
http://www.businessinsider.com/catholic-churchs-chief-exorcist-priest-says-missing-girl-kidnapped-for-vatican-sex-parties-2012-5?IR=T [Accessed: June 28th 2016]

Cannon, D., (1994) *Conversations with Nostradamus: His Prophecies Explained, Vol. 3.* Ozark Mountain Publishing Inc. Ch. 19

Cassette Acme (2012) *I Cloned my pet episode 1* [Online video] June 28th 2012. Available from: https://www.youtube.com/watch?v=a7bw0-5ja5Q [Accessed: August 7th 2016]

CBC News Canada (2009) *Wrongfully convicted Donald Marshall Jr. Dies* [Online] Available from: http://www.cbc.ca/news/canada/wrongfully-convicted-donald-marshall-jr-dies-1.781139 [Accessed: May 16th 2016]

CBS News (2009) *Man Accused of Threatening to Kill Obama* [Online] Available from:
http://www.cbsnews.com/news/man-accused-of-threatening-to-kill-obama/ [Accessed: June 2nd 2016]

CESSqc (2011) *Child Abuse, Pedophiles and Child Protection Service Crimes – Conspiracy of Silence* [Online video] February 20th 2011. Available from:
https://www.youtube.com/watch?v=Ck1cj68xiCA [Accessed: May 22nd 2016]

Change Org (2016) *Stop Human Cloning* [Online] Available from:
https://www.change.org/p/stop-human-cloning-by-sharisse-franklin [Accessed: August 13th 2016]

Cherry, K., (2016) *What is Social Loafing?* [Online] Available from: https://www.verywell.com/what-is-social-loafing-2795883 [Accessed: August 15th 2016]

CherTV (2011) *Cher – The Music's No Good Without You (Official Music Video)* [Online video] October 31st 2011. Available from: https://www.youtube.com/watch?v=6UUfnE4lyIs [Accessed: August 4th 2016]

CherTV (2012a) *Cher – Believe (Official Music Video)* [Online video] March 19th 2012. Available from: https://www.youtube.com/watch?v=ZOm0BruEVT0 [Accessed: August 4th 2016]

CherTV (2012b) *Cher – If I Could Turn Back Time (Official Music Video)* [Online video] September 2nd 2012. Available from: https://www.youtube.com/watch?v=BsKbwR7WXN4 [Accessed: August 4th 2016]

Cialdini, R. B., (2007) *Influence: The Psychology of Persuasion,* Harper Business

Coffin, D. R., (1988) *The Villa in the Life of Renaissance Rome.* Princeton University Press

Crystalinks (c. 2016) *Teutonic Knights* [Online] Available from: http://www.crystalinks.com/teutonicknights.html [Accessed: June 16th 2016]

David Icke (2012) *Is Dead Girl The Victim Of Vatican Sex Parties?* [Online] Available from: https://www.davidicke.com/article/174209/66792-is-dead-girl-the-victim-of-vatican-sex-parties [Accessed: August 6th 2016]

Department of Justice Canada (2016) *Enhancing Safety: When Domestic Violence Cases are in Multiple Legal Systems (Criminal, family, child protection) A Family Law, Domestic Violence Perspective. Part 9: Hearings, Cross-sector Evidence Issues. 9.10 Polygraph Evidence* [Online] Available from: http://www.justice.gc.ca/eng/rp-pr/fl-lf/famil/enhan-renfo/p7.html [Accessed: June 22nd 2016]

Dictionary (2016) *Paramour* [Online] Available from: http://www.dictionary.com/browse/paramour [Accessed: August 3rd 2016]

Donald Marshall Proboards (2012a) *DONALD'S ORIGINAL LETTER TO THE PUBLIC..* [Online] Available from: http://donaldmarshall.proboards.com/thread/75/donalds-original-letter-public [Accessed: July 28th 2015]

Donald Marshall Proboards (2012b) *General Board* [Online] Available from: http://donaldmarshall.proboards.com/board/1/general-board [Accessed: August 13th 2016]

DuckDuckGo (2016) *DuckDuckGo* [Online] Available from: https://duckduckgo.com/about [Accessed: June 3rd 2016]

Dungeons and Dragons (2016) *What is D&D? NEW TO THE GAME* [Online] Available from: http://dnd.wizards.com/dungeons-and-dragons/what-is-dd [Accessed: May 17th 2016]

Ehrsson, H.H., (2013) *Inspirational Lecture –Professor Henrik Ehrsson* [Online video] October 3rd 2013. Available from: https://www.youtube.com/watch?v=iR7HissYN2U&ab_channel=karolinskainstitutet [Accessed: July 2nd 2015]

Encyclopaedia Britannica (2014) *Counter-Reformation* [Online] Available from: https://www.britannica.com/event/Counter-Reformation [Accessed: June 14th 2016]

Encyclopaedia Britannica (2015) *Jesuit Religious Order* [Online] Available from: https://www.britannica.com/topic/Jesuits [Accessed: June 6th 2016]

Encyclopaedia Britannica (2016a) *Mithraism* [Online] Available from: https://www.britannica.com/topic/Mithraism [Accessed: August 28th 2016]

Encyclopaedia Britannica (2016b) *Farnese Family* [Online] Available from: https://www.britannica.com/topic/Farnese-family [Accessed: August 28th 2016]

Epperson, A. R., (1990) *The New World Order*, Publius Press. [Online] Available from: https://ia700406.us.archive.org/27/items/TheNewWorldOrder_342/TheNewWorldOrder.pdf [Accessed: July 7th 2015]

Eric Hastey (2012) *Donald Marshall – RAP Song May 22, 2012* [Online video] June 13th 2012. Available from: https://www.youtube.com/watch?v=mlVMo3C9_Ok [Accessed: August 1st 2016]

Eutraco (no date) *LES SOCIÉTÉS SECRÈTES* [Online] Available from: http://www.eutraco.com/cristal/livre/le%20livre%20jaune%205.pdf [Accessed: August 6th 2016]

Eyes Wide Shut (1999) Film. Directed by Stanley Kubrick. [DVD]. USA: Warner Brothers

Flo Rida (2011) *Flo Rida – Good Feeling [Official Video]* [Online video]. Oct 21st 2011. Available from: https://www.youtube.com/watch?v=3OnnDqH6Wj8 [Accessed: February 18th 2016]

Fueled by Ramen (2008) *Paramore: Decode [OFFICIAL VIDEO]* [Online video] Oct 31st 2008. Available from: https://www.youtube.com/watch?v=RvnkAtWcKYg [Accessed: August 3rd 2016]

Fuller, F., (2008) *Does Time Change Speed* [Online] Available from: http://science.howstuffworks.com/science-vs-myth/everyday-myths/time-dilation.htm [Accessed: May 12th 2016]

Giant Bomb (2016) *Pyramid Head* [Online] Available from: http://www.giantbomb.com/pyramid-head/3005-2442/ [Accessed: June 24th 2016]

Hallen, E., (2014) *The Science of Social Proof: 5 Types and the Psychology Behind Why They Work* [Online] Available from: https://blog.bufferapp.com/the-ultimate-guide-to-social-proof [Accessed: August 14th 2016]

HEREclickPlease (2011) *TROLLS! Government disinfo! Cointelpro* [Online video]. May 7th 2011. Available from: https://www.youtube.com/watch?v=o_JF1jn24Gc [Accessed: May 30th 2016]

Hiduth (2015) *Supriem Rockefeller* [Online] Available from: https://hiduth.com/supriem-rockefeller/ [Accessed: May 9th 2016]

Hiduth (2016) *Hiduth* [Online] Available from: https://hiduth.com/ [Accessed: May 10th 2016]

History (2009) *The Medici Family* [Online] Available from: http://www.history.com/topics/medici-family [Accessed: June 5th 2016]

How Stuff Works Science (c. 2016) *Can humans Survive on air alone?* [Online] Available from: http://science.howstuffworks.com/innovation/edible-innovations/breatharian.htm [Accessed: June 10th 2016]

HR Giger (c. 2012) *HR Giger* [Online] Available from: http://www.hrgiger.com/ [Accessed: June 24th 2016]

Human Beings –vs- Psychopathic Entities (2012) *TRAYVON MARTIN CONSPIRACY Was he sacrificed to donate his heart to Dick Cheney's transplant* [Online video]. April 15th 2012. Available from: https://www.youtube.com/watch?v=-aVUnfcF6-A [Accessed: May 2nd 2016]

Icke, D., (2001) *Children of the Matrix: How an Interdimensional Race has Controlled the World for Thousands of Years –and Still Does.* Bridge of Love

Icke, D., (2004) *And the Truth Shall Set You Free: The 21st Century Edition.* David Icke Books

IMDb (c. 1989) *The Simpsons* [Online] Available from: http://gb.imdb.com/title/tt0096697/ [Accessed: June 24th 2016]

Imperial Teutonic Order (c. 2016) *The History of the Teutonic Order of Saint Mary's Hospital in Jerusalem* [Online] Available from: http://www.imperialteutonicorder.com/id16.html [Accessed: June 15th 2016]

In5d (2010) *Tila Tequila: '3 Dark Man-Made Greys' Sent to Scare Her* [Online] Available from: http://in5d.com/tila-tequila-3-dark-man-made-greys-sent-to-scare-her/ [Accessed: May 2nd 2016]

Independence Day (1996) Film. Directed by Roland Emmerich. [DVD]. USA: 20th Century Fox

innovateus (c. 2013) *What is the function of Reticular Activating System* [Online] Available from: http://www.innovateus.net/health/what-function-reticular-activating-system [Accessed: May 13th 2016]

intheknow7 (2010) *Godlike Productions (GLP) Controlled Opposition / Gatekeepers: BANS (SRI) & Tavistok Postings* [Online] Available from: https://intheknow7.wordpress.com/2010/04/11/godlike-productions-glp-%E2%80%9Ccontrolled-opposition%E2%80%9D-gatekeepers-for-global-mgt-team/ [Accessed: June 3rd 2016]

Investopedia (2015) *How the Rothschild Family Created Their Wealth* [Online] Available from: http://www.investopedia.com/articles/investing/111915/how-rothschild-family-created-their-wealth.asp [Accessed: June 4th 2016]

justking81 (2008) *1980s Heinz Ketchup Commercial* [Online video] April 26th 2008. Available from: https://www.youtube.com/watch?v=GYyBu9xTTHI [Accessed: May 24th 2016]

Канал пользователя gf2045 (2012) *Dmitry Itskov: Welcome to the Global Future 2045* [Online video]. Feb 21st 2012. Available from: https://www.youtube.com/watch?v=9wEZsSIpypg [Accessed: May 5th 2016]

KanyeWestVEVO (2009) *Kanye West – Heartless* [Online video] June 16th 2009. Available from: https://www.youtube.com/watch?v=Co0tTeuUVhU [Accessed: August 1st 2016]

King, S., (1983) *Pet Sematary.* Doubleday

Kipling Society (c. 2012) *IF* [Online] Available from: http://www.kiplingsociety.co.uk/poems_if.htm [Accessed: June 18th 2016]

Kirsch, J.P., (1911) *Orsini* In *The Catholic Encyclopaedia.* New York: Robert Appleton Company [Online] Available from: http://www.newadvent.org/cathen/11325b.htm [Accessed: June 6th 2016]

Krugman (2008) *BRAINWAVE FREQUENCIES DURING WAKING, REM AND NON-REM SLEEP* [Online] http://soundersleep.com/uploads/waves2(w%20pics).pdf [Accessed: May 11th 2016]

LadyGagaVEVO (2011) *Lady Gaga – The Edge Of Glory* [Online video]. Jun 16th 2011. Available from: https://www.youtube.com/watch?v=QeWBS0JBNzQ [Accessed: May 4th 2016]

Mack's Criminal Law (2016) *Polygraph: The Law* [Online] Available from: http://www.mackscriminallaw.com/polygraph-law/ [Accessed: June 22nd 2016]

make-your-goals-happen (no date) *The Reticular Activation System. Your Automatic Goal Seeking mechanism* [Online] Available from: http://www.make-your-goals-happen.com/reticular-activating-system.html [Accessed: May 13th 2016]

MarilynMansonVEVO (2009) *Marilyn Manson – Personal Jesus* [Online video]. October 6th 2009. Available from: https://www.youtube.com/watch?v=Rl6fyhZ0G5E [Accessed: June 30th 2016]

Marshall, D., (2015) *Empowerment by Virtue of Golden Truth. Human Cloning: Specifically REM Driven Human Cloning. Summary Disclosure.* Unpublished.

Marshall, D., (2016a) *Experiences from the Cloning Center. Volume 1: April 5th 2012 to May 24th 2012.* Unpublished.

Marshall, D., (2016b) *Exposing the Illuminati's REM Driven Human cloning subculture. Volume 1: March 25th 2012 to May 18th 2012, Frequently Asked Questions.* Unpublished

Meyer, S., (2005) *Twilight.* Little Brown

Meyer, S., (2006) *New Moon (The Twilight Saga, Book 2).* Little Brown

Meyer, S., (2007) *Eclipse (The Twilight Saga, Book 3).* Little Brown

Meyer, S., (2008) *Breaking Dawn (The Twilight Saga, Book 4).* Little Brown

Moeller, C., (1910) *Hospitallers of St. John of Jerusalem.* In *The Catholic Encyclopaedia.* New York: Robert Appleton Company [Online] Available from: http://www.newadvent.org/cathen/07477a.htm [Accessed: June 8th 2016]

mvoulgaropoulos (2016) *Donald Marshall Feb 2016 2-hour interview* [Online video] March 16th 2016. Available from: https://www.youtube.com/watch?v=dOlsX5cj2tM [Accessed: August 10th 2016]

National Sleep Foundation (2016) *Stages of Human Sleep. What are the stages of human sleep?* [Online] Available from: http://sleepdisorders.sleepfoundation.org/chapter-1-normal-sleep/stages-of-human-sleep/ [Accessed: May 11th 2016]

NBC (2016) *Saturday Night Live* [Online] Available from: http://www.nbc.com/saturday-night-live [Accessed: June 23rd 2016]

News (2008) *Dr Teruhiko Wakayama brings frozen mice back to life as clones* [Online] Available from: http://www.news.com.au/lifestyle/real-life/mice-brought-back-to-life-as-clones/story-e6frflri-1111117939902#ixzz1vHd9qD7G [Accessed: May 2nd 2016]

Nickelback (2013) *Nickelback Hero Official Music Video* [Online video]. September 23rd 2013. Available from: https://www.youtube.com/watch?v=oPr8ZqRHTQo [Accessed: May 26th 2016]

One World Of Nations (2014) *Global Power Structures | The Rothschilds and More: Report #2* [Online] Available from: http://www.oneworldofnations.com/2014/03/global-power-structures-rothschilds-and_30.html [Accessed: June 5th 2016]

Online Etymology Dictionary (2016) *Paramour* [Online] Available from: http://www.etymonline.com/index.php?allowed_in_frame=0&search=paramour [Accessed: August 3rd 2016]

Open Minds (2011) *Phil Schneider's incredible ET claims.* [Online] Available from: http://www.openminds.tv/phil-schneiders-incredible-et-claims/9982 [Accessed: May 9th 2015]

Palais Pallavicini (2016) *The Pallavicini Family* [Online] Available from: http://www.palais-pallavicini.at/en/pallavicini-family.html [Accessed: June 4th 2016]

Paranormal Central (2016a) *Cloning. Is it real? Donald Marshall on Paranormal Central® March 6, 2016* [Online video] March 8th 2016. Available from: https://www.youtube.com/watch?v=CaJBdfp4myQ [Accessed: August 10th 2016]

Paranormal Central (2016b) *Donald Marshall update!! Bigfoot!! Alien Abduction!! Paranormal Central® May 29, 2016* [Online video] May 30th 2016. Available from: https://www.youtube.com/watch?v=Yq5mXvKQctI [Accessed: August 11th 2016]

PC Mag (2011) *What is Siri?* [Online] Available from: http://www.pcmag.com/article2/0,2817,2394787,00.asp [Accessed: August 6th 2016]

Petkova, V. I., and Ehrsson, H.H., (2008) *If I Were You: Perceptual Illusion of Body Swapping,* PLoS ONE, Volume 3, Issue 12, pp. 1-9

Pet Sematary (1989) Film. Directed by Mary Lambert. [DVD]. USA: Paramount Pictures

Project Avalon (2008) *James Casbolt: Underground U.K. bases!* [Online] November 25th 2008. Project Avalon Discussion Forum. Available from: http://www.projectavalon.net/forum/showthread.php?p=86540 [Accessed: May 9th 2016]

Project Camelot (2008a) *Project Camelot Interviews George Green – Part 1 of 2* [Online video]. April 16th 2008. Available from: https://www.youtube.com/watch?v=sSYXrWIA618&ab_channel=ProjectCamelot [Accessed: May 11th 2015]

Project Camelot (2008b) *Project Camelot Interviews George Green – Part 2 of 2* [Online video]. April 16th 2008. Available from: https://www.youtube.com/watch?v=6zSrg0IxHzI&ab_channel=ProjectCamelot [Accessed: May 11th 2015]

Q69573 (2012) *Illuminati Mind Control Victim Gabriela Rico Jimenez Briefly Breaks Free (English Subtitles)* [Online video] August 31st 2012. Available from: https://www.youtube.com/watch?v=yuJqidKLncg [Accessed: May 10th 2016]

Rome Art Lover (c. 2016a) *Rome in the Footsteps of an XVIIIth Century Traveller. Caprarola Gardens of Palazzo Farnese* [Online] Available from: http://www.romeartlover.it/Cimino7.html [Accessed: June 12th 2016]

Rome Art Lover (c. 2016b) *Rome in the Footsteps of an XVIIIth Century Traveller. Caprarola Palazzo Farnese* [Online] Available from: http://www.romeartlover.it/Cimino6.html [Accessed: June 14th 2016]

Rome Tour (2011) *Borgo Santo Spirito, Borgo, Rome* [Online] Available from: http://rometour.org/borgo-santo-spirito-borgo-rome.html [Accessed: June 15th 2016]

SAG-AFTRA (2016) *About Us | SAG-AFTRA* [Online] Available from: http://www.sagaftra.org/content/about-us [Accessed: June 4th 2016]

Salem News (2012) *America's Greatest Child Sex Scandal: Boys Town in Lincoln, Nebraska* [Online] Available from: http://www.salem-news.com/articles/december292012/boys-town-scandal-tk.php [Accessed: May 22nd 2016]

Schneider, P., (1995) *Phil Schneider Documentary of truth about Aliens & UFO's & our Government.* [Online video]. September 21st 2013. Available from: https://www.youtube.com/watch?v=Oljrjxnixtw&ab_channel=AliensAmongUs [Accessed: May 10th 2015]

Schneider, P., (1996) *Phil Schneider's Last Speech ~ Two Months Before His Assassination ~ Aliens & Underground Bases* [Online video]. November 24th 2013. Available from: https://www.youtube.com/watch?v=Slgb5U-OqFM&ab_channel=FallofMedia [Accessed: May 10th 2015]

SGIRA (c. 2016) *Farnese Family* [Online] Available from: http://www.sgira.org/hm/patrons_farnese.htm [Accessed: June 10th 2016]

Society of Jesus (c. 2016) *Father Adolfo Nicolás, Superior General of the Society of Jesus* [Online] Available from: http://www.sjweb.info/curiafrgen/curia_frgen.cfm [Accessed: June 9th 2016]

Soules, M., (2007) *Influence: The Psychology of Persuasion* [Online] Available from: http://www.media-studies.ca/articles/influence_ch4.htm [Accessed: August 14th 2016]

Study (2015) *Social Loafing: Definition, Examples & Theory* [Online] Available from: http://study.com/academy/lesson/social-loafing-definition-examples-theory.html [Accessed: August 15th 2016]

TED (2008) *Philip Zimbardo: The psychology of evil* [Online video] September 23rd 2008. Available from: https://www.youtube.com/watch?v=OsFEV35tWsg [Accessed: May 19th 2016]

TimeMasteryCoach (2013) *Reticular Activating System* [Online video] May 25th 2013. Available from: https://www.youtube.com/watch?v=QCnfAzAIhVw [Accessed: May 13th 2016]

Tila Tequila (c. 2012) *Tila Tequila: Up Close & Personal. Blog Archives* [Online] Available from: http://tilatequila.com/category/blog/ [Accessed: May 30th 2016]

The Alex Jones Channel (2011) *Secret Cloning Projects Exposed* [Online video] July 27th 2011. Available from: https://www.youtube.com/watch?v=LWhEOmWcHNs [Accessed: May 4th 2016]

TheBanglesVEVO (2013) *The Bangles – Walk Like an Egyptian* [Online video] February 7th 2013. Available from: https://www.youtube.com/watch?v=Cv6tuzHUuuk [Accessed: May 21st 2016]

The Canadian Encyclopaedia (2016) *Robert Pickton Case* [Online] Available from: http://www.thecanadianencyclopedia.ca/en/article/robert-pickton-case/ [Accessed: August 18th 2016]

The Chive (2012) *Celebs and their doppelgangers* [Online] Available from: http://thechive.com/2012/01/10/celebs-and-their-doppelgangers-30-photos/ [Accessed: May 6th 2016]

TheFugeesVEVO (2011) *The Fugees – Killing Me Softly With His Song (Official Video)* [Online video] March 26th 2011. Available from: https://www.youtube.com/watch?v=oKOtzIo-uYw [Accessed: June 18th 2016]

The Independent (2013) *How the horrific case of serial killer William Pickton, who may have killed up to 50 women, shone light on the plight of Vancouver's First Nation women* [Online] Available from: http://www.independent.co.uk/news/world/americas/how-the-horrific-case-of-serial-killer-william-pickton-who-may-have-killed-up-to-50-women-shone-8457870.html [Accessed: May 25th 2016]

The Matrix (1999) Film. Directed by The Wachowski Brothers. [DVD]. USA: Warner Brothers

The Naked Scientists (2009) *A rush of blood to the head* [Online] Available from: http://www.thenakedscientists.com/HTML/science-news/news/1754/ [Accessed: February 16th 2016]

The People Under the Stairs (1991) Film. Directed by Wes Craven. [DVD]. USA: Universal Pictures

The Petition Site (2016) *End Human Cloning. REM Driven Human Cloning* [Online] Available from: http://www.thepetitionsite.com/en-gb/952/622/178/end-human-cloning.-rem-driven-human-cloning./ [Accessed: August 13th 2016]

TLC (c. 2012) *I Cloned My Pet* [Online] Available from: http://www.tlc.com/tv-shows/other-shows/videos/i-cloned-my-pet-videos/ [Accessed: August 7th 2016]

Travel Guide China (2016) *Dragon's Personality by Blood Types* [Online] Available from: https://www.travelchinaguide.com/intro/social_customs/zodiac/dragon/blood-type.htm [Accessed: May 17th 2016]

Truth or Lie (c. 2016) *How accurate is a polygraph?* [Online] Available from: http://www.truthorlie.com/accurate.html [Accessed: June 20th 2016]

Twilight (2008) Film. Directed by Catherine Hardwicke. [DVD]. USA: Summit Entertainment

UC Davis Health System (2016a) *HLA Typing/Matching* [Online] Available from: http://www.ucdmc.ucdavis.edu/transplant/learnabout/learn_hla_type_match.html [Accessed: May 4th 2016]

UC Davis Health System (2016b) *Matching and Compatibility* [Online] Available from: http://www.ucdmc.ucdavis.edu/transplant/livingdonation/donor_compatible.html [Accessed: May 4th 2016]

Unconfirmed Sources (2004) *Pentagon Reveals Secret Cloning Program* [Online] Available from: http://unconfirmedsources.com/wp/pentagon-reveals-secret-cloning-program/ [Accessed: May 8th 2016]

UT Dallas (no date) *Elements of Cinematography: Camera* [Online] Available from: http://www.utdallas.edu/atec/midori/Handouts/camera.htm [Accessed: August 12th 2016]

Vatican (c. 2016) *The Roman Curia. The Uniform of the Swiss Guards* [Online] Available from: http://www.vatican.va/roman_curia/swiss_guard/swissguard/divisa_en.htm [Accessed: June 7th 2016]

Vatican Assassins (2010a) *The Pentagon: Jesuit Military Fortress from Spain, to Italy, to the American Empire* [Online] Available from: http://vaticanassassins.org/2010/06/27/the-pentagon-jesuit-military-fortress-from-spain-to-italy-to-the-american-empire/ [Accessed: June 14th 2016]

Vatican Assassins (2010b) *Pic Post: Borgo Santo Spirito; Command Center for the Jesuit Superior General* [Online] Available from: http://vaticanassassins.org/2010/06/22/pic-post-borgo-santo-spirito-command-center-for-the-jesuit-superior-general/ [Accessed: June 15th 2016]

Villa Farnesina (c. 2014) *Villa Farnesina History* [Online] Available from: http://www.villafarnesina.it/?page_id=47&lang=en [Accessed: June 11th 2016]

Vincent Eastwood (2013) *Illuminati Cloning Programs, Sex and Murder Cults and Reptilians! 26Feb2013* [Online video] February 26th 2013. Available from: https://www.youtube.com/watch?v=M_1UiFeV5Jg [Accessed: July 10th 2015]

Vocabulary (2016) *Paramour* [Online] Available from: https://www.vocabulary.com/dictionary/paramour [Accessed: August 3rd 2016]

Warner Bros. Records (2009) *Depeche Mode – Personal (Remastered Video)* [Online video] October 26th 2009. Available from: https://www.youtube.com/watch?v=u1xrNaTO1bI [Accessed: June 30th 2016]

Web Bot Forum (c. 2012) [Online] Available from: http://webbotforum.com/content.php?s=f519364541f50b25eb11aaa5721d3c6a [Accessed: May 4th 2016]

World Wide Hippies (2013) *The Truth About Long Hair* [Online] Available from: http://www.worldwidehippies.com/the-truth-about-long-hair/ [Accessed: June 29th 2016]

xlogold (2006) *Matt Le Blanc –Heinz Ketchup Commercial* [Online video] August 8th 2006. Available from: https://www.youtube.com/watch?v=N_vssdys8lk [Accessed: May 24th 2016]

Zen Gardner (2013) *Jesuit Pope Agenda –Meet The Templars, Knights of Malta And Blackwater / Xe Exterminators* [Online] Available from: http://www.zengardner.com/jesuit-pope-agenda-meet-the-templars-knights-of-malta-and-blackwaterxe-exterminators/ [Accessed: June 9th 2016]

Printed in Great Britain
by Amazon